T0374612

THE I TATTI
RENAISSANCE LIBRARY

James Hankins, General Editor

MANETTI

A TRANSLATOR'S DEFENSE

ITRL 71

GIANNOZZO MANETTI

A TRANSLATOR'S DEFENSE

EDITED BY

MYRON McSHANE

ENGLISH TRANSLATION BY

MARK YOUNG

THE I TATTI RENAISSANCE LIBRARY
HARVARD UNIVERSITY PRESS
CAMBRIDGE, MASSACHUSETTS
LONDON, ENGLAND
2016

printed in the United States of America

Series design by Dean Bornstein

Library of Congress Cataloging-in-publication data

Manetti, Giannozzo, 1396–1459, author.
[Apologeticus. English]
A translator's defense / Giannozzo Manetti ; edited by Myron McShane ;
English translation by Mark Young.
pages cm. — (The I Tatti Renaissance library ; ITRL 71)
English and Latin.
English translation based on the Latin text edited and published
by Alfonso De Petris in 1981 of the Apologeticus, a 5 book,
mid-fifteenth century, treatise by Giannozzo Manetti
in defense of his own translation of Psalms from the original Hebrew.
Includes bibliographical references and index.
ISBN 978-0-674-08865-8 (alk. paper)
1. Bible — Translating — Early works to 1800. 2. Bible. Psalms. Latin — Versions — Early works to 1800. 3. Manetti, Giannozzo, 1396–1459. Apologeticus. 4. Translating and interpreting — Early works to 1800.
I. McShane, Myron, editor. II. Young, Mark, 1964– translator.
III. De Petris, Alfonso, editor. IV. Harvard University Press.
BS449.M3613 2016
220.501 — dc23 2015010877

Contents

Introduction

At the time it was written in the mid-fifteenth century, Giannozzo Manetti's *A Translator's Defense* (*Apologeticus*) was the longest treatise on translation ever written.[1] In fact, the Florentine humanist's justification for his new translation of the Psalms was longer than the combined works of his three celebrated predecessors on translation theory: Cicero, Jerome, and Leonardo Bruni. Certainly, Manetti (1396–1459) was not the first writer since Jerome to have attempted to translate Hebrew into Latin. He may not have even been the first to write a treatise on biblical translation since the renowned Church Father.[2] However, *A Translator's Defense* remains the first extant theoretical work that we possess on translating the Bible in over one thousand years. The eldest son of a wealthy Florentine merchant, Manetti's wide-ranging talents were broad even by the standards of fifteenth-century Italy. A leading humanist of his generation, he was celebrated in Florence for his roles as politician, orator, and diplomat, and he also served as apostolic secretary in Rome and as royal counselor at the court of Naples.[3] In his final six years in Rome and Naples, he was an especially prolific translator. Manetti tackled both secular and sacred texts. In the secular realm, he completed versions of several of Aristotle's lengthy ethical treatises. In the sacred domain, he laid claim to being the first modern translator of the Bible, two generations before Erasmus and Luther, through his translation of the entire New Testament from Greek and the Psalms from Hebrew.[4]

In sharp contrast to his present-day obscurity, Manetti was the subject of no less than four biographies in the years following his death. One of them was even written in verse! By the century's end, a noted humanist ranked him alongside the great polymath

Leon Battista Alberti as one of the two leading figures of the Quattrocento.[5] Despite his extraordinary accomplishments, it is understandable how Manetti receded into obscurity. Although his fame among contemporaries extended as far as Spain, and a handful of works would be published over the ensuing five centuries, most of his oeuvre still languishes in manuscript form.[6] It did not help Manetti's cause that the nineteenth-century founders of the modern study of the Renaissance disliked his Latin style and favored humanism's secular contributions more than its religious ones. However, from the mid-twentieth century onward, his works have attracted increasing attention from scholars.[7]

The *Apologeticus* occupies a privileged position as the first work mentioned in the most well-known account of Manetti's life.[8] Vespasiano da Bisticci's particular emphasis on the *Apologeticus* indicates how important the work is to understanding Manetti. Although an exact date cannot be established, it was likely written around the midpoint of his tenure (1455–59) in the service of King Alfonso of Naples, to whom the work is dedicated. The title of the work draws inspiration from two ancient sources. First, there is an allusion to Plato's *Apology*, where Socrates defends himself and his way of life against his accusers. The Athenian philosopher was a figure close to Manetti's heart, as he wrote the first life of Socrates in Latin.[9] Second, the title recalls a work of the same name by the early Church Father Tertullian. Fittingly, for a treatise on biblical translation, Manetti shares Tertullian's aims in providing a robust defense of Christianity. This allusion to Tertullian also illustrates the enormous influence that patristic literature had on Manetti. One of his teachers, Ambrogio Traversari, was a pioneer in translating the Greek Church Fathers and is the only Italian-born humanist to be named in the *Apologeticus*. Throughout this work, Manetti will cite early Christian writers such as Eusebius and Augustine at length, but another Church Father will play

an absolutely central role—Jerome. When Manetti conceived of retranslating the Bible, he would have had to reckon with the cult status of the patron saint of translators in the Italian Renaissance.[10] After Jerome had completed his biblical translation in the early fifth century, his version had gradually become the one universally adopted in the West. Although Jerome's version would come to be known as the Vulgate only at the Council of Trent in 1546, its ubiquitousness is shown by the fact that it was frequently referred to simply as "our translation (*nostra tralatio*)." Given the status of Jerome's translation, it was no small matter to consider revising it. A little over a decade before Manetti completed his treatise, another of his former teachers, Leonardo Bruni, dean of Florentine humanism, had written a sharply worded warning to a younger correspondent about learning Hebrew. For Bruni, to acquire the language of the prophets was useless, since Jerome had already provided an unsurpassed version of Holy Scripture. To proceed in doing so would foolishly suggest that one might compete with the sanctified Church Father. The moral of Bruni's letter is clear: humanists should not stray into biblical studies.[11] But Manetti did.

Why did our author learn Hebrew? To do such a thing in Italy was nearly unprecedented. Throughout the Middle Ages, not one of the very few who learned Hebrew was Italian. In particular, Manetti's hometown of Florence had a reputation for being hostile to Jews.[12] The earliest reference by a humanist about acquiring Hebrew can be found in a letter of 1416 by Manetti's fellow Florentine Poggio Bracciolini. In describing his rudimentary efforts to learn the language of the prophets, Bracciolini does not see any intrinsic worth in Hebrew other than how it explains the way Jerome translated the Bible.[13] Manetti's principal biographer and close friend, Vespasiano da Bisticci, informs us that Manetti learned Hebrew for two reasons: to read Sacred Scripture in the original language and to dispute with learned Jews about the supe-

riority of Christianity. These stated goals fit well with what is known about Manetti. Though remaining a layman, he had received an education in theology and had acquired a reputation for piety. As for disputing with Jews, Manetti was a vigorous evangelist who, as early as 1448, began a theological work arguing for the superiority of Christianity. Entitled *Against the Jews and the Gentiles,* this incomplete work, ten books of which were finished from an original design of twenty, is in the *Adversus Iudaeos* (Against the Jews) tradition that goes back to the roots of Early Christianity and which flourished unabated in the early Quattrocento.[14]

Manetti's learning of Hebrew may very well have been due to his own reading of Jerome's letters and the prologues to his biblical translations, where the Church Father vigorously champions a return to what he called Hebrew Truth (*Hebraica veritas*).[15] But it may be worth considering another motive. It has been suggested that our Florentine, given the ambitious nature of humanism, wished to compete with a Venetian nobleman by the name of Marco Lippomano. Further evidence has recently come to light regarding letters that Lippomano exchanged in Hebrew with a learned Jew in 1422. Manetti himself tells us that this now little-known humanist and one-time duke of Crete was well versed in Hebrew as well as Latin and Greek. The example Lippomano presented of a trilingual Italian humanist may well have functioned as a stimulus for the Florentine's studies in the language of the prophets.[16]

If Manetti did not receive encouragement in studying Hebrew from Bruni, he would have been exposed to a more favorable opinion on the matter from Traversari, who had acquired manuscripts in Hebrew and may also have inspired his pupil to develop his Hebraic interests. Regardless of what drove him to learn Hebrew, Manetti acquired the language from several teachers. It is alleged that he was able to sing and even converse in Hebrew. With one of

his instructors, a learned Jew by the name of Immanuel de San Miniato, he read the entire Hebrew Bible as well as rabbinical commentaries, many of which he personally owned.[17] Manetti, through his remarkable efforts to master Hebrew, has won recognition as a major figure in the Christian study of Hebrew, otherwise known as Christian Hebraism, in its transition from the Late Middle Ages to the Reformation.

In considering the work itself, it is worthwhile lingering over its complete title, which is *Against the Critics of His New Translation of the Psalms in Five Apologetical Books* (*In V libros adversus sue nove Psalterii traductionis obtrectatores apologeticos*). The emphasis on critics suggests that Manetti's treatise will descend into the kind of bitter tirade that so often arose among humanists competing for position and privilege. But in Book I Manetti quickly abandons a direct confrontation with his critical opposition in order to pursue a broad historical, philological, and translational approach, presenting a unified exposition of the problems inherent in translating the Psalms. Frequently, scholars have discussed only Book V, dealing specifically with translation, although there is no evidence that the last book ever circulated independently. Manetti's earlier historical (Books I and II) and philological analyses (Books III and IV) will act as a lengthy prelude to his direct comments on the art of translation in the final book of the treatise.

At the outset, Manetti is concerned with charges laid against his biblical translation. Specifically, he mentions the attack, echoing Bruni's earlier remarks, that it is both useless and arrogant to compete with Jerome's biblical translations. Manetti never identifies who is actually criticizing his Psalms translation, and none of the criticism survives. This has even led to speculation that the anonymous critics did not exist, thus making the entire work function rhetorically as a proleptic exercise to ward off future criticism of his translation.[18] As a seasoned orator, Manetti may be following the procedures of classical oratory, where the suppres-

sion of the name of an opponent is not unusual.[19] Yet Manetti does in fact provide some indirect clues as to who his critics might be. He claims they are Christians rather than Jews and that they do not possess theological training. Given that Manetti began his biblical translation under the encouragement of Pope Nicholas V himself, it makes sense that the criticism would have come from humanist circles rather than theological ones. But which humanist critics is he alluding to? Three contemporary disputes provide background on the tensions between humanism and theology. In each conflict, Manetti was familiar with at least one of the principals. Poggio Bracciolini, in a celebrated quarrel with Lorenzo Valla, had accused the latter of insulting Jerome.[20] Around the same time, two Greek émigrés, George of Trebizond and Cardinal Bessarion, clashed over the wording of a passage in the Gospels.[21] Interestingly, George of Trebizond also worked in Naples at the court of King Alfonso. In the *Apologeticus,* Manetti cites at length one of George's patristic translations without acknowledgment (2.13–26), while later directly praising Bessarion (5.42), the only living humanist mentioned in the work. Finally, it has been suggested that Leon Battista Alberti's savage satire, *Momus,* is directed at Nicholas V's extravagant building program at Rome and the incompetent experts who surround him. Insofar as Manetti was the pope's biographer, it is not difficult to see that he would be one of the targets of Alberti.[22] If humanists, in general, avoided the shoals of theological speculation, nonetheless there were enough controversies to fuel criticism of Manetti's treatise.

The *Apologeticus* opens with a rhetorical tour de force: thirteen famous authors and thirty-four of their unsparing critics are named. If Homer and Aristotle were opposed in their day, it is not surprising that Manetti himself is now receiving criticism. In listing this impressive catalog, Manetti introduces five major forms of writing: poetry, oratory, history, philosophy, and theology. This schema will be of considerable importance near the end of the

treatise, when there is a discussion of how different subjects conform to different translation styles. After this opening display, he abruptly changes focus from the subject of criticism to biblical history (1.22–42).[23] Manetti argues that the Psalms must be seen within the entire context of the Hebrew Bible. Scripture, subjected to a historical analysis, becomes an object to be examined rather than passively accepted. In his examination, Manetti is critical of received tradition. First, he reports the belief that the seventy Septuagint translators authored the Chronicles. He then goes on to modify this view by referencing his knowledge of Hebrew commentaries. He cites the noted medieval Jewish exegete Shlomo Yitzhaki, of Troyes, best known by the acronym Rashi, that the Chronicles were written by Ezra rather than Greeks (1.38).[24]

In his discussion, Manetti tackles issues pertaining to the organization, genre, and number of psalms, concluding that the Psalter was originally divided into five books (1.48). In asserting that the Psalms should be considered as five books rather than one, it is significant that Manetti sides with Hebrew scholars against Jerome.[25] In doing so, he has recourse to the topos of modesty, a favorite rhetorical device of his. Assuring us that he does not wish to appear arrogant, Manetti claims that he is not qualified to judge between the Hebrews and Jerome. However, he nonetheless implies that Jerome is wrong if one consults the Hebraic text.

Emboldened by correcting one Church Father, he then proceeds to improve upon another. In Eusebius' *Preparation for the Gospel*, the Septuagint, or the Greek translation of the Hebrew Bible, was said to have been preceded by an earlier version. In the *Preparation*, the bishop of Caesarea had reported that Plato, relying on a pre-Septuagintal translation, was none other than an Athenian Moses. In contrast, Manetti believes that such a translation could never have existed, because Greeks of Plato's era, accustomed to the purity of Attic diction, would have been aesthetically

repelled by biblical Hebrew. In this way, the Florentine has sought diplomatically to disagree with two authoritative Church Fathers. He has not accepted patristic accounts passively, but exercised his critical judgment in evaluating their claims. Implicitly, Manetti is arguing that he is a greater authority, at least with respect to certain details, than either Jerome or Eusebius. Having clarified that the Septuagint was the first biblical translation, he will now devote Book II to adjudicating claims of how it was composed and why it diverges from the Hebrew Bible.

Manetti continues his indirect approach in the second book. Instead of stating outright his preference for Jerome's pragmatic evaluation of the worth of the Septuagint, he relates at considerable length the legend of that venerable translation in addition to its later defense as the product of divine inspiration.[26] Only after this extended prelude does he proceed to inform us about Jerome's career and translation. In his quotation of Eusebius' account of the creation of the Septuagint (2.13–26), Manetti relates the extraordinary tale of how seventy-two elders translated the Hebrew Bible at the court of the Alexandrian king Ptolemy Philadelphus. So as not to arouse the suspicion of collusion, the interpreters labored in isolated cells. Lo and behold, each translator, guided by the Holy Spirit, produced the same version! Following this, Manetti discusses the controversy between Augustine and Jerome over the accuracy of the Septuagint. He provides virtually two entire chapters of the *City of God*, a text which Vespasiano claims he had committed to memory, recounting Augustine's view that though the Septuagint contained textual errors, its composition was guided by the Holy Spirit. Suddenly, more than halfway through Book II, he relays Jerome's withering reply to the notion of the Septuagint's divine inspiration: "It is one thing to be a prophet, another to be a translator" (2.48). In other words, the Hebrew original is to be preferred to the inaccurate Greek translation. Once again, Manetti

dissimulates by protesting he cannot arbitrate between Augustine and Jerome's views (2.49–50), when it is clear that his own retranslation of the Psalms bears witness to his preference for the Hieronymian analysis over the Augustinian one in regard to the Septuagint.

Why does Manetti go to the trouble of recounting at length two defenses of the hallowed Greek translation before finally privileging Jerome's skepticism about the legend? First, he is acutely aware that Jerome's translation of the Psalms from the Septuagint has been chosen by the Church of Rome rather than his Hebrew version, which is known as the version *iuxta Hebraeos* (according to the Hebrews).[27] In narrating the credulous accounts of Eusebius and Augustine, he can recount the miraculous story of how the Septuagint came into being and how, through the efforts of Ptolemy Philadelphus, it became the jewel of his renowned Alexandrian library (2.36), without threatening the reverence given to two Church Fathers.

Second, the Septuagint myth points to the ultimate aims and ambitions that Manetti had for his biblical translation. To comprehend exactly what those were, we must turn to the biography he wrote of his one-time patron, Pope Nicholas V (1397–1455). In *The Achievements of Nicholas V,* written shortly after the pontiff's death and hence just before the *Apologeticus,* Manetti tells us that His Holiness wanted to establish a Vatican Library that would rival Ptolemy Philadelphus' fabled library. If the passage where this is mentioned is examined closely, it reveals that, just after the parallel has been drawn between Nicholas V and the Hellenistic king, Manetti proceeds to enumerate the many translations the pope has commissioned for his prospective Vatican Library, ranging from poetry and history to philosophy and theology. So far, so good. In doing this, he suggests a similarity between how his papal patron recruited translators and the Ptolemaic commission of the

Septuagint. However, once these actions have been duly narrated, Manetti suddenly makes a breathtakingly self-promoting gesture. The humble biographer interrupts the narrative dealing with the glories of his subject, Nicholas V, in order to relate his own personal activity under the pontiff. He tells us that on arriving in Rome and seeing other translators busy at work, he decided to contribute by composing his theological work, *Against the Jews and the Gentiles,* and a new translation of the Bible. In placing his own endeavors at the very end of the list of translations that Nicholas had requested, Manetti is clearly implying that his theological work and his biblical translation, when completed, would represent the pinnacle of the pope's quest to imitate the achievements of the Ptolemaic ruler. In ascending order of importance, Nicholas V's library would contain esteemed translations of poetry, history, philosophy, theology and, representing the acme, Manetti's revised Scripture. In other words, just as Ptolemy's Septuagint outshone anything else in the Alexandrian library, so too Manetti's biblical translation would give the greatest luster to Nicholas V's envisioned Vatican Library. Unfortunately for Manetti, Pope Nicholas V's death ended the dream of both a reconstituted Vatican Library — formally established only later by Sixtus IV — and the prominent role his revised translation would play in that envisioned monument to learning. However, though his papal successor did not share Nicholas V's humanist objectives, Manetti was still able to salvage a portion of what he had imagined by moving to the Neapolitan court. Ultimately, with the *Adversus Iudaeos* left incomplete, the Psalms translation represents what he managed to accomplish from his work on the Hebrew Bible, with the *Apologeticus* acting as its defense.[28]

If the treatment here of the Septuagint legend provides insight into Manetti's motives, the second half of Book II is devoted to Jerome's efforts to provide a correct translation of the Psalms. On the one hand, Jerome's translation of the Psalter from Septuagintal

Greek was done to appease traditionalists. On the other hand, to translate *iuxta Hebraeos* provided greater fidelity to Holy Writ. Though Jerome receives the greatest praise possible as a defender of Christianity, Manetti shows that the cherished Church Father ultimately failed to silence Jewish critics as to the inaccuracies of his translation. It will be up to Manetti to provide what Jerome was not able to accomplish, namely, a perfected Latin Psalter.

In detailing Jewish criticism of Jerome, Manetti reveals a darker side to his whole enterprise. Although it must be granted that our author, unlike his contemporaries, took the time to learn Hebrew, thereby exposing himself to the possible criticism that he was too partial to Judaism, he nevertheless indulges in highly defamatory remarks about Jews and their culture and retails fantasies about their implacable vindictiveness. Apologists for Manetti can no doubt take refuge in the rejoinder that it is futile to judge historical actors outside the context of their own times. On this subject, nuance is definitely required. In his polemical work, *Against the Jews and the Gentiles,* Manetti is eager to praise the uprightness of Moses in the biblical past in contrast to the alleged dishonesty of later Jews.[29] Nevertheless, it cannot but be repellent to modern readers that Manetti exploits the knowledge he received from Jewish teachers in order to castigate their own faith, a gesture repeated ad nauseam in the coming century by Christian Hebraists. If it is conventional now to differentiate between doctrinal opposition to Judaism and outright anti-Semitism, our Florentine humanist blurs the distinction.[30]

In Books III and IV of the *Apologeticus,* Manetti is concerned with supplying a correct text of the Psalms. Earlier readers of Jerome's translation were well aware of its deficiencies. Medieval scholars made lists of errors, known as *correctiones*. However, what they failed to do was compare Jerome's translations with the original sources in Greek and Hebrew. The critical use of sources would have to await the arrival of the most radical of Quattrocento

humanists, Lorenzo Valla. It was Valla's crucial insight to evaluate the accuracy of the Vulgate by having recourse to the Greek text. Valla reoriented biblical study away from scholastic interpretation in order to emphasize rhetorical and philological questions. He began this work more than a decade before Manetti undertook his revision of the Psalms. His labors are represented in two works, known as the *Collatio* and the *Annotations*.[31] The latter work would later exert a powerful influence on Erasmus, who on discovering the manuscript, prepared it for publication in 1505, before going on to publish his groundbreaking edition of the New Testament in 1516. On the Hebrew Bible, however, Valla was silent. Manetti was Valla's contemporary and they both overlapped as apostolic secretaries in Rome. Although there is no direct evidence that Manetti knew of Valla's conjectures, it is highly unlikely that he would not have heard of them and very probable that he actually used Valla's work in preparing his own translation of the New Testament.[32]

In Book III, Manetti compares Jerome's Latin translations from the Greek and the Hebrew. If Jerome's Latin version from the Hebrew is a translation, then the saint's version from the Septuagint is a translation of a translation, which explains Manetti's preference for the former over the latter. He proceeds as follows. First, he lists where the Latin version from the Septuagint adds words, phrases, or entire lines that do not correspond to Jerome's version from the Hebrew (following 3.1, *Concerning Additions*). Then he lists those places in the Latin/Greek version that omit words, phrases, or entire lines from the Hebrew version (following 3.42, *Concerning Omissions*). In listing these additions and omissions, Manetti is judging Jerome's translation of the Septuagint in light of his version from the Hebrew. That is to say, he is comparing Latin with Latin. In Book IV, he lists faulty translations and the way in which the titles differ in both versions.

In these rather mechanical analyses, Manetti provides an orderly philological investigation of each one of the one hundred and fifty psalms. It should be noted that Manetti's method here differs considerably from that of Lorenzo Valla in his *Collatio* and *Annotations*. Unlike his fellow humanist, Manetti does not tackle specific textual problems or provide explanatory glosses; nor does his list of verbal variants reveal a particularly critical spirit. Moreover, he does not cite the actual Hebrew text of the Old Testament, as Valla does with the Greek text of the New Testament. Rather, he simply compares one Latin translation (from the Septuagint) with another Latin translation (from the Hebrew). Or does he?

Before verifying what Manetti claims he is doing, it is worthwhile considering how the Psalms translation appears in relation to his treatise. In all three extant manuscripts, the Psalms translation comes before the *Apologeticus*. From the order in which they appear, translation before treatise, it is clear that readers were meant to have read the Psalms first before considering Manetti's defense. The primary source takes precedence over Manetti's arguments in favor of his version. Practice comes before theory. Two of the manuscripts present an unusual reading experience. Each contains a triple translation laid out in columns that comprise, reading left to right, Jerome's translation from the Septuagint followed by Jerome and Manetti's versions from the original Hebrew.[33]

At the beginning of Book III, Manetti shows how Jerome's Septuagintal version of the Psalms contains additions and omissions not found in the Hebrew Bible version. For example, Jerome's Septuagintal version of Psalm 1.2 reads, "Not so the impious, not so (*Non sic impii, non sic*)," whereas his Hebrew version merely reads "Not so the impious," without the repetition of "not so (*non sic*)." All seems in order. When we turn to Book IV, and its discussion of "unsuitable translations (*ea que aliene traducta*)," we would expect to see a comparison of Jerome's two versions of his

translation. Once again, if we use Psalm 1 as an example, Manetti suggests that the first line has an error. The first verse of the Septuagint reads, "Blessed is the man who has not followed the counsel of the impious and has not stood in the path of sinners, and has not sat in the chair of pestilence (*Beatus vir, qui non abiit in consilio impiorum, et in via peccatorum non stetit, et in cathedra pestilentiae non sedit*)." The phrase "chair of pestilence (*in cathedra pestilentiae*)" is said to be incorrect. We might expect that he will correct the "chair of pestilence (*cathedra pestilentiae*)," from the Septuagintal version, with "chair of the mockers (*cathedra derisorum*)," to reflect Jerome's Hebrew version. Instead, Manetti offers us . . . his *own* version from the Hebrew! Instead of Jerome's "chair of the mockers (*cathedra derisorum*)," we have Manetti's "seat of the mockers (*sede derisorum*)."[34] Here, Manetti's cautious indirection transforms into something closer to subterfuge. Essentially, Manetti establishes the expectation that he will be comparing Jerome's versions, when, in fact, he compares Jerome's Septuagintal version with his own. For the conscientious reader, whose reading of the *Apologeticus* would have occurred *after* that of the tricolumnar Psalms translation, the conclusion would be unavoidable. If all three versions are carefully compared, then Jerome's version is being replaced by that of Manetti. If the revered Jerome could not be openly revised, then Manetti will take refuge in this subtle solution.[35] At this point, it is worth noting that Manetti, in his political career in Florence, had frequently been entrusted with sensitive ambassadorial duties. This practical experience may very well have assisted him in expertly navigating the contentious issue of biblical translation in the presence of a standard authority such as Jerome. Compared to the controversies aroused by Valla and, later, Erasmus, in their biblical annotations, Manetti offers a resourceful solution to confronting an entrenched authority. But this is not all.

In providing a corrected version of Jerome, Manetti has greater ambitions than the mere exercise of rhetorical ingenuity. His

translation of the Psalms, as we have seen, was envisaged as part of a complete biblical translation, which, if the commission had been fully executed, would have crowned Nicholas V's blueprint for an authoritative new Vatican Library. The rigorous compilation of corrections, assiduously itemized in the *Apologeticus,* significantly realizes another way in which Nicholas V's foundation for his great collection would have rivaled Ptolemy's Alexandrian library: the preparation of authorized texts. It was well known that the Alexandrian library sought to acquire the best possible texts for its collection and housed editors who scrupulously refined texts such as the epics of Homer. This editorial practice helps to explain why Manetti inserts a digression in Book II relating how the Athenian tyrant Pisistratus established an edition of Homer (2.30–33). He equates the seventy-two editors supposedly hired by Pisistratus with the same number who translated the Septuagint, thereby implying a similarity between the two projects. Manetti, in improving upon Jerome's versions, would have provided an official version of the Psalms for Nicholas V.[36]

After establishing the historical and philological reasons for his translation of the Psalms in the first four books, Manetti is finally able to address the question of translation in Book V. Before doing so, however, he begins with a lengthy introduction dedicated to King Alfonso (5.1–19). Manetti's translation of the Bible may have begun under the patronage of Pope Nicholas V, but his translation and its defense were actually completed under the Neapolitan king. Although Manetti had been asked to stay on in Rome after Nicholas' death, he chose to move to Naples to work for the monarch. This decision underlines the importance of patronage for Renaissance humanists and, considering the lavish compensation he earned at the Neapolitan court, the raw value of money. Manetti was paid, in fact, considerably more than the eminent humanist George of Trebizond, in addition to receiving favorable commercial privileges in Naples. That he chose Alfonso's court

over remaining in Rome or attempting a return to Florence is notable. In addition to financial gain, Manetti had the benefit of working for an early example of the Renaissance prince. It might be tempting to overidealize King Alfonso, as Vespasiano predictably does, but even when allowance is made for the hyperbolic praise typical of the Quattrocento, it is clear that Alfonso had given support to a host of humanists from Biondo Flavio to Panormita.[37] No doubt such support was not disinterested. Humanists helped his regime gain legitimacy and prestige. But if Alfonso did not have the vision of Nicholas V, he was nonetheless a supporter of Valla's philological innovations. The initial relationship between Manetti and Alfonso had been rocky due to several orations penned against the monarch by the Florentine. Eventually, Manetti came round to appreciating the king and dedicated *On the Dignity and Excellence of Man* to him.[38]

After the remarks devoted to Alfonso, Manetti is finally ready to offer his theoretical views on translation. These were not formed in isolation, since he was able to draw on a lengthy tradition of Ciceronian, Hieronymian, and humanist theoretical writings on the subject.[39] Although he will borrow heavily from all three sources, he begins from the humanist perspective. It is worth briefly discussing this background. As is usually the case, it is Petrarch who inaugurates this tradition through his desire to read Homer in the original Greek. Despite failing to learn the Homeric language, Petrarch and his disciple Boccaccio commissioned a Latin prose translation of the Greek epics. On reading this version, both Italian poets felt extremely disappointed with the uninspiring results. The promised translation proved to be less satisfying than imagined.[40] Another of Petrarch's Florentine disciples, Coluccio Salutati, is the first humanist to present actual remarks on how to translate. In a brief letter to a younger correspondent, the future chancellor of Florence urges the would-be translator of Homer not to make the same mistakes as his predecessor. Salutati

counsels Antonio Loschi to avoid the wretched word-for-word version by Leonzio Pilato. Instead, he memorably recommends setting the text ablaze with little fires.[41] But the Florentine statesman, like his protégé Loschi, was ignorant of Greek. In order to remedy this defect, Salutati took a decisive step in the development of Renaissance humanism. He invited the Byzantine scholar Manuel Chrysoloras in 1397 to teach in his native city. Although Chrysoloras would spend only three years in Florence, his presence there meant that many pupils would receive invaluable tutelage in Greek. Two key documents bear witness to this. In a preface from 1416, Cencio de' Rustici reports Chrysoloras' view that translation is either literal or free or follows the sense-unit.[42] Around a decade later, Leonardo Bruni, Chrysoloras' most famous pupil, would compose *On the Correct Way to Translate*, the first surviving treatise on translation since antiquity.[43]

In his opening remarks on translation theory, Manetti borrows liberally from Bruni's work (5.19–36), but without acknowledgment. Indeed, he frequently has recourse to the very words of *On the Correct Way to Translate*. Manetti faithfully records the thoughts of his former master in recommending, for example, that one must have a thorough command of both the source and the target languages and be attuned to the rhythm and uniqueness of the author. What are we to make of this blatant plagiarism? It has been well documented that humanist culture was less fastidious than contemporary scholarship in terms of acknowledging attribution. Viewed in a certain light, Manetti's wholesale use of Bruni can be seen as an act of homage.[44] His use of his teacher's very words suggests that Bruni's remarks on translation had become the consensus by the mid-1450s. And yet Manetti, though reluctant to name Bruni, is in no way hesitant to identify other contemporaries, such as Cardinal Bessarion and Ambrogio Traversari. Moreover, his respect for the elder humanist was not unconditional, for he had embarked several times on redoing biographical

works and translations that Bruni had already completed.[45] If Manetti felt the need to revise Bruni's fairly loose translations of Aristotle, then Book V of the *Apologeticus* should also be seen as a revision of Bruni.

It is clear from reading Manetti's funeral oration for the long-time Florentine chancellor that he esteemed Bruni's talents in translation. But it is instructive to see how the pupil praises his master. Bruni is prized for translating poets, historians, orators, and philosophers,[46] which accounts for four of the five categories of writing that were dealt with at the beginning of the *Apologeticus*. As for the fifth and most prestigious category, theology, Bruni has nothing to say. If Manetti relies on the late humanist for secular writings, he will have to venture himself into the realm of biblical translation, with the assistance of Jerome. But the frequent appeals to Jerome are accompanied by an equal number of overtures toward Cicero.

Literal translation is rejected, on the authority of Horace and Jerome, and translation according to sense is recommended through reference to Cicero. Manetti then praises the philosophical and theological works of Bessarion and Traversari. But Manetti soon transcends the sterile debate between literal and sense-based translation. Crucial to his thinking is the distinction between the relatively free style of translation allowed translators of poetry, oratory, and history, compared to the stricter method recommended to those who translate philosophy and theology.

When it comes to the latter two subjects, Manetti may reject the medieval translations of Aristotle or Pseudo-Dionysius the Areopagite in favor of versions by his contemporaries, but he also follows Cicero, who allows himself less freedom in translating philosophy than he does oratory. In his selective use of Jerome's writing on translation, *On the Best Kind of Translating*, Manetti will privilege the patristic writer's preference for sense translation rather than his more mystical reflections.[47] A quotation such as

"For a translation made from one language into another word for word buries the sense and strangles it as grass destroys crops" (5.61) is emphasized, while more enigmatic utterances from Jerome, like his celebrated "the order of words is also a mystery (*et verborum ordo mysterium est*)," go unnoticed.[48] In general, Manetti counsels that philosophical and theological works ought not be broad and rambling (*lata ac vaga* [5.52]). Frequently, he will resort to spatial metaphors when discussing his precepts. The most arresting passage in Book V occurs when he once again uses the terms *vagus* and *latus* to urge translators not to wander at will over wide and open fields (5.77). He repeats this injunction a third time near the end of the treatise, when advising that it is not fitting that translations of Scripture wander (*vaga* [5.82]). Ultimately, he recommends that translators ought to strive for the golden mean between medieval literalism and Brunian freedom in order not to "incline to or favor either extreme (*ut neutram in partem declinare ac propendere videantur*)," but hew to the "middle and safe way (*sed medium et tutum* [5.77])." But Manetti's middle way is nuanced. For he claims that he wishes to translate the Psalms almost literally (*paene ad verbum*).[49] In so doing, the Florentine reorients the translation of the sacred toward greater fidelity. Manetti's concluding remarks resignedly explain why the Church of Rome prefers the Septuagintal Psalter over a translation *iuxta Hebraeos*. The Septuagint occupies a prestigious position as the first translation, as the one favored by the Apostles, as the version consecrated by legend, and as the one deemed most beautiful. And yet anyone who reads these remarks is well aware that Manetti's translation of the Psalms and his lengthy defense subtly contradict the Church's preference for the Septuagint.

Manetti's pioneering role as a Christian Hebraist and biblical translator, though remarkable, is ultimately only of historical value. His biblical scholarship, preeminent in his time, has long been surpassed. His role as a translation theorist, however, tran-

scends the merely antiquarian. Biblical translation remains a live question, as evidenced by the ongoing translation of Scripture into over two thousand world languages. The last generation has seen an astonishing amount of activity in translation theory — witness the emergence of the discipline known as Translation Studies. Gradually, the picture of early modern translation theory in Latin has come into clearer focus.[50] It is hoped that this edition of the *Apologeticus* will contribute to a greater awareness of how fertile Renaissance translation theory was. And is.[51] Manetti's treatise still remains one of the few extensive treatises to be authored by an actual practicing translator.[52] *A Translator's Defense* still has the power to challenge received ideas on translation, especially translation of the sacred.

This volume had its origins in a presentation I made on Manetti's treatise in a memorable graduate seminar on translation theory at New York University taught by Richard Sieburth. From the outset, Richard has, with his customary generosity, warmly encouraged the publication of this work. For his long dedication to translation theory and practice, this book is dedicated to him. Given the scope and size of Manetti's work, I asked a longtime collaborator, Mark Young, if he would take on the challenge of translating the text. Throughout the process, Mark has shared his fascination with the intricacies of Manettiana. He is most definitely the *miglior fabbro*. I am grateful to the I Tatti Library's two readers. I have adopted Andrew Dyck's helpful suggestions regarding the text, notes, and introduction as well as Daniel Stein Kokin's insightful remarks on the introduction. In addition, I would like to express my thanks to the past and present chairs and directors of graduate studies in French at NYU for their encouragement: Tom Bishop, Benoit Bolduc, Denis Hollier, Lucien Nouis, Judith G. Miller, and Sarah Kay. Timothy Reiss provided meaningful support in the initial stages, as did Emily Apter and

the late Michel Beaujour. Daniel Stein Kokin generously shared a draft version of his valuable article on Marco Lippomano, which introduced me to Beltramo di Mignanello's work. Similarly, David Marsh kindly allowed me to see a draft version of his introduction to a forthcoming edition of Manetti's *Contra Iudaeos* in this series. A doctoral fellowship from the Social Sciences and Humanities Research Council of Canada provided time for research. Natalie Oeltjen at the Centre for Reformation and Renaissance Studies at the University of Toronto provided a welcome sanctuary to conduct research. I would also like to thank Annet den Haan and Stefano Baldassarri for sharing recent research on Manetti. The findings of works from 2014 onward, though cited and consulted with profit, have not been fully integrated due to their appearance after this edition was in press. Dylan, Gloria, Kerry, Lisa, Magdalena, Sean, and Xavier are to be thanked for enduring my endless conversations on a too little-known work. We have benefited from three generations of Manetti scholars among whom I would especially like to thank Paul Botley, whose work introduced me to Manetti, and Alfonso De Petris, whose edition of the *Apologeticus* we have reproduced here. Finally, I must thank James Hankins and the Editorial Board of I Tatti for accepting our proposal for an edition of the *Apologeticus*. I was first introduced to the delights of Quattrocento translation theory through reading James' translation of Bruni's *De interpretatione recta*. For this volume, I have benefitted greatly from his editorial expertise. All errors are ours.

Myron McShane

This project had its beginnings in conversations I had with Myron McShane over the course of several years about Quattrocento humanist Latin texts. I am grateful to Myron for introducing me to this period. This project took root when John Grant suggested to me that Myron and I contact James Hankins about the possibility of our contributing to the I Tatti Renaissance Library. I would like

to thank James for his supportive and thoughtful direction on this project and for his considerable scholarship, specifically his work on Leonardo Bruni. My thanks as well to John for that initial vote of confidence and generous support over the last two years. He has been kind enough to review my translation of Books I, II, and V, and I have adopted essentially all of his many corrections and suggestions. I would also like to express a debt of gratitude to Andrew Dyck for his many improvements to my translation. Any infelicities of course remain my responsibility. I would like to thank my wife, Joanne; my sons, David, Roman, and Marko; and my parents, David and Sandra, for their profound support. The students and the faculty of the Abelard School are to be thanked for their unflagging enthusiasm for debate, consensus, and more debate.

Mark Young

NOTES

1. Since in the work's rubrics the adjective *apologeticus* modifies the individual books in the five-book work, it might seem more proper to refer to the work in Latin as the *Libri apologetici*. De Petris' title of *Apologeticus* is sanctioned, however, by Manetti's own usage at 1.19 and 5.90.

2. The Theban archbishop Simone Atumano (1318?–d. before 1387) composed a work entitled *Biblia Triglotta*, which included versions of the Greek New Testament in Hebrew and Latin, although this work appears to have vanished in the sixteenth century. A manuscript in the Biblioteca Nazionale Marciana may contain an extract from his Greek translation of the Hebrew Bible. On Atumano, see Kenneth M. Setton, *The Papacy and the Levant (1204–1571)*, vol. 1 (Philadelphia: The American Philosophical Society, 1976), 469–71, and Giorgio Fedalto, *Simone Atumano* (Brescia: Paideia Editrice, 2007). There are indications that the fourteenth-century English scholar and Hebraist Adam of Easton (d. 1397) composed a work on translation, *De diversitate translationum* (as well as a complete new

translation of the Hebrew Bible into Latin). Nothing has survived and perhaps never existed. See Judith Olszowy-Schlanger, "Robert Wakefield and the Medieval Background of Hebrew Scholarship in Renaissance England," in *Hebrew to Latin, Latin to Hebrew,* ed. Giulio Busi (Berlin: Aragno, 2006), 81–82.

3. For a detailed summary of Manetti's life, see the first volume dedicated to him in this I Tatti series, *Giannozzo Manetti, Biographical Writings,* ed. Stefano Baldassarri and Rolf Bagemihl (Cambridge, MA: Harvard University Press, 2003), vii–xix, and Simona Foà's entry on him in the *Dizionario biografico degli Italiani* (Rome: Istituto della Enciclopedia Italiana, 2007), 68:613–17 (henceforward *DBI*). For the historical writing, see *Giannozzo Manetti. Historia Pistoriensis,* ed. Stefano Baldassarri et al. (Florence: SISMEL, 2011); on his orations, H. W. Wittschier, *Giannozzo Manetti, Das Corpus der "Orationes"* (Cologne: Böhlau, 1968), and more recently Brian Maxson, *The Humanist World of Renaissance Florence* (Cambridge: Cambridge University Press, 2014); in addition to the lives composed by Manetti in *Biographical Writings,* there are generous excerpts from his papal life, *On the Achievements of Nicholas V,* in Smith and O'Connor's *Building the Kingdom,* 361–484 (complete citations of works cited briefly in this Introduction can be found in the Bibliography). The full Latin text has been edited by Anna Modigliani, *De vita ac gestis Nicolai Quinti summi pontificis* (Rome: Istituto storico italiano per il Medio Evo, 2005).

4. Although Manetti's biblical translations remain currently in manuscript, Annet den Haan's recent dissertation provides a valuable edition of his translation of the New Testament. See "Giannozzo Manetti's New Testament," pt. 3, 1–355. It should be added that the editor of the Amsterdam edition of Erasmus' New Testament translation frequently cites Manetti's New Testament translation. See Erasmus, *Opera omnia,* vol. 6.2, ed. Andrew Brown (Amsterdam: Elsevier, 2001), 5–6.

5. Vespasiano da Bisticci wrote two versions of Manetti's life in Italian, the *Vita di Meser Giannozzo Manetti, Fiorentino* and the *Comentario della vita di Messer Giannozzo Manetti,* the first of which can be found in English in *The Vespasiano Memoirs: Lives of Illustrious Men of the XVth Century,* trans.

W. G. and E. Waters (Toronto: University of Toronto Press, 1997 [a reprint of the original 1926 edition]), 372–94; the Italian texts are in Vespasiano's *Le Vite*, ed. A. Greco (Florence: Istituto nazionale di studi sul Rinascimento, 1976), 1:485–538 and 2:513–627. A Latin adaptation of the lengthier *Comento* is by Naldo Naldi, *Vita Jannotii Manetti* in *Rerum Italicarum Scriptores*, ed. L. A. Muratori (Milan, 1732), 20:521–608. For the life in verse, see *Manettiana: La biografia anonima in terzine e altri documenti inediti su Giannozzo Manetti*, ed. Stefano Baldassarri and Bruno Figliuolo (Rome: Roma nel Rinascimento, 2010), 81–167. The comparison to Alberti is in Paolo Cortesi, *De hominibus doctis dialogus*, ed. and trans. Maria Teresa Graziosi (Rome: Bonacci, 1973), 38.

6. For his reception in Spain, see Jeremy N. H. Lawrance, *Un episodio del proto-humanismo español: tres opúscolos de Nuño de Guzmán y Giannozzo Manetti* (Salamanca: Biblioteca Espagñola del Siglo XV, 1989), and in the European Renaissance, Christoph Dröge, "The Pope's Favorite Humanist in the Land of the Reformation: On the Reception of the Works of Giannozzo Manetti in Sixteenth-Century Germany and France," in *Acta Conventus Neo-Latini Bariensis: Proceedings of the Ninth International Congress of Neo-Latin Studies* (Tempe, AZ: Medieval and Renaissance Texts and Studies, 1998), 217–24. For a list of sixteenth- to nineteenth-century editions of Manetti's works, see Wittschier, *Corpus*, 208–10. A modern bibliography is in Foà, "Manetti," in *DBI*. Recent scholarship on the *Apologeticus* includes Fubini, "L'ebraismo"; Bergquist, "Christian Hebrew Scholarship"; and Arjo Vanderjagt, "*Ad fontes!*: The Early Humanist Concern for the *Hebraica veritas*, in *Hebrew Bible/Old Testament: The History of Its Interpretation*, ed. Magne Saebø, 2 vols. (Göttingen: Vandenhoeck and Ruprecht, 2008), 2:154–89.

7. On the nineteenth-century devaluation of Manetti, see the influential remarks of one of the founders of modern humanist philology, Georg Voigt, *Die Wiederbelebung des classischen Alterthums* (Berlin: Reimer, 1859), 172. The positive revaluation of Manetti in English begins with Trinkaus, *Image and Likeness*, who followed Sebastiano Garofolo's foundational study, "Gli umanisti italiani del secolo XV e la Bibbia." Both works concentrate on the *Apologeticus*. A notable example of widespread interest in our author is the publication of the proceedings of an international con-

ference on diverse apects of his *oeuvre, Dignitas et excellentia hominis: Atti del Convegno internazionale di studi su Giannozo Manetti,* ed. Stefano Baldassarri (Florence: Le Lettere, 2008).

8. Vespasiano, *Vite,* 1:486.

9. The life of Socrates is in Manetti, *Biographical Writings,* 176–233. On this work, see James Hankins, "Manetti's Socrates and the Socrateses of Antiquity," in *Dignitas et excellentia hominis,* 203–19.

10. See Eugene Rice's *Saint Jerome in the Renaissance* (Baltimore: The Johns Hopkins University Press, 1985), in particular chapter three, "The Cult," 49–83.

11. The letter, dated September 12, 1442, is translated in Gordon Griffiths, James Hankins, and David Thompson, eds., *The Humanism of Leonardo Bruni* (Binghamton, NY: Medieval and Renaissance Texts and Studies, 1987), 333–36; Latin text in Leonardo Bruni, *Epistolarum Libri VIII, recensente Laurentio Mehus* (1741), ed. James Hankins, 2 vols. (Rome: Edizioni di Storia e Letteratura, 2007), 2:160–64 (IX.12). It is discussed in Botley, *Latin Translation,* 101–2, and Trinkaus, *Image and Likeness,* 578–80.

12. On the medieval study of Hebrew, see the classic study by Beryl Smalley, *The Study of the Bible in the Middle Ages,* 3rd ed. (Oxford: Blackwell, 1983), and, in particular for the Psalms, Deborah Goodwin, *Take Hold of the Robe of a Jew: Herbert of Bosham's Christian Hebraism* (Leiden: Brill, 2006). For views on the Jews in Manetti's hometown, see Umberto Cassuto, *Gli Ebrei a Firenze nel età del Rinascimento* (Florence: Tipografia Galletti e Cocci, 1918), 9–10.

13. A translation is in P. W. G. Gordan's *Two Renaissance Book Hunters: The Letters of Poggio Bracciolini to Nicolaus de Niccolis* (New York: Columbia University Press, 1974), 24–31; Latin text in Poggio Bracciolini, *Lettere,* ed. Helene Harth (Florence: Olschki, 1984–87), 1:128. Discussed in Botley, *Latin Translation,* 104, and Dröge, "*Quia morem Hieronymi in transferendo cognovi,*" 69–71.

14. *Against the Jews and Gentiles* (*Contra Iudaeos et Gentes*) is an important companion piece to the *Apologeticus* and tells us much about Manetti's views on Jews. It exists only in manuscript (Vatican City, Biblioteca

Apostolica Vaticana, Urb. Lat. 154) except for a translation of Book VI in Manetti, *Biographical Writings*, 133–63. See the forthcoming bilingual edition of *Contra Iudaeos* in this I Tatti series, ed. Stefano Baldassarri and David Marsh (Cambridge, MA: Harvard University Press). For its date, see De Petris, "*L'Adversus Judeos et gentes* di Giannozzo Manetti," ser. 2, *Rinascimento*, 16 (1976): 193–205 = *Ripercorsi filosofici e letterari*, 615–32 . See also Trinkaus, *Image and Likeness*, 726–34; Dröge, *Giannozzo Manetti als Denker*, 62–81; and G. Fioravanti's "L'Apologetica anti-giudaica di Giannozzo Manetti," *Rinascimento*, ser. 2, 23 (1983): 3–32. For an overview of the *Adversus Iudaeos* tradition, see Fioravanti's "Polemiche antigiudaiche nell'Italia del Quattrocento: un tentativo di interpretazione globale," in *Ebrei e Cristiani nell'Italia medievale e moderna: Conversioni, scambi, contrasti, Atti del VI Congresso internazionale dell'AISG S. Miniato, 4–6 novembre 1986*, ed. Michele Luzzati et al. (Rome: Carucci, 1988), 75–92.

15. See the correspondence between Jerome and Pope Damasus in Jerome, *Letters*, tr. Charles Mierow (Westminster, MD: Newman Press, 1953), and Latin text in *CSEL* 54: 103–10. For a useful discussion of *Hebraica veritas*, see Andrew Cain, *The Letters of Jerome: Asceticism, Biblical Exegesis and the Construction of Christian Authority* (Oxford: Oxford University Press, 2009), 53–67.

16. On his praise of Lippomano's learning, see Manetti, *Biographical Writings*, 156, as well as Biondo Flavio, *Italia Illustrata*, trans. Catherine Castner (Binghamton: CEMERS, 2005), 160. Christoph Dröge has emphasized the importance of Lippomano in four publications: *Giannozzo Manetti als Denker*, 18–20; "*Quia morem Hieronymi in transferendo cognovi*," 71; "Zur Idee der Menschenwürde in Giannozzo Manettis 'Protesti di giustizia'," *Wolfenbütteler Renaissance-Mitteilungen* 14 (1990): 117–20; and "The Pope's Favorite Humanist," 217–24. His insight has been confirmed by G. Busi and S. Campanini, who reproduce the Hebrew correspondence in "Marco Lippomano and Crescas Meir. A Humanistic Dispute in Hebrew," in *Una manna buona per Mantova = Man tov le-Man Tovah. Studi in onore di Vittore Colorni per il suo 92° compleanno*, ed. Mauro Perani (Florence: Olschki, 2004), 169–202. Lipomanno may have also acquired Arabic by means of Hebrew. See Daniel Stein Kokin, "Isaac ha-Cohen's

Letter to Marco Lippomano: Jewish-Christian Exchange and Arabic Learning in Renaissance Italy," *Jewish Quarterly Review* 104 (2014): 194–233. On Lippomano, see Margaret King, *Venetian Humanism in the Age of Patrician Dominance* (Princeton: Princeton University Press, 1986), 389–90. On Italian Renaissance Hebraism, G. Busi, *L'enigma dell' ebraico nel Rinascimento* (Torino: Aragno, 2007).

17. On Immanuel, see Cassuto, *Gli Ebrei,* 222. On Manetti's Hebrew learning and library, see Trinkaus, *Image and Likeness,* 581; and Dröge, *Giannozzo Manetti als Denker,* 28–33, and "*Quia morem Hieronymi in transferendo cognovi,*" 68.

18. Trinkaus, *Image and Likeness,* 595.

19. See Catherine Steel, "Name and Shame? Invective Against Clodius and Others in the Post-Exile Speeches," in *Cicero on the Attack,* ed. Joan Booth (Classical Press of Wales: Swansea, 2007), 105–28.

20. On this quarrel, which dated from 1452–53, see Salvatore Camporeale, "Poggio Bracciolini versus Lorenzo Valla: The *Orationes in Laurentium Vallam,*" in *Perspectives on Early Modern and Modern Intellectual History: Essays in Honor of Nancy S. Struever,* ed. Joseph Marino and Melinda W. Schlitt (Rochester: University of Rochester Press, 2001), 27–48. Interestingly, both combatants use Manetti as a mouthpiece in their writings. See Botley, *Latin Translation,* 90–91.

21. On this dispute, see John Monfasani, *George of Trebizond: A Biography and a Study of His Rhetoric and Logic* (Leiden: Brill, 1976), 91–101.

22. See Smith and O'Connor, *Building the Kingdom,* 220–21.

23. Manetti's overview of the text of the Hebrew Bible is, of course, composed within the scholarly limitations of its time. For a current guide, see Emanuel Tov, *Textual Criticism of the Hebrew Bible,* 3rd ed. (Minneapolis: Fortress, 2012).

24. See *Rashi's Commentary on Psalms,* ed. Mayer Gruber (Leiden: Brill, 2004), 68–69.

25. For current views on the composition of the Psalms, see Peter Flint and Patrick Miller, *The Book of Psalms: Composition and Reception* (Leiden: Brill, 2005).

26. On the relationship between history and legend in the Septuagint, see Tessa Rajak, *Translation and Survival: The Greek Bible of the Ancient Diaspora* (Oxford: Oxford University Press, 2009), 24–63. See also Abraham Wasserstein and David J. Wasserstein, *The Legend of the Septuagint: From Classical Antiquity to Today* (Cambridge: Cambridge University Press, 2006).

27. Complicating matters further, there is an additional version sometimes attributed to Jerome, known as the Gallican Psalter, based on the Septuagint, which became incorporated into the Vulgate. On the various versions of the Psalter, see Sidney Jellicoe, *The Septuagint and Modern Study* (Oxford: Oxford University Press, 1968), 250–54.

28. For the relevant passages in Manetti's life of Nicholas V, 2.15–17, see Smith and O'Connor's bilingual edition of Book II in *Building the Kingdom*, 377–81. My interpretation is indebted to the admirable discussion in Smith and O'Connor, "What Do Athens and Jerusalem Have to Do with Rome?," *Building the Kingdom*, 91–117.

29. Dröge, "*Quia morem Hieronymi in transferendo cognovi*," 68–88.

30. For a perspective on Christian appropriation of Jewish texts, see Robert Bonfil's *Jewish Life in Renaissance Italy*, trans. Anthony Oldcorn (Berkeley: University of California Press, 1994). On anti-Semitism in this period, see Heiko Oberman, *The Roots of Anti-Semitism in the Age of Renaissance and Reformation*, trans. James Porter (Philadelphia: Fortress Press, 1984).

31. For an overview of the topic, see Monfasani's succinct remarks in "Criticism of Biblical Humanism, 15–38. A useful introduction to Valla's philological contribution to the evaluation of the Vulgate is in Jerry Bentley, *Humanism and Holy Writ* (Princeton: Princeton University Press, 1983), 32–69. Christopher Celenza provides an excellent discussion of Valla's prefaces to the *Collatio*, along with Latin-English versions, in his "Lorenzo Valla's Radical Philology: The Preface to the *Annotations to the New Testament* in Context," *Journal of Medieval and Early Modern Studies* 42 (2012): 365–94. The text of the earlier *Collatio Novi Testamenti* is edited by A. Perosa (Firenze: Sansoni, 1970), and the *Annotationes* can be found in Lorenzo Valla, *Opera omnia* (Torino: Bottega d'Erasmo, 1962 [reprint of 1540 edition]), 1:801–95.

32. For a careful discussion of Valla's likely influence on Manetti, see den Haan's "Giannozzo Manetti's New Testament: New Evidence," 731–47. Monfasani, "Criticism of Biblical Humanism," 32, and Garofalo, "Gli umanisti italiani del secolo XV e la Bibbia," 364, also believe that Manetti was well acquainted with Valla's annotations. Bentley, *Humanism and Holy Writ*, 58, rejects direct influence, while Botley, *Latin Translation*, 94, sounds a note of caution.

33. Manetti's tricolumnar arrangement has earlier precedents in the Quattrocento. For example, the Sienese Arabist Beltramo di Leonardo Mignanelli (1370–1455) prepared a comparative version of two Latin translations of the Psalms alongside an Arabic version in his *Liber de variantibus Psalterii* in 1443. On this work, see Stein Kokin, "Isaac ha-Cohen's Letter," 205. For an overview of the subject of multicolumn translations, see Belén Bistué, *Comparative Translation and Multi-version Texts in Early Modern Europe* (London: Ashgate, 2013).

34. Dröge conveniently prints Jerome's two translations from the Septuagint and *iuxta Hebraeos*, along with Manetti's version (from the manuscript Vatican City, Biblioteca Apostolica Vaticana, Pal. lat. 41), in the appendix to *Giannozzo Manetti als Denker*, 146–66.

35. Charles Trinkaus was the first to recognize Manetti's procedure, in *Image and Likeness*, 2:595. It is clear, however, by studying Dröge's examples, that Manetti employs a variety of strategies. On certain occasions, he differs from both Hieronymian versions. At other times, he follows Jerome's Hebrew version. One would require a complete edition of Manetti's translation of the Psalms, still unedited, to fully describe his modus operandi. For a list and location of the twenty of his *Psalms* that have been edited, see Botley, *Latin Translation*, 100, n. 165.

36. See Smith and O'Connor, *Building the Kingdom*, 105, who follow the brilliant insight of Silvia Rizzo on the way in which Manetti echoes the aims of the Alexandrian Library; see her article, "Per una tipologia delle tradizioni manoscritte di classici latini in età umanistica," in *Formative Stages of Classical Traditions: Latin Texts from Antiquity to the Renaissance*, ed. Oronzo Pecere and Michael D. Reeve (Spoleto: Centro di studi sull'alto medioevo, 1995), 371–407 at 389–91. On Pisistratus and related matters,

see Gregory Nagy, "Homer and the Evolution of a Homeric Text," in his *Homeric Questions* (Austin: University of Texas Press: 1996), 65–112.

37. On the role of the Neapolitan king as a cultural patron, see the chapter titled "A Renaissance King," in Alan Ryder's *Alfonso the Magnanimous* (Oxford: Oxford University Press, 1990), 306–57.

38. He later dedicated a treatise to him on the earthquake that struck Naples in 1456. For a useful discussion of Manetti's relations with Alfonso, see Jerry Bentley, *Politics and Culture in Renaissance Naples* (Princeton: Princeton University Press, 1987), 121–26. For Manetti's salary (900 ducats) in comparison to George of Trebizond's (600 ducats), see 60.

39. On Ciceronian translation theory, see Siobhan McElduff, *Roman Theories of Translation: Surpassing the Source* (New York: Routledge, 2013). On Jerome, see Lawrence Venuti, "Genealogies of Translation Theory: Jerome," in *The Translation Studies Reader*, 3rd ed. (New York: Routledge, 2012), 483–502.

40. For an account in English, see Robin Sowerby, "Early Humanist Failure with Homer (1)," *International Journal of the Classical Tradition*, 4.1 (1997): 37–63. The classic work on Petrarch, Boccaccio, and their Homeric translator is Agostino Pertusi, *Leonzio Pilato fra Petrarca e Boccaccio* (Rome: Istituto per la Collaborazione Culturale, 1964). A recent in-depth study is the series of essays entitled *Petrarca e il mondo greco*, ed. Michele Feo et al., 2 vols. (Florence: Le Lettere, 2002).

41. The letter is translated by Edward Dolin in Douglas Robinson, *Western Translation Theory: From Herodotus to Nietzsche* (Manchester: St. Jerome Publishing, 2002), 53. The Latin text can be found in the *Epistolario di Coluccio Salutati*, ed. Francesco Novati (Rome: Forzani, 1893), 2:355–56.

42. The letter is reproduced in Ludwig Bertalot, *Studien zum italienischen und deutschen Humanismus* (Rome: Storia e letteratura, 1975), 2:133, with discussion in Marianne Pade, *The Reception of Plutarch's Lives in Fifteenth-Century Italy*, 2 vols. (Copenhagen: Museum Tusculanum Press, 2007), 1:98.

43. An English translation is in Griffiths et al., *Humanism of Bruni*, 217–29. The Latin text, with Italian translation, is in Leonardo Bruni, *Sulla*

perfetta traduzione, ed. and trans. Paolo Viti (Naples: Liguori Editore, 2004), 74–123.

44. Stefano Baldassarri, "Teoria e prassi della traduzione nell' *Apologeticus* di Giannozzo Manetti," *Journal of Italian Translation* 3 (2008): 7–31.

45. Botley, *Latin Translation*, 80.

46. The Latin text of Manetti's funeral speech, the *Oratio funebris*, can be found in Leonardo Bruni, *Epistolarum libri VIII*, ed. Mehus, 1:lxxix–cxiv. Paolo Viti discusses Manetti's imitation of Bruni in "Giannozzo Mannetti e l'orazione funebre," in *Dignitas*, 311–32.

47. Kathleen Davis' English translation of Jerome's work is included in *The Translation Studies Reader*, ed. Lawrence Venuti, 3rd ed. (London: Routledge, 2012), 21–30. The Latin text can be found in Jerome, *Liber de optimo interpretandi*, ed. G. J. M. Bartelink (Leiden: Brill, 1980).

48. Glyn P. Norton provides a brief description of how Manetti demystifies Jerome in "Cultural Exchange and Translation in the European Renaissance," *Übersetzung: ein internationales Handbuch zur Übersetzungsforschung*, ed. Harald Kittel et al. (Berlin: De Gruyter, 2004–11), 2:1375–83, at 1378. He expands on this point in his groundbreaking *The Ideology and Language of Translation in Renaissance France and Their Humanist Antecedents* (Geneva: Droz, 1984), 47, as well as in "Humanist Foundations of Translation Theory (1400–1450): A Study in the Dynamics of Word," *Canadian Review of Comparative Literature* 8 (1981): 173–203.

49. This phrase can be found in the title of Manetti's translation of his Psalms (Vatican City, Biblioteca Apostolica Vaticana, MS Pal. lat. 41, 3v).

50. In addition to translations of Bruni and Manetti, there is also the late Renaissance treatise of Daniel Huet, discussed in *Translation Theory in the Age of Louis XIV: The 1683 De optimo genere interpretandi (On the Best Kind of Translating) of Pierre-Daniel Huet (1630–1721)*, ed. and trans. James DeLater (Manchester: St. Jerome, 2002), along with generous excerpts of Laurence Humphrey's *Interpretatio linguarum* [The Translation of Languages] (1559), in *English Renaissance Translation Theory*, ed. Neal Rhodes (London: MHRA, 2013), 263–94.

51. Glyn P. Norton has done much to emphasize the creativity of Manetti's translation theory in "Cultural Exchange," 1378, as well as in *Ideology and Language*, 44–54, and "Humanist Foundations," 173–203.

52. To this day, most contemporary works on translation theory, such as George Steiner's well-known *After Babel*, 3rd ed. (Oxford: Oxford University Press, 1998), are written by nontranslators. On the other hand, although highly influential essays on translation theory have been written by practicing translators such as Friedrich Schleiermacher and Walter Benjamin, these theoretical writings are notably brief. For translations of the essays by Schleiermacher and Benjamin, see Venuti, *Translation Studies*. One notable exception is the philosopher Jacques Derrida, who in addition to authoring works on translation theory, such as *Le monolinguisme de l'autre* [Monolingualism of the Other] (Paris: Galilée, 1996), has also translated a major work by Edmund Husserl.

IANNOZII MANETTI
AD ALFONSVM CLARISSIMVM
ARAGONVM REGEM
QVINQVE LIBROS ADVERSVS SVE
NOVE PSALTERII
TRADVCTIONIS OBTRECTATORES
APOLOGETICOS

FIVE APOLOGETIC BOOKS
AGAINST THE CRITICS
OF HIS NEW TRANSLATION OF
THE PSALTER
BY GIANNOZZO MANETTI,
DEDICATED TO
ALFONSO, KING OF THE
ARAGONESE

LIBER PRIMVS

1 Cum novam quandam totius Psalterii de hebraica veritate in latinam linguam traductionem, anno iam propemodum elapso, absol-
vissem atque id opus, qualecunque sit, huic tam claro tamque
glorioso Alfonsi regis nomini cum maxima reverentia dedicatum,
ad maiestatem tuam transmisissem, a non nullis partim ignavis,
partim doctis hominibus, sed in sacris ac divinis Litteris parum
eruditis, me in eo opere quodam arrogantie crimine insimulatum
2 ac reprehensum et obiurgatum fuisse audivi. Id enim solum obtrectatores mei (quantum ego, diligenter et accurate totam rem
perscrutatus, haurire et intelligere potui) hac generali sententia
obicere videbantur, quippe quamcunque aliam sacrorum librorum
sive de hebreo sive de greco idiomate in romanam linguam translationem, post celebratas illas et decantatas Hieronymi nostri utrinque hebraice ac grece in latinum eloquium fideliter eleganterque
conversas, superfluam quandam et supervacaneam atque arrogan-
tem cum fuisse tum quoque fore asserebant. Quod cum ego mecum crebro animadverterem, ac quale id ipsum iniuste et temerarie
reprehensionis mee genus esset sepenumero paulo diligentius con-
siderarem, profecto mecum satis inique atque impie admodum
haud immerito agi putabam.

3 Nam cum pro multis et magnis ac piis et devotis laboribus lu-
cubrationibusque meis ad defensionem sacrarum latinarum litterarum adversus non nullas falsas hebreorum virorum de codicibus
nostris incusationes ac calumnias duntaxat conversas, singularia
quedam laudum et commendationum atque honorum premia de-
berentur, ita male de his obtrectatoribus meis non dico hebreis,
sed christianis hominibus merebar, ut contraria vituperationum et
ignominiarum atque infamiarum damna reportarem. Equo tamen

BOOK ONE[1]

When about a year ago I had finished a new translation of the 1
complete Psalter from the original Hebrew into Latin, and I had
dedicated that work — whatever it is worth — with the greatest
reverence to the renowned and glorious name of King Alfonso,
and I had sent it to Your Majesty, I heard that several men — some
idle, others scholarly but with little training in sacred and divine
literature — had in a certain work made accusation against me with
much censure and denunciation for arrogance. My critics, as far as 2
I was able to understand and digest their position after I had examined the whole matter carefully, seemed to object along the following general lines: they maintained that any other translation of
the sacred books from either Hebrew or Greek into the Roman
language had been and would be unnecessary and therefore arrogant, given the precedence of the celebrated and acclaimed translations of Jerome, faithfully and elegantly made from both Hebrew
and Greek into accomplished Latin. While I often thought about
this and pondered again and again more thoroughly the unjust
and thoughtless charge against me, I began to think with good
cause that I was being treated very unfairly and unscrupulously.

For although distinctive rewards of praise, commendation, and 3
honor were owed to me for my intensive, pious and devoted labors and late nights in defense of the sacred Latin texts against some malicious attacks of Jews and their false accusations and calumnies about our texts, I was recompensed so poorly by my critics — I do not mean Hebrews, I mean Christians — that I took away the opposite penalties of censure, disgrace, and infamy. Nevertheless, I

animo illa quecunque et qualiacunque essent, pro virili mea ferenda ac tolleranda propterea non iniuria esse censebam, cum quia mihi ipsi sincere et pure veritatis conscius eram, tum etiam quia ea a malivolis quibusdam invidisque et ignaris hominibus provenire non dubitabam.

4 Ad hec accedebat quo equiori animo ac facilius huiusmodi adversus me maledicta perferrem, quia nullis unquam egregiis quaruncunque rerum sive grecis sive latinis scriptoribus, memoria ab antiquitatis origine repetita, in quocunque scribendi genere (quasi id naturale hominibus esset, ut alii in hac presertim cuiuslibet digne scriptionis excellentia aliis inviderent) detractores defuisse memineram. Ut enim a poetis incipiam, quos omnium aliorum scriptorum, hebreis duntaxat exceptis, primos fuisse manifestum est, Homero et Hesiodo, Terentio ac Virgilio, ut duobus precipuis utriusque lingue paribus multis aliis omissis contenti simus, quanquam consensu pene omnium quisque illorum in poemate ceteris excellere videretur, plures obtrectatores non defuere.

5 Nam et Homero Xenophanes Colophonius philosophus, et Zoilus quidam nescio quis greco cognomine *Mastix* (quod latine *Verberonem* significat), et Galba denique imperator plurimum obtrectavere. Quorum primus ita ei detrahebat, ut illud Hieronis, Sicilie tyranni, audire mereretur. Nam cum ipse apud predictum Hieronem, tenuitate patrimonii coactus, vix se duos servos alere posse conquereretur, ita respondisse fertur: 'At Homerus, cui tu detrahis, plures quam decem milia vel mortuus alere et educare videtur.' Secundus adversus eius libros grece conscripsit. Tertius ipsius carmina ita execratus est, ut de abolendis illis aliquando cogitaret, idem sibi imperanti licere testatus quod Platoni, homini privato quamvis docto et erudito, antea licuisset, qui illum e civitate quam constituebat, cum ceteris poetis eiciendum atque expellendum esse existimavit.

believed, and rightly so, that I for my part should calmly bear and endure all of these criticisms, both because I knew the plain truth of the matter, and also because I did not doubt that malicious, envious, and ignorant men had leveled these charges.

Moreover, I was able to endure the slanders more calmly and 4
more easily because I remembered that all outstanding Greek and Latin writers going back to antiquity, on all topics and in all genres, had had their detractors, as though it were human nature for excellent writing in particular to spark envy. Let us start with the poets, since they were obviously the earliest authors (excluding Hebrew ones), and let us be content with two preeminent writers from each language, even if we have to omit many others. Homer and Hesiod and Terence and Vergil had several critics, although there was almost universal agreement that they surpassed all other poets.

In particular the philosopher Xenophanes of Colophon, and a 5
certain Zoilus who had the Greek cognomen Mastix (which in Latin means "whip"), and finally the emperor Galba, especially disparaged Homer. Xenophanes' criticism of Homer led to his hearing these well known words from Hiero, king of Sicily. For when he appeared at Hiero's court, driven there by his meager patrimony, and complaining that he was barely able to feed his two slaves, Hiero responded: "But Homer, whom you disparage, is able to nourish and educate more than 10,000 men, even though he is dead."[2] Homer's second critic wrote in Greek against his books. The third, Galba, so execrated Homer's poems that he thought at one time of banishing them. He swore that, as emperor, he should be permitted to do what had been permitted to Plato, a private albeit a learned man, who thought that Homer and other poets must be driven out and expelled from the new city that he was founding.

6 Id etiam ipsum Hesiodo evenisse legimus, atque eadem et Terentio et Virgilio contigisse non dubitamus. Quippe Terentio Lanuinus quidam obtrectare non destitit, quin immo ut eum a scribendo deterreret, illi ipsi tria scribenti vitia obiciebat. Primo nanque quod eas quas e greco vertebat fabulas, sibi soli ac si sue essent nec ab illo traducte fuissent impudenter arrogabat. Deinde de bonis grecis malas in conversione latinas effectas. Postremo fabulas ab eo sive scriptas sive traductas tenui esse oratione scripturaque levi criminabatur.

7 Nec Virgilio quoque obtrectatores defuere. Nam et Numitorius et Carbilus et M. Vipranius et Herennius et Petilius Faustus et Evangelus quidam et Anneus Cornutus mirum in modum varieque obtrectarunt. Alii nanque *Bucolicum* carmen a Theocrito Siracusano, alii *Georgica* ab Hesiodo et ab Arato, alii *Eneida* ex utrisque celeberrimis Homeri *Iliados* et *Odyssee* poematibus pleraque usurpasse obiecere. Et non solum ab Homero, ut est communis fere omnium eruditorum hominum consensus, sed etiam a Pindaro et ab Apollonio, *Argonauticorum* scriptore, et a Sophocle et Eschilo,
tragediarum auctoribus, et a Partenio insuper grammatico, suo
8 grecarum litterarum preceptore; et non modo a grecis, sed a latinis
preterea poetis cum plurima usurpasse obiurgabant, siquidem ab Ennio, a Nevio, a Pacuvio, ab Accio, a Furo, a Varo, a Lucretio denique multa illum suscepisse dictitabant. Nec his obiurgationibus contenti, alia quedam probra adiungebant, quod scilicet non nulla ab aliis usurpata ieiune exiliterque disseruerat, ac etiam

We read that this very thing happened to Hesiod, and we are 6
certain that the same things befell both Terence and Vergil. For a certain Lanuvinus did not cease belittling Terence and in fact taunted him with three faults in his writing to make him give it up. First, he charged that Terence shamelessly appropriated for himself alone the plays that he translated from Greek as though they were his own and had not been translated by him. Then he charged that Terence had translated fine Greek plays into terrible Latin ones. Finally, he charged that the plays written by Terence or translated by him were jejune in style and thin in content.[3]

Vergil as well had his critics. For Numitorius, Carvilius, Mar- 7
cus Vipsanius, Herennius, Petilius Faustus, a certain Evangelus and Annaeus Cornutus all disparaged him in astonishing and different ways.[4] Some objected that in the *Eclogues* he had appropriated poetry by Theocritus of Syracuse, others that in the *Georgics* he had appropriated works by Hesiod and Aratus, still others that in the *Aeneid* he had appropriated most of the two greatest poems, the *Iliad* and the *Odyssey* of Homer. And not only poems by Homer, as is the general consensus of almost all the learned, but also that he had appropriated poetry from Pindar and Apollonius, the author of the *Argonautica;* and poetry by Sophocles and Aeschylus, writers of tragedies; and in addition from the grammarian Parthenius, who taught him Greek literature. And not only from the 8
Greeks, but they charged that he had also filched from Latin poets besides, since they insisted that he had taken much material from Ennius, Naevius, Pacuvius, Accius, Furius, Varus, and finally from Lucretius. Not content with these criticisms, they added other reproaches, namely that he had treated the material he usurped from others with little energy or verve, and also that he had

parum proprie plura absurdeque tractaverat, atque ea ipsa in me-
9 dium adducebant, quale est illud:

> candida succinctam latrantibus inguina monstris
> Dulichias vexasse rates

et aliud:

> quis aut Euristea durum
> aut illaudati nescit Busiridis aras

et tertium:

> Et inamabilis unda de Stigia palude canens;

et quartum:

> per tunicam squalentem auro latus haurit apertum;

et quintum:

> Ipse Quirinali lituo parvaque sedebat
> succinctus trabea

et sextum:

> et mala mentis
> gaudia

et septimum:

> Dedalus, ut fama est, fugiens Minoia regna
> prepetibus pennis ausus se credere celo;

et octavum, cum Veneris et Vulcani concubitum commemorat; ac plura alia huiusmodi, que brevitatis gratia omittere quam hoc loco explicare maluimus. Hec quidem vergilianorum, ut aiunt, errorum annotamenta falseque calumnie cum ad manus Asconii Pediani,

handled many things improperly and preposterously, and they adduced these very points such as the following: 9

> Scylla, girded about her shining thighs with barking dogs,
> harassed the Dulichian ships;[5]

and again,

> Who does not know harsh Eurystheus
> or the altars of unpraised Busiris;[6]

and third,

> And the unlovable wave gray from the Stygian marsh;[7]

and fourth,

> His sword drank from his unprotected side through the tunic
> squalid with gold;[8]

and fifth,

> He himself was seated with the augur's staff
> and dressed in a short robe;[9]

and sixth,

> The evil pleasures
> of the mind;[10]

and seventh,

> Daedalus, as the story goes, fleeing the kingdom of Minos,
> dared to entrust himself to the sky on swift feathers;[11]

and eighth, when he relates the lying together of Venus and Vulcan. There are many other criticisms of this kind. In the interest of time I have preferred to pass over them rather than go into detail here. But when this list of alleged Vergilian errors and slanders landed in the hands of Asconius Pedianus, a famous

egregii rhetoris, pervenissent, vehementi quadam mentis indignatione stomachoque indignabundo commotus, sese continere non potuit, quin librum quemdam in maximi poete defensionem quasi apologeticum scriberet, quem titulo *Adversus Vergilii* obtrectatores inscripsit prenotavitque.

10 Quid de oratoribus grecis latinisque dicemus? Nonne ipsi etiam quamvis in arte dicendi admodum excellerent, obtrectatores habuere, quippe Demades et Eschines Demosthenem, ac versa vice Demosthenes Demadem atque Eschinem vehementer emulatus est, quemadmodum ex pluribus aliis eorum scriptis et precipue ex duabus illis celeberrimis ac nobilissimis et *Contra Ctesiphontem* et *Pro Ctesiphonte* orationibus inter seque contrariis plane aperteque deprehenditur? Neque Cicero Hortensio, neque Hortensius Ciceroni, pluresque alii huiusmodi oratores quibusdam eius generis in obtrectando pepercisse videntur. De quo quidem in principio *De finibus bonorum et malorum* idem Cicero inter cetera his pene verbis apprime conqueritur: Quod scilicet varium quoddam reprehensionis nostre genus vitare non poteramus, nisi omnino nihil scriberemus.

11 Tuchididi insuper et Herodoto, Livio ac Sallustio, optimis grecis latinisque historicis, idem ut eorum scripta a quibusdam emulis reprehenderentur, evenisse legimus. Nam et Grecos mendacia historiis scripsisse ac verbosos prolixosque nimis extitisse obiectum fuisse novimus. Et Tuchidides quoque Herodotum in *Historiarum* suarum commentariis parumper carpsisse legitur. Et Crispus Sallustio nimiam dicendi brevitatem et T. Livio superfluam quandam enarrandi amplitudinem non nulli arrogantes impudentesque alienorum scriptorum censores attribuisse videntur. Sallustium enim a pluribus invite atque inscite ab Asinio Pollione reprehensum quod transfretationem transgressum dixisset, Aulus
12 Gellius in libris *Noctium Atticarum* idoneus testis est; ac eisdem grecis historicis Livioque presertim nostro vitio datum fuisse

teacher of rhetoric, he became exceedingly vexed and lost his temper. He was not able to contain himself and so wrote a book in defense of this greatest of poets, as though he were writing a forensic speech for the defense. He entitled it *Against the Detractors of Vergil*.[12]

What shall I say about the Greek and Latin orators? Did they 10
not have critics, even though they were so superb in the art of speaking? For Demades and Aeschines tried hard to imitate Demosthenes, and in turn Demosthenes tried to imitate Demades and Aeschines. This can be plainly discerned from many of their writings but especially from the two very famous and accomplished opposing forensic speeches *Against Ctesiphon* and *For Ctesiphon*. Cicero as well criticized Hortensius, and Hortensius criticized Cicero, nor did many other such orators spare their colleagues.[13] Cicero complains about this at the beginning of *On Ends* in more or less these words: only by writing nothing at all could we have avoided this wide-ranging kind of criticism.[14]

Moreover, we read that the same thing happened to Thucydi- 11
des and Herodotus, and Livy and Sallust, the best Greek and Roman historians: rivals censured their writings. We know that the Greeks were faulted for including lies in their histories[15] and for being too wordy and long-winded. Thucydides is also said to have briefly criticized Herodotus in the commentaries of his *Histories*.[16] Also, several arrogant and shameless critics of others' writings have charged Sallust for extreme conciseness, and Titus Livy with redundant narrative prolixity. Aulus Gellius in his *Attic Nights* provides good evidence that many criticized Sallust reluctantly and that Asinius Pollio criticized him ineptly for saying that the sea-
crossing had been crossed.[17] We know that it was considered a 12
fault of these same Greek historians and especially our own Livy

cognovimus, quod ducum et imperatorum prestantissimorumque
aliorum virorum contiones et orationes mediis gestarum rerum
narrationibus admiscuissent, ac si ea ipsa perscribere a proprio
quodam et peculiari cunctorum historicorum officio et munere vel
maxime abhorrere putaretur. Nec defuerunt etiam usque ad tempora nostra qui livianum dicendi genus, utpote rude quoddam et
rusticana quoque patavinitate nescio qua conditum, carperent lace-
13 rarentque. Et quod maius ac profecto mirabilius est, philosophi
ipsi, qui preter singularem quandam philosophie sue doctrinam,
vite probitatem profiteri videbantur, nequaquam hac mutue ob-
trectationis peste caruere. Siquidem Plato Xenophontem, et e contrario Xenophon Platonem emulatus est. Et Aristoteles, non modo
philosophus, sed aliorum etiam philosophorum—pace cunctorum
dixerim!—facile princeps, precipua doctrinarum suarum excellentia pluribus emulis carere non potuit, qui adversus eum non nulla
scripserunt: ac presertim Theocritus quidam Chius, qui suo quodam nobili, sed amaro epigrammate inter cetera illi integerrimo
atque accuratissimo philosopho obscenitatem atque desidiam ob-
iecisse exprobrasseque videtur; et alter quoque philosophus Eubo-
lides Milesius, quem inimico adversus eum animo in plurimis
14 ipsum Laertius Diogenes reprehendisse testatur. Et Senecam,
acerrimum Stoicorum, Quintilianus rhetor et commemoratus A.
Gellius grammaticus non solum ipsum in suo genere dicendi, sed
etiam in eius doctrina obiurgare ac reprehendere ausi sunt. Quorum utrunque predictus Aulus Gellius maxime fecisse cognoscitur.
Nam totam illius doctrinam utpote puerilem ac inanem et insul-
sam omnino pervertere atque penitus contumeliosis sane verbis
labefactare conatus est. Et idem Aulus Gellius Plinium Secundum, virum prestantissimum scriptoremque nobilissimum, quod
multa prodigiosa in libris *Historie Naturalis* Democrito philosopho
falso tribuisset, reprehendere et obiurgare non dubitavit.

that they included the speeches and orations of leaders and generals and other extraordinary men in the midst of the narration of
actual deeds, as if to write such things were thought to be greatly
at odds with the distinctive and proper duty and function of all
historians. Right up to our own time there have been those who
have censured and carped at the Livian style of diction as crude
and seasoned with a certain rustic Paduan quality.[18] What is more, 13
and this is quite remarkable, philosophers themselves, who, in addition to the extraordinary teaching of their philosophy were seen
to profess a moral life, were by no means free from this destructive
behavior of criticizing each other. For Plato tried to outdo Xenophon, and Xenophon tried the same thing with Plato. Even Aristotle, not only a philosopher but easily the first of all other philosophers—with due respect to them all!—was unable to avoid
several rivals despite the special excellence of his teachings. They
wrote several things against him, especially Theocritus of Chios,
who hurled against that most upright and exacting philosopher
the charges of lewdness and sloth in one of his famous if bitter
epigrams.[19] Diogenes Laertius asserts that another philosopher,
Eubulides of Miletus, was also hostile to Aristotle and criticized
him on many points.[20] Then there is Seneca, the most penetrating 14
of Stoic philosophers. The rhetorician Quintilian and the aforementioned grammarian Aulus Gellius both dared to criticize and
revile him not only for his style, but also for his teaching. Of these
two, Aulus Gellius is known to have done this especially. For he
tried to overthrow all of Seneca's teaching as childish and vacuous
and entirely tasteless, and he tried to topple it in quite insulting
terms.[21] Likewise Aulus Gellius did not hesitate to revile and
criticize Pliny the Elder, a great man and famous writer, for falsely
attributing many unnatural events to the philosopher Democritus
in his books of *Natural History*.[22]

15 Et denique (quod ceterorum omnium maximum, et id quod iusta admiratione refertum videri debet!) divinarum litterarum professores, et quidem christiani ac religiosissimi homines, huius vicissitudinarie emulationis nequaquam expertes evasere. Siquidem Augustinus ac Rufinus Hieronymum pluribus sacrarum litterarum locis vehementer reprehenderunt ac totam illam Veteris Testamenti translationem eius, utpote non necessariam, sed superfluam quandam ac inutilem perpetue—quantum in ipsis fuit—infamie, postquam ediderat, damnare non dubitarunt; ante vero quam ederet, amice exhortabantur, ne in traducendis sacris veteribus litteris aliquatenus laboraret, quemadmodum duabus precipuis Augustini ad eum epistolis plane aperteque deprehenditur.

16 Quibus quidem et aliis huiusmodi eius obtrectatoribus ipse pluribus prefationum suarum locis acribus verbis et non sine ingenti quadam animi indigna tione respondit, atque in epistolis quoque suis ab huiusmodi obtrectatoribus sese defendere tutarique non cessat. Nam et quodam predictarum prefationum loco: Obtrectatores, inquit, mei asserunt me in Septuaginta interpretum sigillatione nova pro veteribus cudere, ita ingenium quasi vinum probantes, et reliqua. Et alibi ita ait: Que audientis vel legentis utilitas est nos laborando sudare et alios detrahendo laborare? Et in prefatione sui de hebraica veritate Psalterii ad Sophronium, ita scribit: 'Unde impulsus a te, cui et que non possum debeo, rursus me obtrectatorum latratibus tradidi.' Et in libro *De optimo genere interpretandi* eadem repetit pluraque alia subiungit; et in volumine *Epistolarum* ad Augustinum vel dehortantem a transferendo vel iam traducta carpentem, acriter vehementerque respondere non dubitavit.

17 Quid tandem de novellis sacrarum disciplinarum doctoribus referemus? Nonne Franciscus Mayronensis Aquinatem Thomam, virum cum sanctimonia vite tum plurimarum quoque doctrinarum

Finally—and this is the most important and most surprising of 15
all—the professors of divine letters, who were also very devout Christians, have by no means failed to participate in such mutual rivalry. For Augustine and Rufinus vigorously criticized Jerome in many passages of the sacred texts, and they did not hesitate to condemn his entire translation of the Old Testament (as much as they could) to everlasting infamy as unnecessary, redundant, and useless, after he had published it. But before he published it, they encouraged him in a friendly way not to carry through with his translation of the sacred old texts, as can easily be discerned in
two letters in particular from Augustine to Jerome. Jerome re- 16
sponds angrily to these and similar critics in several passages of his prefaces often and not without a large amount of indignation, and in his letters he also does not cease from defending and protecting himself from them. At one point in one of his prefaces he says: "My critics maintain that I hammered out new things to take the place of the old on the embossed work of the Seventy translators. They assess ability as they do wine" etc.[23] And elsewhere he says: "What use is it to the reader or listener that I am sweating with effort while their effort goes into detraction?"[24] In the preface of his Psalter from the original Hebrew, he writes the following to Sophronius: "Urged on by you, to whom I owe what I am unable to pay, again I handed myself over to those barking critics."[25] In his book *On the Best Kind of Translating* he repeats the same things and adds many others. As well, in the volume of his letters to Augustine, who was either dissuading him from translation or criticizing what he had translated, he did not hesitate to respond fiercely and aggressively.[26]

What, finally, shall I say about the more recent teachers of the 17
sacred teachings? Did not Francis of Meyronnes vigorously attack Thomas Aquinas in many places and especially in [Francis' commentary on] the *Sentences* [of Peter Lombard], even though Aquinas was a man filled with the holiness of life and was also expert

generibus apprime affluentem, pluribus locis ac presertim sanctarum *Sententiarum* libris admodum insectatus est? Quapropter si plerisque tam grecis quam latinis quaruncunque rerum artiumve scriptoribus obtrectatores (quasi ita natura comparatum esset!) nunquam defuisse manifestum est; id nobis his novis depravatisque temporibus pariter accidere nec miramur nec etiam nimis moleste ferimus, quod effugere et evitare nullo modo poteramus, ceu apud Ciceronem, ut supra diximus, scriptum legimus, nisi nihil omnino scripsissemus.

18 Licet vero hec et cetera huiusmodi maledictorum in nos genera equo, ut scripsimus, animo ferenda et tolleranda ob commemoratas causas esse foreque constituerimus atque ita feramus tolleremusque, puram tamen ac sinceram sacrarum litterarum nostrarum veritatem adversus quoscunque tam pios (hoc est catolicos) quam impios (id est incredulos infidelesque) obtrectatores atque, ut ita dixerim, impugnatores aperto, ceu dicitur, marte non iniuria de-
19 fendere ac protegere tutarique decrevimus. Nam si Aristoteli, philosophorum, ut diximus, magistro et principi, adversus Thalem Milesium, Anaximandrum, Anaximenem pariter Milesios, Anaxagoram Clazomenium, Parmenidem, Melissum, Democritum Abderitem, Leucippum, Prothagoram, Archelaum, Pythagoram Samium reliquosque antiquissimos sapientie amatores et (quod longe maius est) adversus Socratem, fulgidum quoddam humanarum virtutum iubar et oraculo Apollinis omnium sapientissimum iudicatum, et (quod mirabilius etiam videri debet) contra Platonem preceptorem suum pro simplici quadam ac seculari et ethnica, ut
20 ita dixerim, veritate scribere licuit, quid nos christiani homines pro defensione catolice fidei ac sacre divineque veritatis conservatione facere debemus? An eam per silentium et taciturnitatem nostram turpiter impugnari ac sine aperta virilique protectione tam abiecte perire permittemus, cum gentiles ethnicosque philosophos pro

in many areas of study?[27] So if it is clear that many Greek and Latin authors in every branch of learning never lacked critics—as if this has been ordained by nature!—neither am I surprised that this likewise happens to me in these more recent and debased times, nor am I greatly annoyed since, as I noted above with Cicero, I could in no way avoid or escape this fate unless I had written nothing at all.[28]

Although I have decided that I must and will endure with 18
equanimity this and other kinds of abuse for the reasons cited above, and am doing so now, nevertheless, I have with justification resolved to defend and protect in open warfare, as the saying goes, the pure and sincere truth of our sacred letters against every critic and attacker, both pious—that is, Catholic—and impious—that
is, unbelievers and infidels. For if Aristotle, the master and chief 19
of philosophers, can write against Thales of Miletus, Anaximander and Anaximenes, both also of Miletus, Anaxagoras of Clazomenae, Parmenides, Melissus, Democritus of Abdera, Leucippus, Protagoras, Archelaus, Pythagoras of Samos and other ancient lovers of wisdom[29] and—what is greater by far—against Socrates, that shining light of human virtue and judged by the oracle of Apollo to be the wisest of them all,[30] and, what is even more amazing, against Plato his teacher,[31] on behalf of a simple and
secular and what I may call pagan truth, what ought we Christian 20
men to do to defend the Catholic and sacred faith and preserve divine truth? Or shall we permit it through our silence to be wickedly maligned and to perish so abjectly without an open and manly defense, while we witness the pagan philosophers battling

humana veritate scriptis suis tam acriter dimicasse ac pugnasse intellexerimus? Vera est enim illa celebrata tritaque predicti Aristotelis sententia veritatem amicitie absque dubitatione preferendam fore, quam quidem in primo *Ethicorum* his verbis expressisse videtur:

> Quanquam hec questio perardua sit ob amicos viros, qui ideas introduxerunt, sed pro defensione veritatis etiam propria delere oportere presertim philosophos magis forsan existimandum est. Nam cum ambo sint amici, pium est veritatem in honore preferre.

21 Quas ob res his et huiusmodi rationibus adducti, sacram profecto et catolicam ac divinam veritatem his brevibus ac particularibus scriptis nostris maioris brevitatis causa protegere, et paulo post prolixis quibusdam et generalioribus protectionibus ac defensionibus explicande veritatis gratia, omnipotentis Dei favoribus auxiliisque adiuti ac suffulti, defendere tutarique constituimus.

22 Sed ut tota huius tante tamque saluberrime rei veritas paulo evidentius elucescat, haud inutile fore existimavimus si non solum de compilatione Psalterii, de qua quidem principalis questio inpresentiarum accidere oririque videtur, sed de cunctis quoque aliis hebraicarum litterarum scriptoribus, qui in sacro canone continentur, eorumque interpretibus non nulla memoratu digna paulo altius ab origine repetemus. Quocirca primo de antiquis hebreorum et quidem sacrorum librorum scriptoribus, deinde de quibuscunque dignis eorum traductoribus, nunc quo a nobis brevius fieri poterit, alias vero, cum plus otii dabitur, si Deus adiutor noster erit, multo latius et uberius disseremus. Ab hebreis ergo divinorum codicum compositoribus merito incipientes, non ab re fuerit iuxta precipuum sui canonis ordinem eos singillatim recensere. Proinde Hebrei veteres sacros libros ceteris omnibus scriptis suis longe preferentes atque sine ulla comparatione dignissimos fore

and fighting so fiercely in their writings for secular truth? For that celebrated and well-worn saying of Aristotle is correct: truth should be preferred to friendship without hesitation. He suggests this in the first book of the *Nicomachean Ethics* with these words:

> Although this investigation is made difficult because the men who introduced the Forms are our friends, it ought rather to be thought that philosophers especially should even destroy their own creations in defending truth. For although both are friends, it is pious to prefer and honor truth.[32]

Prompted by these considerations, I decided, in the interest of 21
greater brevity, to defend the very sacred and Catholic and divine truth with these short and particular writings, and a little later, supported and assisted by the favor and aid of omnipotent God, to defend and protect it with longer and more general defenses.[33]

But in order for this magnificent and beneficial truth to shine 22
more clearly, I thought that it would be very useful to go back further in time and investigate from the beginning not only what should be said about the compilation of the Psalter, concerning which this present inquiry has emerged, but also about all the other writers of Hebrew texts who are included in the sacred canon, as well as their translators. Hence I shall first discuss the ancient writers of the Hebrew sacred books, then whatever translators were worthy of them. On this occasion I shall go through these topics with greater brevity; at some other time, when I have more leisure at my disposal, I shall go into them with much greater depth, with God's help. Thus beginning, and rightly so, with the Hebrew authors of the divine books, it will be pertinent to review them one by one according to the particular order of their canon. Likewise, the ancient Hebrews, preferring their sacred books by far to all their other writings and believing them incomparably the most worthy, wisely and beautifully divided these writ-

existimantes, scripta ipsa triplici sancte dignitatis gradu optime simul ac pulcherrime distinxerunt et cuncta illa viginti quatuor voluminibus comprehenderunt.

23 Primum igitur scriptorum suorum gradum Lex divina obtinere non dubitatur, que quinque libros continens Thora hebraice nuncupatur. Secundus est Profetarum, quos ipsi Neviin dicunt atque octo codicibus comprehenduntur. Tertius Agiographa continet, que illi Chedovin quasi Spiritu Sancto dictata vocaverunt atque in undecim libros partiti sunt. Moyses ergo, ut a vetustiori scribendi genere incipiamus, cunctorum scriptorum, quorum volumina vel apud Hebreos vel apud Grecos vel apud Latinos reperiantur, primus, hebreis parentibus in Egypto natus ac per hoc, cum ibi educaretur, omni Egyptiorum sapientia apprime eruditus, Amiramis et Iocabel filius fuit. Hic quinque illos tam celebres tamque divinos libros gesta Hebreorum a conditione orbis usque ad extremum vite sue tempus continentes, ea sevissima ac turbulentissima prime egyptiaceque captivitatis tempestate conscripsit; quos Hebrei suo idiomate Thora (id latine Legem, ut diximus, significat) titulo prenotarunt atque eosdem Greci unico verbo a numero librorum Pentateucum appellaverunt (quod in latinum conversum, quinque libros significare videtur).

24 Secundus vero gradus Prophetas continet, quorum primus est liber Iosue, quem composuit quidam nomine Iosue, filius Nun. Hic est ille qui in ducatum israelitici populi ob incredibilem quandam virtutum suarum excellentiam predicto Moysi successisse traditur atque una cum Septuaginta illis senioribus, quos Moysi ipsi ad gubernandum regendumque eundem israeliticum populum a principio datos fuisse ac per diversa postea tempora successisse constat, commemoratum librum scripsisse perhibetur. Sequitur deinde Iudicum codex, quem Samuelem prophetam simul cum predictis

ings into three distinct levels of sacred authority and arranged them all in twenty-four volumes.

There is no doubt that the first level is the Divine Law. This 23
contains five books and in Hebrew is called the Torah. The second level is the Prophets, which they call Nevi'im and is made up of eight books. The third contains the Hagiographa, which they call Ketuvim as though dictated by the Holy Spirit, and they divided it into eleven books. To start with the oldest genre: Moses was the first of all the writers whose books may be found either among the Hebrews, the Greeks, or the Latins. Born to Hebrew parents in Egypt and raised there, he was therefore extremely learned in all the wisdom of the Egyptians. He was the son of Amram and Jochebed. He wrote those five renowned and divine books that contain the deeds of the Hebrews from the founding of the world to the very end of his life, at that very difficult and tumultuous time of the first Egyptian captivity. The Hebrews in their language call these books the Torah (in Latin this means the Law, as I have said) and with a single word based on the number of books the Greeks call them the Pentateuch (pentateuch translated into Latin means five books).

The second level contains the Prophets. The first book is 24
Joshua, which a certain Joshua, son of Nun, wrote. He is the one who is recorded to have succeeded Moses in the leadership of the Israelites because of his extraordinary prowess. It is agreed that he wrote this book together with the Seventy Elders who were given to Moses from the beginning to govern the Israelites and who later succeeded one another at various times. The book of Judges follows. Samuel the prophet together with the Seventy Elders is said to have written it to the halfway point of the book, which in Hebrew is entitled Samuel, and which contains events up to his

Septuaginta usque ad dimidium pene libri, qui hebraice *Samuel* inscribitur, et singula gesta usque ad eius mortem complectitur ⟨scripsisse perhibetur⟩: reliquam vero alterius fere dimidii partem post mortem Samuelis solos commemoratos Septuaginta, graves quosdam idoneosque auctores, continuasse et absolvisse legimus.

25 Quartus sequitur liber Regum, quorum digna memoratu atque profecto mirabilia gesta predicti Septuaginta perpetuis hebraicarum litterarum monumentis mandaverunt. Quintus Esayas. Sextus Hieremias. Septimus Ezechiel. Ultimum unum Duodecim Prophetarum volumen, quos omnes unico titulo Tereassar ad numerum librorum appellaverunt (quod lingua caldea in latinum interpretatum, duodecim plane aperteque significat), atque eos ipsos Latini in duodecim libros distinxerunt et a parvitate suorum voluminum in comparatione aliorum maiorum prophetarum Duodecim Minores cognominaverunt.

26 Esayas, libri sui scriptor, nobili ac regio genere Hierosolimis ortus, Amos cuiusdam (non illius qui parvam prophetiam scripsit, sed alterius Amos etiam prophete) filius, sub Ozie, Ioatan, Acaz, Ezechie, Hebreorum regibus, scripsisse ac prophetasse traditur, ac demum a Manasse, commemorati Ezechie filio, illum interimere vel maxime cupiente, at cum ipse divino quodam omnipotentis Dei miraculo cedri arbore coram mirabiliter adaperta occultaretur, una cum predicta arbore serra sectus, hoc sevo et inhumano ac profecto immani et inaudito mortis genere damnatus, interimitur.

27 Hieremias pariter prophetie sue librum scripsit. Hic fuit Elchie cuiusdam prophete filius, Anathothites in vico quodam hoc nomine nuncupato, qui a Hierosolimis tribus passuum milibus distabat, sacerdos a sacerdotibus natus; proinde nobili genere ortus, quoniam tribus sacerdotalis ob singularem eius dignitatem tribui regie coniuncta erat, et in matris quoque utero sanctificatus, hic sub tribus regibus Iosia et Ioathan, eius filio, ac Ieconia, filio Ioachim, prophetavit, licet ipse Iosie solius mentionem ex eo fecisse videatur, quia reliqui duo tribus duntaxat mensibus regnaverunt.

death. We read that the Seventy alone, serious and capable authors, continued and completed the remaining part of the second half after the death of Samuel.

Fourth is the Book of Kings, whose memorable and extraordinary deeds the Seventy entrusted to everlasting monuments of Hebrew letters. Isaiah is the fifth, Jeremiah the sixth, Ezekiel the seventh. Last is the book of twelve prophets, all of which they named Tereassar after the number of the books. (When translated from Aramaic to Latin, *tereassar* means twelve.) The Romans separated them into twelve books and called them the Twelve Lesser because they are shorter in comparison with the other major prophets. 25

Isaiah, the writer of his own book and born from a noble and royal family of Jerusalem, was the son of Amoz (not that Amos who wrote the "minor prophecy," but another one who was also a prophet). He wrote and prophesied under Uzziah, Jotham, Ahaz, and Hezekiah, kings of the Hebrews. Manasseh, the son of Hezekiah, was particularly eager to kill Isaiah. When Isaiah was hidden in a cedar tree that had strangely opened through a divine miracle from almighty God, he, together with the tree, was cut with a saw by Manasseh and died, condemned to this cruel, savage, and unprecedented kind of death. 26

Jeremiah also wrote a book of his own prophecy. He was the son of Hilkiah, a prophet, and was born a priest from a family of priests from Anathoth, a village three miles from Jerusalem. Born from a noble family—since the priestly tribe had been joined to the royal tribe on account of its extraordinary standing—and sanctified in his mother's womb, he prophesied under three kings, Josiah, his son Jehoahaz, and Jeconiah, son of Jehoiakim, although he mentions only Josiah since the two others reigned for only three months. 27

28 Ezechiel prophetie sue librum scripsisse non dubitatur. Hic fuit Buzi cuiusdam sacerdotis ac prophete filius, atque una cum Ioachin rege captivus in Babiloniam usque perductus, in ea captivitate in loco quodam Caldeorum iuxta fluvium nomine Cobar prophetasse ac prophetiam suam scripsisse perhibetur. Ultimus in hoc secundo sacrarum litterarum gradu Duodecim Prophetarum liber collocatur et ponitur, quorum variis titulis unum eorum volumen prenotatum, ut diximus, scriptum fuisse manifestum est. Illorum primus in ordine ponitur Osee: hic fuit Beri cuiusdam prophete filius ac Esaie temporibus floruit et sub eisdem regibus prophetavit. Ioel secundus prophetie sue scriptor, Fatuelis etiam prophete filius, temporibus quoque Esaie et Osee prophetasse ac scripsisse traditur.

29 Amos tertius, non Esaie pater, ut supradiximus, quanquam et ille etiam propheta fuerit, licet prophetiam non scripserit, ut hic noster Thecue opido quodam, unde Thecuites, a loco nativitatis cognominatus, quod sex passuum milibus a Bethleem distabat, temporibus Esaie et Osee prophetasse scribitur. Ille nanque Esaie pater nobili ac regia stirpe oriundus, huius vero genitor ex ignobili et pastorali genere fuit; atque uterque diversis apud Hebreos caracteribus annotatur. Hunc Amasias sacerdos pluribus frequenter plagis affecit, et non multo post Ozias, eius filius, vecte quodam per tempora crudeliter admodum impieque transfixit ac demum interemit.

30 Abdias quartus prophetiam suam et ipse conscripsit. Hunc Hebrei illum esse dicunt, qui sub rege Sammarie nomine Achab, cuius pecunie minister erat, cum impiissima Iezabel passim quoscunque prophetas occideret, centum ex illis in speluncis, quo salutis sue causa confugerant, pavisse scribitur et ob hoc tam singularis ac tam precipue pietatis sue munus prophetandi gratiam divinitus suscepisse creditur. Ionas in ordine quintus prophetie sue scriptor extitit. Hunc Hebrei veteres catolicique doctores nostri celeberrime illius mulieris Sareptane, quem Helias

There is no question but that Ezekiel wrote the book of his own prophecy. He was the son of the priest and prophet Buzi. Having been led as a captive to Babylon along with King Jeconiah, he is said to have prophesied and written his prophecy in that captivity in a certain place of the Chaldeans beside the river Chebar. The book of Twelve Prophets is placed last in this second rank of sacred letters. As I said, it is clear that a single volume of theirs was written, noted with various titles. The first of these in order is Hosea. He was the son of a certain prophet Beeri. He flourished in the time of Isaiah and prophesied under the same kings. Joel is second and is the writer of his own prophecy. He was son of the prophet Pethuel and is recorded to have written and prophesied in the same era as Isaiah and Hosea. 28

Amos is third, but not that Amoz, father of Isaiah, as I mentioned above.[34] That Amoz was also a prophet, but he did not write a prophecy, as did our subject, who was surnamed Tekoites after the town Tekoa, his birthplace, six miles from Bethlehem. He is recorded to have prophesied in the time of Isaiah and Hosea. Furthermore, the father of Isaiah was born of a noble and royal family, whereas the father of this Amos was born from modest pastoral folk. Also, the two names are spelled differently in the Hebrew alphabet. Amasias the priest beat Amos repeatedly and not much later Amasias' son, Ozias, cruelly and impiously pierced his temples with a bar and killed him. 29

The fourth is Obadiah, who also wrote his own prophecy. The Hebrews say that he was minister of finance under king Ahab of Sumer, at the time when that most irreverent Jezebel killed several prophets indiscriminately. He fed a hundred of these in caves, where they had fled for safety. Because of this service of extraordinary piety, he is thought to have received the blessing of prophecy from Heaven. Jonah is fifth in order and is the author of his prophecy. The ancient Hebrews and our own Catholic teachers say that he was the son of that very famous woman Sareptana, and 30

propheta de morte ad vitam suscitavit, filium fuisse predicant, non Amathi patris, ut in textu exprimi videtur, si ad litteram intelligatur.

31 Hunc talem nostri prophete patrem non nulli extitisse tradidere. Quod paulo diligentius et accuratius considerantibus nequaquam verum propterea esse videbitur, quia vidua illa que mater eius fuisse creditur, non de israelitico, sed de gentili populo fuerat. Proinde eius virum pariter gentilem extitisse iure dubitare et ambigere non possumus. Ethnicis enim et alienigenis hominibus prophetie spiritus non dabatur, sed solis fidelibus et sanctis viris servabatur. Unde alterum duorum consequi necessarium est, vel quod Ionas iste noster non fuerit illius Sareptane vidue vel predicti Amathi filius.

32 Nam certa quedam et expressa cum Hebreorum tum doctorum
quoque nostrorum sententia est patres prophetarum, quorum nomina in principio sacrorum librorum exprimuntur, pariter sicut et
filios fuisse prophetas; itaque Amathi propheta ac fidelis et non
gentilis fuisset. Quocirca illi opinioni, utpote et veriori et universa-
liori, quod vidue filius fuerit magis [potius quam] adhereo, et nomen Amathi in textu expressum ad mysticum veritatis, ut hebraice
significat, intellectum mea quidem sententia traducendum non
33 iniuria existimo. Hunc cuiuscunque filius fuerit, temporibus Ro-
boam, regis Israel, scripsisse ac prophetasse prodidere. Hic est ille
qui in periclitatione cuiusdam naufrage navis, qua cum ceteris ve-
hebatur, salutis gratia in mare proiectus, a cete pisce absortus et
devoratus est, in cuius ventre per universum triduum (mirabile et
incredibile dictu nisi sacris litteris contineretur!) vivus perseveravit
ac quarto demum die eodem illius piscis ventre, in quo per totum
triduum continue vixerat, omnino integer penitusque illesus in lucem exivit evasitque.

that the prophet Elijah revived him from death to life, but that he was not the son of Amittai, as is indicated in the text, if it is understood literally.[35]

Several have related that this man was in fact the father of our 31
prophet. But if one investigates more diligently and carefully, it is clear that this is by no means true for the following reason: the woman who is believed to have been his mother was a widow of gentile, not Israelite stock. So we have no justification for doubting that her husband was also gentile. For the spirit of prophecy was not given to heathen and gentiles, but was saved for the faithful and holy alone. So one of two things must follow: either our prophet Jonah was not the son of the famous Sareptana or he was not the son of the aforementioned Amittai.

For there is a specific and explicit belief among both the He- 32
brews and our own teachers that the fathers of the prophets whose names are indicated at the beginning of the sacred books were also prophets. So Amittai would have been a prophet true to his faith and not a gentile. Therefore, I prefer this opinion, as one that is truer and more widely held, that Jonah was the son of the widow, and I think with justification that the name Amittai indicated in the text must be referred to a mystical understanding of the truth,
as indicated by the Hebrew. The tradition is that this man, of 33
whomever he was the son, wrote and prophesied in the time of Jeroboam, king of Israel. When the vessel on which he and others were traveling was in danger of being wrecked, he is the one who was thrown into the sea for the vessel's safety, then swallowed and gulped down by a whale. He stayed alive for three full days in its stomach (an amazing and incredible thing to say, if it were not written in the sacred texts!) and finally on the fourth day he emerged, whole and unharmed, into the light from the belly of the fish, where he had lived continuously for three days.

34 Micheas Morasthites, hoc est in Morasthi opido natus, prophetie sue scriptor, tempestate Ioathe, Achaz et Ezechie, regum Iuda, in libris De gestis Regum ac Paralipomenon scripsisse ac prophetasse legitur. Naun de loco quodam nomine Helcesei oriundus, et ipse in ordine septimus, prophetiam suam scripsit, cum ante adventum regis Assyriorum, qui Israeliticum populum in suas Syrie regiones captivum traduxerat, prophetasse Hebreorum traditiones asserere et confirmare videntur.

35 Abacuch octavus, et ipse prophetiam propriam litteris mandavit. Hic est propheta ille qui ad Danielem, dum in lacu leonum captivus esset, cum cibariis illis tam oportunis tamque necessariis alendi gratia missus fuisse fertur. Sophonias, ut ceteri eius college, prophetiam suam scripsisse non dubitatur. Hic gloriosa quadam maiorum suorum stirpe ortus est; siquidem patrem Chusi nomine, Godoliam avum, Amasiam proavum, Ezechiam atavum, celeberrimos reges simul atque egregios prophetas, habuisse non immerito gloriari potest, ac Iosie, iusti piique principis Iudee, temporibus floruisse traditur.

36 Aggeus, huius ordinis decimus, prophetie sue scriptor fuit. Hic ad Zorobabel et ad Iesum, filium Iosedech, summum illius temporis sacerdotem, ab omnipotenti Deo missus est, ut eos de illis, que propemodum eventura erant, plane aperteque admoneret. Zacharias penultimus prophetiam suam et ipse conscripsit. Hic Barachie patris filius et Abdonis avi, prophetarum, nepos fuit, ac secundo Darii, Medorum regis, anno simul cum Aggeo prophetasse ac scripsisse narratur. Malachias omnium ultimus, de cuius vita et moribus nihil certum ab aliquo idoneo auctore scriptum fuisse legimus. Illa vero que de angelo quodam in corpore assumpto ⟨narrantur⟩, quemadmodum eius nomen de hebreo in latinum conversum significare videtur, vel quod fuerit Esdras scriba, ceu a quibusdam traditur, utpote frivola quedam et inania penitus omittantur.

Micah the Morasthite, that is, born in the town of Morasthi, writer of his own prophecy, wrote and prophesied in the time of Jotham, Ahaz, and Hezekiah, kings of Judah, according to the books of Kings and Paralipomena. Nahum, born in a place called Elkoshi, is seventh in order, and wrote his own prophecy. The accounts of the Hebrews assert and confirm that he prophesied before the arrival of the king of the Assyrians, who had led the Israelite people as captives into his own regions of Syria. 34

Habakkuk is eighth, and he wrote his own prophecy. He is the prophet who was sent to Daniel with timely and necessary comestibles while Daniel was captive in the den of lions. Zephaniah, as with the rest of this group, clearly wrote his own prophecy. He was born of a glorious line of ancestors. He is justly able to boast that Cushi was his father, Gedaliah his grandfather, Amariah his great-grandfather, and Hizkiah his great-great-grandfather. They were famous kings and extraordinary prophets. The tradition is that he flourished under Josiah, a just and pious prince of Judah. 35

Haggai, tenth of this group, was the writer of his own prophecy. Omnipotent God sent him to Zerubbabel and to Joshua, son of Josedech, the high priest at that time, so that he could clearly warn them about what was impending. Zechariah is penultimate, and he also wrote his own prophecy. He was the son of Berechiah and grandson of Iddo, both prophets, and he prophesied and wrote in the second year of Darius, king of the Medes, at the same time as Haggai. Malachi is the last of all, but I have read that no reliable author has written anything certain about his life or character. What is related about his receiving an angel in his body, as his name, translated from Hebrew into Latin, seems to indicate,[36] or that he was the scribe Ezra, as some relate, I will entirely omit as being frivolous and unsubstantiated. 36

37 Cum igitur de primo ac secundo sacrorum librorum ordine non nulla breviter attigerimus, reliquum est ut de tertio *Agiographorum* deinceps pauca dicamus. Hic igitur tertius divinorum librorum ordo in undecim varios diversosque codices distinguitur ac per hoc totum Testamentum vetus viginti quatuor voluminibus continetur. Huius tertii gradus primus in ordine Paralipomenon liber accedat, quod quidem nomen grece Pretermissa significat, quoniam illa subiungere subtexereque conspicitur que in libris Regum antea omissa fuisse videbantur; et apud Hebreos huiusmodi *Diureagianum* titulo prenotatur. Que quidem dictio in latinum ad proprietatem traducta *Verba Dierum* manifeste interpretatur, sed per tropum dicendi, quo unaqueque lingua peculiariter abundat, apud nos *Gesta*
38 *temporum* paulo elegantius significare perhibetur. Huius libri auctores predicti Septuaginta extitisse creduntur, licet secundum sententiam Rabi Salomonis ab Esdra scriba legisque doctore scriptus fuisse videatur. Is enim cum non nulla que ad vetus Testamentum pertinebant, a prioribus scriptoribus vel omnino pretermissa vel ieiune et exiliter tractata conspicaretur, ea in hunc librum congessit; nec defuerunt etiam qui certum quendam huius operis scriptorem ignorari faterentur. Hunc Psalterium sequitur, cuius David rex plerunque ac pene omnino compilator extitisse non dubitatur. De quo quidem opere ad extremum paulo diligentius atque uberius disseremus, cum id ipsum ad nostrum propositum vel maxime spectare ac pertinere videatur.

39 Accedit Proverbiorum liber, quem Salomon, commemorati David regis filius, scripsisse traditur. Quarto loco *Iob* in ordine ponitur, cuius auctorem Moysem, divine legis latorem, fuisse Hebrei traditionibus suis memorie prodiderunt; atque eam quorundam nobilissimorum principum ac amicissimorum inter se virorum disputationem (per sententias in medium adductas atque hinc inde collatas et comparatas), ut certa quedam et vera ac expressa de Providentia divina, de qua veteres philosophi satis dubitasse et ab invicem acriter contendisse ac inter se certasse creduntur, sententia

Since I have briefly talked about the first and second category 37
of the sacred books, next it remains to say a few things about the third category, the Hagiographa. This third category of divine books is divided into eleven varied and diverse books, and so the whole Old Testament contains twenty-four volumes. The first book of this third group, called Paralipomena, comes next. This is the Greek for "omitted," since the material that had been left out earlier in the books of Kings is attached here. Among the Hebrews this section is entitled *Divrei ha-Yamim*.[37] When this word is properly translated into Latin, it is rendered as *Words Of the Days*, but by a figure of speech, of which every language has its own special store,[38] we can render it a little more elegantly as *The Deeds
of the Times*. The authors of this book are believed to have been the 38
aforementioned Seventy, although Rabbi Salomon believes that its author was the scribe and doctor of law, Ezra.[39] When Ezra noticed that there were several things pertaining to the Old Testament that had been either entirely overlooked by earlier writers or had been drily and thinly treated, he gathered these things into this book. However, several authorities maintained that the writer of this work was not known for certain. The Psalter is next. Almost everyone agrees that King David was the compiler. I will discuss this book more carefully and in more detail in the concluding section, since it is particularly relevant to my project.

The book of Proverbs comes next. Tradition holds that Solo- 39
mon, son of King David, wrote it. Job is placed fourth. The Hebrews have handed down in their traditions that Moses, who delivered the divine law, was the author. They also maintain that this debate among certain noble princes and mutual friends, by means of opinions brought forward and compared, took place so that a reliable, true, and clear idea about Divine Providence, about which the ancient philosophers harbored doubts and contended fiercely

ad utilitatem totius humani generis innotesceret; licet non nulli catolici sacrique doctores nostri longe aliter de commemorati libri auctore sentire videantur, qui eam predicti dialogi disputationem a Iob quodam non Hebreo origine, sed viro gentili ac proselito, quemadmodum re vera gesta fuerit, conscriptam fuisse arbitrantur.

40 Quartus subtexitur Ruth, quem libellum Hebrei veteres eisdem traditionibus suis a predictis Septuaginta senioribus litteris mandatum scribere non dubitarunt. Cantica canticorum per ordinem in medium afferantur; hunc parvum codicem a commemorato Salomone scriptum fuisse constat. Chinoth insuper hebreis sacrarum litterarum lectoribus offertur, cuius scriptor Hieremias propheta ille celeberrimus fuit; atque id nomen ex hebreo in latinum conversum non ab re Lamentationem significat, quoniam ibi futurum Hierosolime excidium multum admodum deploratur.

41 Octavus in ordine Ecclesiastes adventat, cuius scriptorem predictum Salomonem, ille ipse de se loquens, in principio voluminis sui fuisse testatur, atque hebraice Coeleth inscribitur, quod latine Contionatorem significat, quia ad humanum genus diversis ex locis in unum, ut ipse fingit, hinc inde collectum inter se solum varias tamen personas gerentem disputationem, non ut in dialogis per diversos collocutores fieri consuevit, de summi boni constitutione instituisse profitetur. Librum Hester titulo prenotatum, a Septuaginta commemoratis senioribus compilatum Hebreorum traditiones asserere et confirmare videntur.

42 Daniel decimus in Agiographorum ordine sequitur, qui pleraque prophetie sue loca caldeo sermone, licet hebraicis caracteribus, conscripsit. Esdras ultimo loco non iniuria collocatur et ponitur. Hic enim fuit ille peregregius Legis et Prophetarum ac totius sacre scripture doctor, qui hunc divinorum librorum catalogum in eo in quo nunc apud Hebreos cernimus ordine, optime digessisse ac pulcherrime instituisse perhibetur. Nam cetera omnia que de Tobia, Iudith ac Sapientia, vulgo Salomonis inscripta, et de

one with another, could be made known for the benefit of all mankind. However, several of our Catholic theologians seem to think far differently about the author of this book, since they believe that a certain Job, who was not a Hebrew but a gentile recently converted, wrote this debate just as it truly happened.

Next in line is Ruth. The Hebrews of old in the same accounts 40
did not hesitate to write that this short book was written by the Seventy Elders. The Song of Songs [Song of Solomon] may be adduced as next in order. The consensus is that Solomon wrote this small volume. Chinoth is presented next to Hebrew readers of sacred letters. The famous prophet Jeremiah wrote this. This word translated from Hebrew into Latin means Lamentation, appropriately, since the future destruction of Jerusalem is deeply lamented there.

Eighth in order is Ecclesiastes. The writer of this book is the 41
aforementioned Solomon. He attests this at the beginning of the book where he talks about himself. In Hebrew this book is entitled Coeleth. In Latin this signifies the Preacher, since he proclaims that for the human race, collected, as he devises in his fiction, from various places, he has established a debate about the nature of the supreme good with himself playing various roles, not, as is the general practice, conducted by various interlocutors.[40] The accounts of the Hebrews assert and confirm that the book entitled Esther was compiled by the Seventy Elders.

Daniel follows as the tenth in order of the Hagiographa. He 42
wrote most passages of his own prophecy in Aramaic but used Hebrew letters. Esdras properly assumes the final place. He was the most outstanding teacher of the Law and Prophets and of all sacred literature. He is credited with so perfectly arranging and establishing this catalog of divine books in the order in which we now see the Hebrews have them. For since Tobias, Judith, and Wisdom (commonly ascribed to Solomon), and Ecclesiasticus

Ecclesiastico, qui liber a Iesu quodam, Sirach filio, compositus fuisse traditur, et de duobus denique Machabeorum codicibus, utpote apocripha et incerta et ab Hebreis veteribus repudiata, inpresentiarum missa faciamus et ad nostrum David, unde longius digressi sumus, parumper redeamus.

43 De hoc Psalterii sacro divinoque opere, quod a David, clarissimo Israel rege, plerunque constat fuisse compositum, tria in primis breviter admodum querenda esse videntur. Primo enim utrum huius Psalterii titulus unum vel plures libros continere videatur; secundo utrum carminibus vel soluta oratione editum fuisse appareat; tertio utrum omnes psalmi in hoc Psalterii volumine contenti sint numero centum quinquaginta nec plures nec pauciores reperiantur, et utrum omnes a David solo compositi fuisse credantur. Nos igitur ad singula queque eo ordine quo proposita sunt, declarande veritatis gratia brevissime respondebimus.

44 Quinque et non unum solum esse Psalterii libros vetus quedam et certa cunctorum Hebreorum opinio est, ita trita ac vulgata, ut de hoc apud eos nullatenus ambigatur. Quod tribus rationibus maxime probare et confirmare videntur. Primo nanque aiunt quod in antiquis et in emendatis eorum codicibus talis librorum distinctio reperitur; secundo subiungunt quod ab Esdra, commemorato Legis et Prophetarum interprete, in ordinatione, quam de cunctis hebrei canonis codicibus fecisse traditur, huiusmodi librorum invenitur facta divisio; tertio dicunt quod Hebrei veteres hoc idem traditionibus suis plane aperteque confirmant.

45 Cui quidem opinioni Hieronymus noster adversari ac repugnare atque longe aliter sentire videtur. Nam unum duntaxat librum fuisse opinatur; idque ipsum in ea prefatione, quam in principio

(traditionally considered to have been written by a certain Jesus, son of Sirach), and finally the two books of Maccabees have been rejected as apocryphal and uncertain by the Hebrews of old, let us renounce them for the present and return for the moment to our subject, David, from whom I have digressed too far.

Concerning the sacred and divine work of the Psalter, which is generally agreed to have been composed by David, the distinguished king of Israel, three things in particular should be quite briefly investigated. First, whether the title Psalter seems to comprise one or several books; second, whether it was published as poetry or prose; and third, whether the total number of psalms contained in this book of the Psalter is one hundred and fifty and not more or less; and whether all are thought to have been composed by David alone. In order to disclose the truth, I will respond very briefly to each of these in the order in which they were proposed. 43

There is a longstanding and firm belief among all the Hebrews that there are five books of the Psalter and not one only. This is so trite and commonplace that there is not the slightest debate about it among them. They substantiate this on three grounds. In the first place they assert that such a division of books is found in their old and emended manuscripts. Second, they add that such a division of books is found to have been made by Ezra, the aforementioned interpreter of the Law and the Prophets, in the arrangement that he made for all the manuscripts of the Hebrew canon. Third, they maintain that the ancient Hebrews clearly and distinctly confirm the same in their accounts. 44

Our Jerome opposes and resists this belief and thinks quite differently, for he thinks that there was just one book. He attempts to assert and establish this idea on several grounds in the preface 45

sue Psalterii de hebraica veritate in latinum sermonem ad Sophronium traductionis ⟨ponit⟩, pluribus rationibus asserere et approbare conatur. Quarum prima ac principalissima est celebrata veterum, ut ipse inquit, Hebreorum ac maxime Apostolorum auctoritas, qui semper in Novo Testamento Psalmorum librum et non libros nominant, ubicunque illius oportune meminisse inveniantur; secunda est vetus ipsius operis titulus, qui antiquitus inscribitur Liber Hymnorum.

46 Atque his duabus rationibus suam de unitate libri opinionem asserere et confirmare vel maxime nititur. Quo quidem facto, plura alia in eadem prefatione contenta ad confutationem alterius de pluralitate librorum opinionis convertit et dirigit. Que quidem omnia cum brevitatis tum quoque evitande arrogantie causa omittenda esse duximus, ne forte tantorum litigiorum idonei iudices censoresque fieri velle videremur, si varias utriusque sententie rationes unum in locum colligeremus atque invicem compareremus. Et tamen in translatione nostra vulgatam omnium eruditorum Hebreorum opinionem, ut in cunctis eorum codicibus reperitur,
47 sequi et imitari maluimus. Atque ut ita faceremus, certa quadam vere sincereque interpretationis lege cogebamur, cum ita in ea lingua expresse scriptum comperiremus, e qua in latinum eloquium traducere profitebamur, licet apud grecos, secundum celebratam illam Septuaginta duorum interpretum traductionem, unus duntaxat liber habeatur. Quam quidem opinionem et Hieronymus, ut supradiximus, his verbis in eadem ad Sophronium prefatione confirmare videtur, ubi ita inquit:

> Scio quosdam putare Psalterium in quinque libros esse divisum, ut ubicunque apud Septuaginta interpretes scriptum est: *γένοιτο γένοιτο* id est *fiat, fiat,* finis librorum sit, pro eo quod in hebreo legitur Amen, Amen. Nos autem Hebreorum auctoritatem secuti et maxime Apostolorum, qui semper

that he wrote to Sophronius, at the beginning of his translation of the Psalter from the original Hebrew into Latin. His first and primary point is the well-known authority of the Hebrews of old, as he himself says, and especially of the Apostles, who always speak in the New Testament of The Book of Psalms, and not Books, whenever they have occasion to mention it. His second point is the ancient title of the work itself, which since antiquity has been written as The Book of Hymns.

With these two arguments in particular he endeavors to assert 46
and confirm his belief about the unity of the book. After this, he devotes many other arguments contained in the same preface to refuting another belief about the plurality of the books. But I have decided, both for the sake of brevity and in order not to appear arrogant, to leave out these arguments. If I were to collect the different arguments regarding both beliefs into one place and compare them to each other, I might seem to desire being made a qualified judge and arbiter of such significant controversies, and I would prefer to avoid that. Nevertheless, in my translation I have preferred to follow and imitate the common view of all Hebrew
scholars as found in all their manuscripts. I was compelled by a 47
fixed law of true and honest translation to proceed this way, since I discovered that it had clearly been so written in the language that I was claiming to translate into Latin. However, among the Greeks, according to that celebrated translation of the Seventy-Two Translators, one book alone is indicated. Jerome also, as I said above, appears to support this belief with the following words in the same preface to Sophronius, when he says:

> I know that some men think that the Psalter has been divided into five books, so that the end of each book is indicated wherever the Seventy Translators write *genoito, genoito* that is, *fiat, fiat,* for Amen, Amen, which is read in Hebrew. We, however, following the authority of the Hebrews and

> in novo testamento Psalmorum librum nominant, unum volumen asserimus.

Ac per hunc modum de primo quod a nobis superius querebatur, hec inpresentiarum dixisse sufficiat.

48 Ad secundum deinde procedentes, dicimus quod David Psalmos versibus et non prosa oratione composuerit. Id ex eo probari vel maxime potest, quod hebreis scriptum litteris carmine et non soluta oratione doctis eruditisque hominibus ostendatur. Apud Grecos quoque a pluribus sacris doctoribus David poeta appellatur; quod nisi carminibus scripsisset, profecto nunquam hoc poete nomen sortitus fuisset, quod quidem solis carminum poematumque conditoribus tribuebatur servabaturque. Ad hec accedit Hieronymi nostri auctoritas, qui de hac Psalterii compilatione pluribus locis loquens, cum suavitate carminum tum non nullis tam grecis quam latinis et quidem peregregiis poetis in hunc modum atque eiusmodi verbis alicubi conferre et comparare non dubitavit: 'David, Synphonides noster, Pindarus et Alceus, Flaccus quoque atque Catullus atque Serenus, Christum lira predicat, et in decacordo Psalterio ab inferis excitat resurgentem.'

49 Tertio de numero Psalmorum querendum restat, in quo quidem non plures nec pauciores etiam quam centumquinquaginta Psalmos in volumine Psalterii integro et non depravato sive hebreo sive greco sive latino contineri profitemur et dicimus. Si vero apud Grecos aut apud Latinos huiusmodi numerus forte variatus ac diversus fuisse reperiretur, certum quoddam manifestumque erratum foret. Atque huiusmodi erroris due duntaxat cause esse fierique possent.

especially the Apostles, who always refer in the New Testament to the Book of Psalms, assert that there is one volume.[41]

Let this suffice for the present concerning the first question posed above.

Proceeding to the second point, I say that David composed his psalms in verse and not in prose. This point can be proved, above all, from the following: it is clear to learned and erudite men that what was written in Hebrew characters was in verse and not in prose. Furthermore, many sacred teachers among the Greeks call David a poet. If he had not written in verse, he certainly never would have obtained the name of poet. This title was granted and reserved for the authors of songs and poetry only. Our Jerome lends his authority here. Speaking in many places about the compilation of the Psalter, he does not hesitate to compare it in the sweetness of its poetry to some famous Greek and Latin poets with these words and similar ones elsewhere: "David, our Simonides, Pindar and Alcaeus, Flaccus and Catullus and Serenus, with his lyre predicts Christ and on his ten-stringed psalter summons him from the dead as he rises again."[42] 48

Thirdly, the question remains concerning the number of psalms. I assert and maintain that there are neither more nor less than one hundred and fifty psalms contained in the complete and uncorrupted volume of the Psalter, whether the Psalter is in Hebrew, Greek, or Latin. If, however, a different number than this is discovered among the Greeks or among the Latins, this would be a clear and obvious error. There are only two possible causes for such an error. 49

50 Quarum prima esset quod in greca scilicet atque latina lingua interdum ex uno plures, et versa vice ex pluribus unum psalmum effectum fuisse legimus. Hoc tametsi verum videatur, tale tamen est, ut predictus centumquinquaginta numerus nullatenus exinde variatus fuisse cernatur. Nam si ex uno duos, profecto ex duobus pariter unum factos non ignoramus. Altera forte in quibusdam mendosis falsisque codicibus reperiri posset. Etenim si psalmus ille celeberrimus, qui trito ac vulgato verbo incipit 'Beati immaculati in via,' et reliqua, cum hebraice per distinctos alphabeti caracteres in totidem rubra capitula presertim apud Latinos videatur facta distinctio, non tamen diversi psalmi nec esse neque videri debent. Proinde centum quinquaginta duntaxat psalmos esse constat, quos omnes, ut alteri superioris questionis parti suo ordine respondeatur, solus David nequaquam composuisse traditur.

51 Nam non nulli alii quorundam psalmorum certi auctores conditoresque extitere; atque illos eorum omnium testamur auctores, quorum nomina in variis titulis exprimuntur: David scilicet et Asaph et Idithum et Filiorum Chore, Eman Ezaraite, Moysi et Salomonis et reliquorum; et licet non nulli alii quorundam, ut diximus, psalmorum auctores extiterint, libri tamen inscriptio a maiori et digniori parte proprium unius nomen assumpsit atque David solius titolo inscribitur.

52 Verum cum in plura a nostro proposito minime aliena paulo longius progressi fuisse videamur, non ab re pariter fore existimavimus si, antequam ad diversos sacrarum litterarum interpretes accedamus, de huiusmodi Psalterii Psalmique nominibus pauca quedam inpresentiarum recitaverimus. Hoc divinorum hymnorum (sic enim grece inscribitur opus) propterea tali Psalterii nomine

The first cause would be that we sometimes read that in Greek or Latin several psalms have been generated from one psalm and, vice versa, one psalm compiled from several. Although this may be true, nevertheless it remains the case that the aforementioned number of one hundred and fifty is thereby in no way changed. For if we are aware that two psalms have been made out of one, we are surely equally aware that one psalm has been made from two. Another cause may perchance be discovered in certain faulty and mistaken codices. For in that famous psalm which begins with the timeworn and well-known phrase "Blessed are the undefiled in the way" etc.,[43] divisions are rendered in Hebrew by distinct letters of the Hebrew alphabet, while among the Latins divisions are rendered by the same number of red-letter headings. Nevertheless, these divisions ought not to be, or seem to be, different psalms. Accordingly, it is agreed that there are only one hundred and fifty psalms. As to who wrote them all — to respond in order to the second part of my earlier query — tradition says that David was by no means the sole author. 50

For there were several other identifiable authors of certain psalms. I maintain that the authors of all of them are those whose names are indicated in the various headings, namely David, Asaph, Jeduthun, the sons of Korah, Heman the Ezrahite, Moses, Solomon, and the rest. Although there were some other authors of certain psalms, as I said, nevertheless, the heading of the book has taken the specific name of one person, because he wrote the greater and more esteemed part, and so David alone is indicated in the title. 51

But since I have digressed a little too far into several matters by no means alien to our topic, I thought that it would be equally apposite if, before I turn to the different translators of sacred letters, I now rehearse a few points about the names *Psalter* and *psalm*. This collection of divine hymns — for this is how it is entitled in Greek — was called by the name of psalter because many 52

nuncupatum fuisse creditur, quia plerique psalmi ad pulsationem psalterii vocibus concinentibus cantati fuisse perhibentur. Psalterium enim erat musicum quoddam instrumentum desuper concavum, et decem duntaxat cordas continebat; cuius quidem instrumenti consonis pulsationibus una cum suavibus diversorum cantuum vocibus omnes psalmi secundum varia tempora diversimode canebantur, et, prout erant, diversimode vel cantandi vel sonandi varia nomina sortiri videbantur.

53 Quatuor preterea modi fuisse traduntur, quibus ad celebrandos psalmos incedebatur: aut enim sola psalterii pulsatione sine ullis humanis vocibus sonabatur, aut symphoniis sine fidibus canebatur, aut mixtim sonando canendoque agebatur ac isto modo bifariam fiebat. Nam fidium interdum pulsatio precedebat et vocis modulatio sequebatur, aut versa vice predicta vocis modulatio precedebat et pulsatio sequebatur. Primus modus Psalmus licet improprie appellabatur, secundus Canticum absolute, tertius Canticum Psalmi, quartus Psalmus cantici nuncupabatur; atque secundum has variorum modorum diversitates multiplices quorundam psalmorum tituli plane aperteque cernuntur.

54 Nunc ad diversas interpretationes parumper accedamus. Plures sacrarum litterarum in grecum eloquium traductiones fuisse constat. De quibus singillatim pauca quedam ad hoc nostrum propositum vel maxime pertinentia disseremus, ut tota res, quoad brevius fieri poterit, clarius et evidentius elucescat. Certa et expressa Eusebii Cesariensis in libro *De preparatione evangelica* sententia est, ante celeberrimam illam ac famosissimam Septuaginta duorum interpretum traductionem, aliam suo et expresso titulo carentem
55 extitisse. Ad cuius quidem sententie adstructionem, hebrei cuius-

psalms are said to have been sung by voices in harmony with the plucking of the psalter. The psalter was a musical instrument that was hollowed out above and had only ten strings. By the harmonious plucking of this instrument together with the sweet voices of different songs, all the psalms were sung in different rhythms,[44] and they were named according to the different ways they were to be sung or performed.

Moreover, they say that there were four ways to perform the 53
psalms: either they were sounded by the simple plucking of the psalter, without human voice, or they were sung in harmony without strings, or they were performed by mixing instrumental music with voice, and the performance became double as follows. Sometimes the plucking of the strings preceded and the modulation of the voice would follow, or the other way around, the voice would start and the plucking of the strings would follow. The first was, albeit improperly, called "psalm," the second just "song," the third "song of the psalm," and the fourth "psalm of the song." The titles of certain psalms clearly reflect the diverse and multiple possibilities of the various modes.

Now let us turn for a moment to the different translations. It is 54
agreed that there were several translations of sacred literature into the Greek language. In regard to these I will say a few things that are of particular relevance to my topic, so that the entire subject, at least insofar as it can be done briefly, may be more clearly elucidated. In his book *The Preparation for the Gospel,* Eusebius of Caesarea gives as his certain and explicit opinion that, before the very famous and renowned translation of the Seventy-Two Translators,
there existed another translation lacking its own explicit title. To 55

dam doctissimi viri auctoritatem in medium lucemque producit, cuius verba in quodam eius libro *Ad Philometorem* hec fuisse dicit:

> Legem nostram in multis Plato secutus est; aperte nanque in pluribus diligenter singula examinasse videtur. Mosayca enim volumina ante Alexandrum, Macedonie regem, eiusque imperium traducta fuere. Unde et plura excerpsit, quemadmodum et Pythagoras philosophus ille antea acceperat,

et reliqua. Huiusmodi sententiam Eusebius per auctoritatem cuiusdam pythagorici approbare et confirmare videtur, qui nihil aliud esse Platonem quam Moysem attica lingua loquentem scri-
56 bere ausus est. Quod efficere nequaquam potuisset, cum prisci Greci ob elegantiam dicendi, cuius avidissimi erant, hebrearum litterarum cognitione penitus caruissent. Que quidem lingua veluti barbara quedam et immanis ab omni politiori elegantia longe abhorrere illis presertim temporibus videbatur, quibus grece facundie studia apprime florebant solaque in singulari honore ac precipuo pretio habebantur, nisi alia quedam quam hec predicta Septua-
57 ginta duorum iam pridem fuisset facta translatio. Non plures enim quam quadraginta anni inter predictum Alexandrum (ante cuius etatem prima illa, si qua fuit, alia translatio in lucem prodiisse fertur) et Ptolemeum cognomine Philadelphum (cuius quidem temporibus hanc ipsam Septuaginta seniorum traductionem factam fuisse constat). Ceterum illa prima, si qua fuit, ante Septuaginta interpretum traductionem, etiamsi priusquam Alexander regnaret facta fuerit, quibus tamen temporibus in lucem venerit incertum est. Hec vero, que dicitur Septuaginta, ante adventum Christi Salvatoris nostri per trecentos quadraginta circiter annos edita fuisse traditur.

58 De qua quidem traductione, quoniam res maxima est et ad nostrum propositum plurimum pertinere spectareque videtur ac duas diversas et pene inter se contrarias Hieronymi et Augustini,

support his opinion he adduces the authority of a certain learned Hebrew, and in a certain book of his, *To Philometor*, he cites his words as follows:

> Plato followed our law in many respects. In many passages he clearly examined aspects of it in detail. For the volumes of Moses had been translated before Alexander, king of Macedonia, and his empire. He excerpted many portions from this translation, just as the famous philosopher Pythagoras had received them earlier,[45]

and so on. Eusebius supports this opinion with the authority of a certain Pythagorean who dared to write that Plato was nothing
else than Moses speaking in the Attic tongue.[46] Plato would by no 56
means have been able to do this, since the ancient Greeks, for the sake of stylistic elegance, which they avidly pursued, utterly lacked knowledge of Hebrew literature. The Hebrew tongue was thought to be uncivilized and savage, far removed from any polished form of elegance, especially in those times when the study of Greek eloquence was particularly intense and was alone held in special honor and great esteem, unless a translation other than the one of
the Seventy-two had been made even earlier. For there were not 57
more than forty years between Alexander — before whose time that first translation, if there was one, is said to have seen the light — and Ptolemy Philadelphus, in whose time it is agreed this translation of the Seventy elders was made. But it is uncertain at what time that first translation, if there was one earlier than that of the Seventy translators, was published, even if it was made before Alexander ruled. The one that is called the Septuagint is said to have been published about 340 years before the advent of Christ our Savior.

But since this translation is of great importance and highly rel- 58
evant to our project and has generated two different and almost opposing opinions from Jerome and Augustine, the most learned

doctissimorum gravissimorumque virorum, opiniones habet, paulo altius ab origine repetemus. Quod quidem ut pro singulari et precipua divinarum rerum dignitate cum uberius agere tum satius disserere valeamus, ea omnia, que ad hoc nostrum institutum aliquatenus pertinere existimabimus, in sequentem librum oportunius ac convenientius congeremus.

EXPLICIT LIBER PRIMVS FELICITER

and weighty men, I will trace the matter a little further back to its origin. In order to be able to treat this topic more fully and discuss it more adequately in line with the unique and special dignity of divine matters, it will be more apt and convenient for me to collect for the following book what I deem pertinent to this project of mine.

BOOK ONE ENDS WITH GOOD FORTUNE

LIBER SECVNDVS

1 Post mortem Alexandri, ob rerum a se gestarum magnitudinem cognomento Magni, Macedonie regis, cum sine liberis decederet legitimisque heredibus careret, universum Orientis imperium, quod quasi totum ab eo vivente possidebatur, in varias partes divisum atque distributum plures cum greci tum latini quoque scribunt historici. Nam cum plurimi clari eius duces armis et bellis atque victoriis diutius assueti, admodum prepotentes essent; unusquisque quanto plus poterat, tanto magis sibi imperii arrogabat.
2 Unde in parva temporis intercapedine factum est ut Egyptus, viribus occupata, ad Ptholemeum quendam perveniret, qui cognomine Lagi, quoniam Lagi cuiusdam filius fuerat, appellatus est. Hic fuit Ptholemeus ille qui predictum Alexandrum in asiaticum bellum magnis exercitibus contendentem secutus, postquam ipsi mortuo in Egypto, ut diximus, successerat, eius gesta grecis litteris mandavit, quemadmodum Arrianus in prefatione librorum, quos de gestis commemorati regis conscripsit, plane aperteque testatur, cum illum et Aristobolum, alterum earundem rerum scriptorem, precipue inter ceteros historicos se imitatum fuisse commemoret.

3 Hic igitur genuit filium, quem Ptholemeum paterno nomine, Philadelphum vero cognomine nuncupavit, qui profecto ditissimus atque opulentissimus rex fuit, ac preter multa commemorandaque rei militaris facinora, quibus plurimum excelluisse videtur, ad construendas bibliothecas grecisque codicibus undique referciendas (mirum in modum supra quam dici potest!) animum adiecit. Quocirca Aristobolum quendam ac Demetrium Phalereum, duos eruditissimos ac preclarissimos viros, huic tanto ac tam arduo operi magna cum expendendi et erogandi auctoritate facultateque prefecit.

BOOK TWO

Many Greek and Latin historians write that with the death of 1
Alexander, king of Macedonia—who had the sobriquet "the Great" because of his formidable accomplishments—the entire empire of the east, which Alexander had possessed almost in its entirety while alive, was divided into sections and apportioned, since he died without children and without legitimate heirs. Since most of his renowned generals, long inured to warfare and victory, were exceedingly powerful, each of them took for himself as large a
share of the empire as his power allowed. As a result, Ptolemy, 2
who had the cognomen Lagu since he was the son of a certain Lagus, forcibly seized Egypt in a short period of time. This was the Ptolemy who followed Alexander into Asia, where he fought with large armies and who, having succeeded Alexander in Egypt when the latter died, as I said, wrote about his exploits in Greek. Arrian clearly indicates this in the preface to the books he wrote about the king's exploits, where he plainly attests that among other historians he had particularly imitated Ptolemy and Aristobulus, a second narrator of the same events.[1]

He fathered a son, whom he named Ptolemy after himself, and 3
also gave him the cognomen Philadelphus. This Philadelphus was an extremely wealthy and splendid king, and in addition to his many impressive military accomplishments, an area he seems to have particularly excelled in, he also devoted himself to building libraries that he planned to cram full of Greek texts from all over. An extraordinary proposal! Accordingly, he placed a certain Aristobolus and Demetrius of Phaleron, two most learned and renowned men, in charge of this magnificent and difficult project, with great power to spend and requisition.[2]

4 Hic est Demetrius ille, Theophrasti discipulus, qui cum patria
pulsus esset iniuria, ad predictum Ptholemeum, cunctorum doctissimorum virorum accommodatum atque honestissimum recep-
taculum, exul se contulit atque ab eo honorifice susceptus est. Hi
duo peregregii huius dignissimi operis prefecti, tantam grecorum
voluminum copiam multis bibliothecis Alexandrie et quidem magnis ingentibusque antea constructis pro sua admirabili et pene incredibili diligentia ac immensis infinitisque sumptibus collocarunt,
ut ad ducenta diversorum librorum milia (mirabile et incredibile
5 dictu!) recenserentur. De quo quidem cum Ptholemeus perficiendi
iam cepti operis avidissimus, predictos bibliothecarum commis-
sarios diligenter percontaretur, responsoque de tanta codicum con-
gerie ac de spe magni futuri incrementi accepto si non modo a
Grecis, sed a barbaris etiam ac maxime ab Hebreis nova et inusi-
tata volumina accuratissime eruerentur, avidior effectus, eisdem
illis nuper commisit, ut a Iudeis presertim divine legis libros et
sacras eorum Scripturas quoquo modo habere recipereque cu-
rarent. Sed etiam ipse quo facilius votis suis potiretur, pro regio
officio habendi curam assumpsit.

6 Proinde et ad Eleazarum, Onie filium, nobilissimo ac regali genere ortum, siquidem et Iaddus avus et pater et Simon quoque
frater maior natu Iudeorum maximi pontifices regesque fuere, tunc
temporis principem sacerdotum atque pontificem, pro codicibus
sacris bonisque ac fidis illorum interpretibus utriusque lingue, hebree scilicet ac grece, peritissimis scripsit. Nec epistolis duntaxat
contentus, legatos quoque suos amplis cum mandatis variisque et
sumptuosis muneribus ex Alexandria Hierosolimam usque transmisit, quibus inter cetera iniunxit ut commemoratum Eleazarum
magna cum reverentia venerarentur atque honorarent observarent-
7 que. Illi deinde ita verbis et gestibus honorato regiisque salutatio-
nibus atque exhortationibus impartito, tam humiliter sua mandata

This is the Demetrius, a student of Theophrastus, who, when 4
he had been driven from his country unjustly, went as an exile to
Ptolemy—the appropriate and honorable port of refuge for all
learned men—and he was graciously received by him. These two
exceptional supervisors of this worthy project, by working incred-
ibly hard and spending vast sums, delivered so many Greek texts
to the many libraries—including many enormous ones built earlier—that as many as 200,000 volumes of various books were tal-
lied, as incredible as that is to imagine! When Ptolemy, who was 5
most eager to complete the work already in hand, kept asking
these supervisors about their work, they reported how large a
number of volumes had been collected and about their hopes for
even more, if new and rare volumes not only written by Greeks
but also by non-Greeks, and in particular the Hebrews, were meticulously hunted down. Ptolemy became even more eager and
commissioned them afresh to exert themselves in whatever way
they could to acquire and obtain from the Jews, in particular,
books of divine law and their sacred scriptures. In fact, so that he
could achieve his wishes more easily, he himself personally undertook the responsibility of acquiring them through his royal office.[3]

Accordingly, he wrote to Eleazar, the son of Onia, a man de- 6
scended from a distinguished royal line—Iaddus, his grandfather,
his father, and his older brother Simon were the high priests and
kings of the Jews—who at that time was the head priest and pontifex. Ptolemy asked Eleazar about sacred books and about experts
in both languages, namely Hebrew and Greek, who could provide
faithful translations. Nor was he content simply with letters. He
also sent his representatives from Alexandria to Jerusalem with
honorable commissions and a variety of lavish gifts. Among other
things, he enjoined them to honor, respect, and attend to Eleazar
with great deference. Then, after honoring him with words and 7
deeds, and having repeated the king's greetings and exhortation to
Eleazar, they very humbly explained their assignment to obtain

exponerent, ut quoquo modo ab eo regia postulata reportarent.
Que quidem cum legati regis diligentissime simul atque accuratissime coram predicto Eleazaro exposuissent, dici non potest quantum sibi et honores et munera et postulata regia placuerint grataque fuerint. Ita enim placuere grataque fuere, ut primo epistole a
rege suscepte gratissime responderet, postulata deinde legatorum
libentissime exaudiret ac insuper plures sacrarum Scripturarum
suarum codices hilariter iocundeque transmitteret, et demum Septuaginta duos seniores, hebree et grece lingue peritissimos, viros
senos e singulis duodecim tribubus electos, in unum congregaret
atque interpretationis faciende gratia ad ipsum regem Alexandriam
8 usque destinaret. Quibus sic in unum congregatis commisit, ut,
preter regias venerationes mansuetasque et humiles exhortationes,
ipsum sacrosanctum legis et prophetarum opus probe et integre
atque fideliter interpretarentur, ut ex suo interpretandi officio vere
ac sincere fungerentur, simul atque maiestati regie impensius grati-
ficarentur; legati igitur ab Eleazaro cum eiusmodi pontificalibus
mandatis abeuntes, ad regem Ptholemeum Alexandriam conten-
derunt. Quos ubi eo applicuerunt, dici non potest quantis rex et
quam magnis honoribus eos prosecutus est.

9 Postquam vero paucorum dierum spatio quieverunt, arduum
illud et ingens interpretandi opus magnanimiter ac seorsum et
singillatim, ut eis a rege iniunctum fuerat, aggressi sunt. Quod a
Ptholemeo de industria factum fuisse legimus, ut singuli seorsum
interpretarentur, ne qua forte inter interpretandum future traductionis suspitio oriretur. Per hunc igitur modum cum dolo agendi
suspitione penitus ablata, non solum ipsa interpretatio integra
atque incorrupta merito haberi putarique posse videbatur; sed
etiam si forte ab aliquo interprete uspiam, ut fit, erratum varia-
tumque fuisset, per accuratam quandam cunctarum aliarum inter-
10 pretationum collationem ab integro undique emendabatur. Singulis igitur cellulis cuique sua separatim assignatis ministrisque et

from him and bring back, in whatever way possible, what the king demanded. When the king's legates had carefully and precisely explained their mission to Eleazar, it is impossible to say how pleased and gratified he was with the honors, the gifts, and the requests from the king. He was so pleased and gratified that he first responded most graciously to the letter received from the king; then he happily attended to the requests of the legates and with great joy sent many of his own volumes of the sacred Scriptures; finally, he gathered together seventy-two elders extremely knowledgeable in Hebrew and Greek, six chosen from each of the twelve tribes, and sent them straight to the king himself in Alexandria to make their translation. He ordered them, once they had 8
gathered together, to show reverence to the king and to address him with gentle humility, but especially to translate the holy work of the law and the prophets correctly, honestly, and faithfully. In this way they would both discharge their office of translation faultlessly and at the same time more deeply gratify his royal majesty. So the legates departed from Eleazar with these orders from the high priest and headed to Ptolemy at Alexandria. When they arrived there, it is impossible to say how many extraordinary honors the king bestowed upon them.

After they rested for a few days, they embarked upon that diffi- 9
cult and monumental task of translation, each one working alone, as had been commanded by the king. We read that this procedure was deliberately arranged by Ptolemy so that no suspicion about the resulting translation might arise during the process of translating. In this way, then, the suspicion of acting deceitfully was entirely removed, and not only was the translation itself able to enjoy the reputation of being honest and genuine, and rightly so, but even if by chance, as happens, one translator made an error somewhere or diverged [from the others], it was fully corrected afresh
by a careful comparison of all the other translations. Therefore 10
each translator was assigned his own separate cell, an attendant,

his omnibus, que ad uniuscuiusque victum necessaria putabantur, abunde subministratis (mirabile profecto ac prorsus incredibile dictu!), non magno quodam plurimorum dierum intervallo tota traductio eodem temporis momento expleta ac perfecta et absoluta fuit, et (quod etiam mirabilius videri debet!) cum hinc inde omnium interpretationum accurata quedam et exacta collatio fieret, profecto non multe et in tam ingenti variorum traductorum numero diverse, sed unica et sola reperta est.

11 Quod cum humanitus fieri non potuerit, a Spiritu Sancto factum fuisse ii soli aiunt atque asserere et confirmare videntur, qui hanc ipsam, de qua disserimus, interpretationem ita divinitus provenisse contendunt, ut nullus ne unus quidem minimus error reperiri possit et valeat. Si qui vero in aliquibus eorum additamentis et in quibusdam quoque omissionibus et in plerisque etiam alienis interpretationibus forte apparere extareque videntur, eos tales non esse errores neque pro erroribus ullatenus habendos plane aperteque dicunt, cum quicquid eiusmodi evenerit, divinitus a Spiritu
12 Sancto profluxisse confirmant. Fieri enim potuit, quemadmodum ipsi aiunt, ut postquam hec translatio per ea que supradiximus, Spiritus Sancti favoribus incepta, expleta et absoluta fuerit; quod omnipotens Deus in mentibus illorum interpretum eatenus inspiraret ut sic interpretarentur, veluti in mentibus prophetarum tanto antea inspiraverat ut ita prophetarent. Ad hec accedebat ut, post plura seculorum curricula, Apostoli et Evangeliste ea ipsa interpretatione non nunquam allegationibus suis usi fuisse videantur; quorum profecto neutrum evenisset, si qua errata in illa forte reperirentur. Quod cum ita fuisse dicant, integram nimirum et incorruptam eam ipsam translationem fuisse esseque constat.

and everything else thought necessary for the sustenance of each was richly provided—an extraordinary and incredible accomplishment! After no great interval of several days had passed, the entire translation was realized and completely finished at the identical moment in time, and—what ought to seem even more amazing—when a careful and detailed comparison of all the translations was made, rather than many different translations resulting from so many individual translators, a single translation emerged.

Those who argue that the translation I am discussing was so 11
divinely produced that not a single error, even the slightest, could be found seem to maintain and assert that, since this could not have happened through human agency, it was achieved by the Holy Spirit alone. However, if there seem to be any errors either in material added or left out, or even in a number of unsuitable translations, they say in plain and explicit terms that such variations are not errors and should not be considered errors in any way at all, since they maintain that anything of that kind flowed
by divine agency from the Holy Spirit. For, as they themselves say, 12
it was possible that, since this translation was begun, completed, and finished, in the way I described above, with the favor of the Holy Spirit, Omnipotent God so stirred inspiration in the minds of those translators that they translated in such a way as he had previously stirred inspiration in the minds of the prophets to prophesy as they did so long before. Moreover, after the course of many ages, the Apostles and Evangelists seem to have used this translation sometimes with their own modifications. Certainly neither of these things would have happened if any errors were found in that translation. Since they say that this was so, it is agreed that this translation itself without a doubt was and is complete and genuine.

13 Atque hec omnia pluraque alia commemoratus Eusebius, in eodem *De preparatione evangelica* libro, his verbis asserere et confirmare videtur, que hoc loco explicande et declarande veritatis gratia non iniuria ponere curavi. Sic enim inquit:

Cum iam Salvatoris nostri tempora viderentur proprius ad-
venire conducebatque saluti maxime omnium gentium, quecunque a prophetis scripta fuerant, intelligere per linguam
grecam, quam fere omnes intelligunt, iudaicam scripturam
universis proposuit; aut enim post Salvatoris nostri tempora
non habuissemus Iudeis ex invidia occultantibus, aut corrup-
tiores nobis dedissent, aut si recte habere potuissemus, in
14 suspitionem traductores facile vocarentur. Salvator ergo noster, qui ut Deus omnia previdebat, optima dispositione usus,
Ptholemeo, Egyptiorum regi, traducendorum librorum cupi-
ditatem iniecit; quod Aristeus vir doctus, utpote qui rebus
aderat, diligenter conscripsit. Fuit autem traductio facta temporibus secundi Ptholemei, qui Philadelphus vocatur, sed
Aristei verba opere pretium est audire. 'Demetrius,' inquit,
'Phalereus in regia bibliotheca constitutus, grandem a rege
pecuniam accepit, ut undique ad illam bibliothecam vel
15 emendo vel transcribendo libros congregaret. Meminique a
presente rege interrogatum quot iam libri in bibliothecis
essent, dixisse: "Plures quam centum milia, sed brevi tempore non erunt fortasse pauciores quam quingenta milia, si
non ab universa Grecia solum (quod feci!) verum etiam ab
aliis gentibus ac precipue a Iudeis, quorum doctrina perutilis
mihi esse videtur, quam plura possumus congregemus." "Et
que nam," rex inquit, "causa te detinuit, ne Iudeorum libros,

Mentioning all these things and more in the same book, *Preparation for the Gospel,* Eusebius seems to claim and assert them with the following words that I have appropriately taken care to set down here in the interest of presenting the truth. He says the following: 13

> Since the era of our Savior seemed to be drawing closer and it was in the interest of the utmost salvation of all peoples to understand in the Greek language, which almost everyone understands, whatever had been written by the prophets, he made the Jewish scripture available to all men. For after the era of our Savior, we would not have got possession of it due to the Jews hiding it away out of envy, or they would have given us damaged copies, or if we had been able to get them, suspicion could easily have been cast on the translators.
> Therefore, our Savior, who, as God, foresaw all things, ar- 14
> ranged everything perfectly and planted in Ptolemy, king of the Egyptians the desire of translating the books. Aristeas, a learned man, wrote about this diligently, since he was present during these events. The translation was made in the time of the second Ptolemy, called Philadelphus, but it is worthwhile hearing the words of Aristeas: "Demetrius of Phaleron," he said, "having been assigned to the royal library, received a large sum of money from the king, to gather books from far and wide for the library, either by way of
> purchase or transcription. I remember that he was asked by 15
> the king in person how many books were now in the libraries and he said: 'More than 100,000, but in a short period of time there will perhaps not be fewer than 500,000, if we collect not only as many books as possible from all of Greece (which I have done!) but also from other nations and especially from the Jews, whose teaching seems to me especially useful.' 'And why have you been held back from either buying

> que regio nobis finitima est, aut emeris iam aut transcripseris, presertim cum ad hanc rem tanta tibi prestetur pecunia quantam petieris?" Tum Demetrius: "Traductione opus est," inquit, "Propria enim lingua et diversis utuntur quam Egyptiis caracteribus."'

et reliqua eiusmodi.

16 Quibus quidem inter eos habitis, rex Demetrio precepit ut traducendorum librorum singularem et precipuam curam assummeret. Omnia enim tanta diligentia faciebat, ut res minimas petitionibus atque mandatis aptissime scriptis ageret. Quare ipse quoque cuncta ut gesta sunt, diligentissime conscripsit; atque epistolam quandam de his rebus in hunc modum Philadelpho misit. Sed antequam verba epistole apponam, in numero codicum superius allegato non iniuria vitio librariorum sive grecorum sive latinorum erratum fuisse arbitror, presertim cum apud A. Gellium, sexto *Noctium Atticarum*, ita scriptum legerimus:

17 > Libros Athenis disciplinarum liberalium publice ad legendum prebendos primus posuisse dicitur Pysistratus tyrannus. Deinceps studiosius accuratiusque ipsi Athenienses auxerunt; sed omnem illam postea librorum copiam Xerses Athenarum potitus, urbe ipsa preter arcem incensa, abstulit absportavitque in Persas.

Hos porro libros diversos multis post temporibus

> Seleucus rex, qui Nicanor appellatus est, referendos Athenas curavit. Ingens postea numerus librorum in Egypto a Ptholemeis regibus vel conquisitus vel confectus est ad milia ferme voluminum septuaginta; sed ea omnia bello priore Alexandrino, dum diripitur ea civitas, non sponte neque opera consulta, sed a militibus forte auxiliariis incensa sunt.

> or transcribing the books of the Jews, whose region borders ours, especially since as much money as you requested is available for this undertaking?' And Demetrius replied: 'These books must be translated, for they use a language and characters different from Egyptian characters.'"[4]

And so on.

After this exchange, the king ordered Demetrius to take special and personal charge of the translation of the books. He managed everything with such extraordinary diligence that he handled the smallest matters with appropriate written requests and orders. So he diligently wrote everything up as it was completed. He sent the following letter about these things to Philadelphus. But before I quote the words of the letter, I think, with some justification, that the number of books indicated above is inaccurate through a mistake made by scribes, either Greek or Latin, especially since we have read in the sixth book of Aulus Gellius' *Attic Nights* the following: 16

> Pisistratus the tyrant is said to have been the first to make books of liberal studies available to be read by the public at Athens. Then the Athenians themselves assiduously and carefully increased the number of books. But afterward Xerxes, once he controlled Athens and had burned the city except for the citadel, carried off that abundance of books to Persia.[5] 17

After much time had passed,

> King Seleucus, who was called Nicanor, made sure these various books were brought back to Athens. Afterward, the Ptolemaic kings collected or produced a huge number of books, as many as 70,000 volumes, but all of these were burned unintentionally and without orders but by chance by auxiliary soldiers in the First Alexandrian War while the city was being plundered.[6]

18 Sed ad Demetrii epistolam parumper redeamus, cuius verba hec sunt:

> Regi magno Demetrius S. D. Quoniam precepisti, o Rex, quod undecunque possim, in bibliothecam tuam utiles libros congeram, certiorem te facio Iudeorum disciplinas et legis litteras eorum lingua conscriptas utiles mihi quidem videri. Feruntur enim abiecte non nulla translata, tante tamen admirationis, ut integra et divina sola legum sanctio Iudaica videatur. Sic enim etiam Echatheus Abderites propter sanctitatem legis nec a poetis gentium tactam arbitratur, nec diligenter ab historicis dispositam. Si ergo tibi videtur, o Rex, scribatur ad Pontificem Iudeorum, ut de singulis tribubus seniores viros, legis peritos et probos, sex mittat, ut diligenti examine id eligamus, in quo plures conveniant traductores. Ista quippe res digna mihi videtur Maiestate tua. Felix sis perpetuo.

19 Quocirca rex iniunxit ut ad Eleazarum, tunc principem sacerdotum, pro hac re suo nomine per predictum Demetrium scriberetur ac multa et quidem pretiosa dona cum omnibus Iudeorum captivis gratis ad eum transmitterentur. Que quidem omnia ut iniunxerat, diligenter accurateque gessit. Exemplum epistole huiusmodi est:

> Rex Ptholemeus Eleazaro Pontifici salutem. Non ignoras multos Iudeorum habitare in regione nostra, qui a Hierosolimis Persarum violentia, tempore quo illi regnabant, abstracti fuerunt; quorum cum multi una cum patre nostro in Egyptum ingrederentur, maiori mercede in legionibus conscripti sunt, cunque fideles repperisset, in presidiis collocavit, ut eorum formidine animos Egyptiorum conservaret.

But let us return briefly to the letter of Demetrius, the words of 18
which are:

> Demetrius greets his great king. Since you ordered me to gather from wherever I could books useful for your library, I can inform you that the teachings of the Jews and the books of law, written in their own language, seem to me useful. To be sure, some are reported to have been poorly translated, nevertheless, they are so admirable that the legislation of the Jews alone seems pure and divine. Echatheus of Abdera also thinks that because of the sanctity of their law it has not been touched by the gentile poets and has not been carefully set out by historians. Therefore, if you think fit, O King, let a letter be sent to the priest of the Jews that he send six elders from each tribe, knowledgeable in the law and upright, so that we may select through careful consideration the translation which most translators agree upon. This indeed seems worthy of your Majesty. May you be blessed for ever.[7]

Therefore the king ordered Demetrius to write to Eleazar, then 19
the chief priest, in his own name about this and he ordered that many precious gifts be sent to him, together with all the Jewish prisoners, free of cost. Demetrius did all that he had ordered diligently and meticulously. Here is a copy of the letter:

> King Ptolemy greets Eleazar the High Priest. You are not unaware that in our territory live many Jews, who were violently dragged off from Jerusalem by the Persians when they governed there. When many of them came into Egypt together with our father, they were enrolled in the legions at a better wage. Whenever he found them trustworthy, he placed them in the royal guard so that he might retain the allegiance of the Egyptians through fear of the Jews.

20 Nos etiam postquam regni habenas suscepimus, eos adhuc multo humanius tractantes, plures quam centum milia redemimus ac convenienti mercede eorum dominis deposita gratis liberavimus, ac siquidem impetu multitudinis perperam gestum est, totum correximus atque emendavimus. Putavimus enim Deo Optimo Maximo gratum fore, qui tantum regnum cum pace ac gloria nobis commendavit. Multos etiam florentis etatis volentesque militare cum dignitate aliqua in exercitu nostro constituimus, et nonnullos etiam apud nos admisimus. Quia igitur volumus et tibi et Iudeis tam presentibus quam futuris gratissimum facere, decrevimus ut lex vestra litteris grecis ab hebraica lingua traducatur, ut vestra quoque volumina cum regiis libris in bibliotheca nostra inveniantur.

21 Recte igitur facies et nostro studio condigne, si viros probos ac seniores peritos legis et lingue grece non ignaros, sex ab unaquaque tribu elegeris. Oportet enim, quando res maxima est, illud eligatur in quo plures convenerint traductores. Hac enim re gesta non parvam nos gloriam consecuturos arbitramur. Ac de his rebus latius tecum loquentur Andreas cubicularius et Aristeus, qui et primitias ad vasa et sacrificia in templum portant argenti atque auri pondus non contemnendum. Scribe tu quoque ad nos de quibuscunque volueris. Gratum enim id nobis erit et amicitia nostra dignum, et quamprimum fieri curabimus quodcunque postulaveris. Vale.

22 Ad hec Eleazarus sic rescripsit: Eleazarus Pontifex amico vero Ptholemeo salutem. Si tu et Arxinoe regina et soror et filii vestri valetis, bene est et, ut volumus, fit; ipsi quoque valemus. Magno gaudio affecti sumus, cum per litteras tuas

After we assumed the reins of the kingdom, we treated them much more humanely still and redeemed more than 100,000 of them. By providing their masters with an agreed-upon compensation, we freed them without obligation to ourselves, and if mistakes were made because of the rush of the crowd, we adjusted and corrected the total amount paid. For we thought that this would be pleasing to the greatest and best God, who entrusted this great kingdom to us with peace and glory. We enrolled many young men in our army with some standing who wished to serve in the military, and we received many of them into our estate. Therefore, because we want to do something most pleasing for you, and for present and future Jews, we have decreed that your law be translated from Hebrew into Greek, so that your volumes, too, may be found in our library along with the royal books. 20

Therefore, you will act rightly and in harmony with our desire if you choose six reliable elders from each tribe who know the law and the Greek language. Since this endeavor is so extraordinary, the translation that the greater number of translators agrees upon should be chosen. We believe that with this accomplishment we will achieve no small praise. Andreas, my secretary, and Aristeas will discuss this in more detail with you. They are bringing a significant amount of silver and gold as firstfruits for your dishes and sacrifices for your temple. Write to us as well about anything you wish. It will be a pleasure for us and in keeping with our friendship, and we will see that whatever you request will be done as soon as possible. Farewell. 21

Eleazar wrote back the following in response: Eleazar the High Priest greets his true friend Ptolemy. If you and your queen and sister Arsinoe and your sons are well, that is excellent and is as we wish. We are also well. We were filled with great joy when we learned through your letter of your 22

bonam erga Iudeos voluntatem tuam cognoverimus. Itaque vocato populo tuam epistolam publice legimus, ut scirent quantam in Deum nostrum habes pietatem; ostendimusque viginti aureas phialas quas misisti, et argenteas triginta et crateras quinque et mensam argenteam ad sacrificandum et ad alia facienda, quibus templum egeret, argenti talenta centum, que Andreas et Aristeus, viri probi et divini ac te digni, abs te nobis tradiderunt, quibus latius diximus que visa sunt. Omnia enim que tibi conferunt, etiamsi preter naturam essent, tui tamen petentis gratia efficere parati sumus.

23 Nam plurima ac maxima et que oblivisci nunquam poterimus, nostro generi beneficia contulisti. Quare illico pro regina et filiis et amicis tuis Deo sacrificia obtulimus; universusque populus oravit ut cuncta tibi ad votum succedant regnumque tibi cum gloria Dominus, omnium Deus, conservet. Preterea ut divine legis commode ac secure fiat traductio, sex ab unaquaque tribu seniores elegi, quos ad te cum libris destinavi. Recte igitur facies, optime rex, Scriptura exquisitissime traducta, si curaveris ut ad nos viri redeant. Vale.

24 Multis deinde hac de re hinc inde dictis explicatisque post iam traductam Scripturam, hec subiungit: Lectitata igitur examinataque lectione, seniores interpretum ac sacerdotes et multi eorum principes coram rege congregati ac propositis in medium libris magna voce dixerunt: 'Quoniam probe ac sancte divina Scriptura traducta est, decens modo est, iustissime rex, ut caveatur ne quis pervertere aliquid audeat.' Quod cum omnes uno consensu approbassent, iussit rex secundum morem suum maledicere. Maledixerunt ergo ut

goodwill toward the Jews. We called together the people and read out your letter publicly, so that they could know how much piety you have for our God. We showed them the twenty golden dishes you sent and thirty pieces of silver and five mixing bowls and the silver table for sacrificing and for doing other things which the temple needs, the hundred talents of silver which Andreas and Aristeas, two upright, spiritual men who are worthy of being in your service, gave to us from you. We told them in more detail about what was required. For we are prepared to do all things that help you, even if they were beyond our ability, since you request them.

For you have bestowed many extraordinary kindnesses on 23
our people, ones we will never be able to forget. In turn, we have offered sacrifices to God for your queen, sons, and your friends. All the people have prayed that all things come about as you wish and that the Lord, God of all, preserve your kingdom for you with glory. Furthermore, in order that the translation of the divine law be done properly and appropriately, I have selected six elders from each tribe whom I have sent to you with books. Therefore, best of kings, you will act correctly if you ensure that these men return to us once the Scripture has been expertly translated. Farewell.

Then, when many points had been discussed and ex- 24
plained among them, after the translation of the Scripture was finished, the following was added: After a reading had been given and pondered, the elders among the translators and the priests and many of their leaders gathered before the king and, after having placed the books on display, said in a loud voice: "Since the Scripture has been properly and piously translated, it is only fitting, most just king, that care be taken lest anyone dare to corrupt any part of it." When everyone unanimously approved of this, the king ordered a curse to be pronounced according to his custom. So they

> solent, si quis addiderit, subtraxerit aut mutaverit aliquid, rectissime id agentes ut divina scriptura perpetuo inviolata servaretur.
>
> 25 His ita gestis mirabili rex affectus est gaudio, ut lecta sibi universa fuerunt, et admiratus legislatoris prudentiam, ita Demetrio dixit: 'Quonam modo fieri potuit, ut nullus neque poetarum neque historicorum de tot tantisque rebus gestis ullam unquam mentionem fecerit?' Cui Demetrius: 'Divina,' inquit, 'hec lex est, et a Deo data, ut vides. At idcirco si qui tetigerunt, a Deo percussi, resilierunt.' Siquidem audivit affirmavitque se audisse a Theopompo quod ceperat non nulla e iudaica Scriptura translata greca oratione ornare; et illico perturbatione quadam et mentis et animi perculsus, magno studio orasse Deum ut revelare dignaretur cuius rei gratia id sibi acciderat, audivisseque per somnium orationis lenocinio venerandam sacre Scripture dignitatem inquinanti talia sibi provenisse.
>
> 26 'Ego quoque,' ipse inquit, 'a Theodecto, tragediarum poeta, accepi quod cum non nulla e iudaica Scriptura ad fabulam quandam transferre vellet, luminibus captus fuerit. Qui quoniam credidit hac de causa id sibi evenisse, magno tempore penitentiam egit. Et tandem sibi visum fuisse restitutum.' Tunc rex magna cum diligentia sanctam Scripturam iudaicam servari iussit.

Sed de his satis. Patet igitur per ea, que ab Eusebio sumpsimus et paulo superius pene ad verbum recitavimus, hanc ipsam celeberrimam sacrarum Scripturarum traductionem, nulla inter interpretes collatione facta, seorsum et separatim inceptam et absolutam

> pronounced a curse, as they were wont, on anyone who added to, removed, or changed any part of the translation, acting most properly so that the divine Scripture would be kept inviolate forever.
>
> After they had done this, when everything was read to the 25
> king, he was filled with marvelous joy. In admiration of the wisdom of the lawmaker, he said to Demetrius: "How could it happen that no poet or historian ever made mention about so many extraordinary deeds?" Demetrius replied to him: "This law is divine and given by God, as you see. Therefore, if anyone touched it, they were struck by God and recoiled." Indeed he heard and asserted that he had heard from Theopompus how he had begun to adorn in Greek some materials translated from Jewish Scripture. His mind and soul being immediately shaken, he had entreated God with great zeal that He might deign to reveal to him why this had happened to him, and he heard through a dream that such things had happened to him because he was sullying the venerable dignity of the Sacred Scripture with the meretricious embellishments of language.
>
> "I also," he himself said, "heard from Theodectus, the tra- 26
> gedian, that when he wished to transfer some elements from Jewish Scripture into a certain play, he was blinded. Since he believed that this happened to him for that reason, he repented for a long time. And finally his sight was restored to him." Then the king ordered that the holy Jewish Scripture be preserved with great care.[8]

But that will suffice on this point. And so it is clear, through the things I have taken from Eusebius and recited just above almost word for word, that this very famous translation of the sacred Scriptures was begun and completed separately, and that no

27 fuisse. Quod utrum verum fuerit an non me ignorare fateor, presertim cum Hieronymum, virum eruditissimum ac trium clarissimarum linguarum peritissimum, longe aliter sentire manifestissime videam, ceu paulo post latius et uberius declarabitur.

28 Eam tamen, quecunque fuerit, opinionem ab homericis *Iliadis* et *Odyssee* poematibus originem habuisse non iniuria arbitror. Celebrata enim omnium eruditorum grecorum hominum sententia est predicta Homeri poemata per omnes eorum libros grecis titulis rapsodias inscribi: quod quidem nomen in latinum eloquium
29 conversum proprie consutum cantum significare videtur. Nam Homerus oculis captus, eius carmina que in dies componebat, veteri poetarum ritu ad liram publice in propatuloque cantabat. Quod cum per omnes celebratas totius Grecie urbes variis, ut fiebat, temporibus factitasset; hinc inde pro diversitate locorum, ubi poeta ille cecinerat, tales versus dispersi reperiebantur, ac per hunc modum passim in tenebris usque ad Pisistrati, Atheniensium tyranni, viri eruditissimi, tempora iacuerant, qui quidem litterarum utpote doctissimus et in primis carminum amantissimus, ingentem sibi gloriam subtili quodam et acri ingenio in hunc modum parare
30 vendicareque excogitavit. Nam celeberrimis diversorum preconum vocibus per totam pene Greciam enuntiari predicique iussit ut quicunque ad se aliquos Homeri versus afferrent, certa et indubitata premia singulorum pro numero versuum allatorum reportarent. Unde cum promisse mercedes quotidianis delatoribus exhiberentur, factum est ut brevi tempore ingens eorum versuum numerus et non nullorum quoque alienorum qui questus gratia afferebantur, in unum congregarentur. Quod cum fecisset, duos et Septuaginta eruditissimos viros e tota Grecia delegisse atque Athenas convocasse scribitur. Quibus cunctos Homeri versus iam antea collectos singillatim ac seorsum prebuit commisitque ut propositis laboribus atque industrie singularibus premiis quisque privatim

collations were performed among the translators. I confess that I 27
do not know whether this happened or not, especially since I see that Jerome, a very learned man and expert in the three most distinguished languages, clearly thinks far differently, as will be shown a little later in more detail.

Nevertheless, I think, with some justification, that this belief, 28
for whatever it is worth, had its origin in the Homeric poems, the *Iliad* and the *Odyssey*.[9] For it is the widespread opinion of all the most learned Greeks that these poems of Homer were divided into books designated with Greek titles as "rhapsodies." Indeed, when this designation is properly translated into Latin, it seems to
mean "a song sewn together."[10] For having lost his sight, Homer, in 29
the ancient manner of poets, sang in public to the lyre the poems that he composed day by day. He did this at various times throughout all the famous cities of the whole of Greece. These verses were found scattered here and there in the various places where the poet had sung them, and in this way had lain everywhere in obscurity down to the time of Pisistratus, the tyrant of Athens, a learned man. As one well read in literature and particularly fond of poems, with fine-tuned and keen genius, he con-
trived to lay claim to great glory in the following way. He ordered 30
various heralds to travel throughout almost all of Greece and repeatedly announce that whoever brought any verses of Homer to him would receive guaranteed rewards in proportion to the number of verses brought. Since the promised payments were made daily to those who brought verses, the result was that in a short time a huge number of Homer's verses, and also verses from others which were brought to make a profit, were gathered together in one place. When he had done this, it is written that he chose seventy-two of the most learned men from all of Greece and summoned them to Athens. He supplied them individually with all

pro se, ut sibi satius convenire videbatur, in ordinem compositio-
31 nemque redigeret. Quocirca per hunc modum delecti viri arduum iniuncte commissionis opus magnanimiter aggressi, ubi singuli quique suum proprium officium diligenter accurateque exolverunt, ad statutum locum et tempus conferendi gratia convenerunt, ac diligentissima quadam atque accuratissima cunctorum operum vicissim collatione habita, in hanc demum omnes uno animo unaque sententia, que nunc extat, ipsorum carminum dispositionem et ordinem convenere, rapsodiamque grece, ut dictum est, de facti nomine cognominavere atque huiusmodi inscriptionem predictis poematibus addiderunt, quam usque ad hec nostra tempora in cunctis priscis novisque codicibus servatam fuisse cernimus legimusque.

32 Hanc ipsam Grecorum hominum de Homeri poematibus opinionem maiores nostri latine lingue illustratores, in quibus principalis est Cicero, maxime confirmasse videntur. Hic enim in tertio *De oratore* quodam loco verba hec ponit:

> Quis doctior illis eisdem temporibus aut cuius eloquentia litteris illustrior fuisse traditur quam Pisistrati, qui primus Homeri libros confusos antea sic disposuisse dicitur, ut nunc habemus? Non fuit ille quidem civibus suis utilis, sed ita eloquentia floruit, ut litteris elegantiaque prestaret,

quanquam Laertius Diogenes in primo *De vita et moribus philosophorum* huiusmodi homericorum poematum, ut ita dixerim, resarcitionem Soloni, uni ex septem sapientibus, in *Vita* eius, magis quam Pisistrato attribuisse videatur.

33 At si id verum fuit quod superius recitavimus, quemadmodum scriptum legimus, profecto illi quod de Septuaginta duobus commemoratis sacrarum litterarum interpretibus ab Eusebio scribitur, simile quiddam esse videbitur. Ceterum quidnam Hieronymus et

the Homeric verses that had been collected, explained the task and the compensation for hard work, and commissioned each of them privately to restore the verses for him, as they saw fit, to the order of the original composition. Hence the men chosen in this way 31
undertook the difficult project imposed on them with great spirit, and when they had each diligently and carefully completed his own proper assignment, they met for a conference at an appointed place and time. After a very exacting and careful comparison was conducted of all their labors, they all finally unanimously agreed on the arrangement and order of all the songs which remains to this day, and they called it in Greek a rhapsody, as it is said, from the nature of their work,[11] and added this designation to the poems. I perceive and read that this designation has been preserved up to our times in all the old and new codices.[12]

Our ancestors, the distinguished practitioners of the Latin lan- 32
guage, seem to have agreed wholeheartedly with this opinion of the Greeks about the poems of Homer, and first among them is Cicero. For in a passage of the third book of *On the Orator,* he says:

> Who is considered to have been more learned in those times or whose eloquence in literature was more brilliant than that of Pisistratus? He it was who first arranged the previously disordered books of Homer in the order we have now. Not that he was helpful for the citizenry, but he was so eloquent that he was preeminent in letters and elegance.[13]

And yet Diogenes Laertius in the first book of *On the Lives of the Philosophers* seems to have attributed the "stitching" together, so to speak, of Homer's poems to Solon, one of the seven wise men, in his *Life,* rather than to Pisistratus.[14]

But if what I have reported above was true, just as I read it, 33
certainly it will appear to be similar to what was written by Eusebius about the seventy-two translators of the sacred texts. What

Augustinus, duo christiane religionis lumina, de hac ipsa celeberrima Septuaginta interpretatione senserint, paulo post referemus, si non nulla quasi de industria ommissa, prius de predicto Ptholemeo Philadelpho illustrandi nominis sui causa breviter in medium attulerimus.

34 Hieronymus enim in *Explanatione super Danielem* de hoc ipso Ptholemeo disserens, sic inquit:

> Iste est Ptholemeus Philadelphus secundus rex Egypti, filius Ptholemei superioris, sub quo Septuaginta interpretes Alexandrie Scripturam sanctam in grecum dicuntur vertisse sermonem, et Eleazaro pontifici multa Hierosolimam et in templum donaria vasa transmisit ut sacre Scripture interpretationem ab eo impetratam ac deinde absolutam in admirabilem bibliothecam suam reconderet, cui bibliothece prefuit Demetrius Phalereus idem apud Grecos orator et philosophus, tanteque potentie fuisse narratur, ut Ptholemeum
> 35 patrem vinceret. Narrant enim historie habuisse eum peditum ducenta milia; equitum viginti, curruum duo milia; elephantos, quos primus adduxit ex Ethiopia, quadringentos; naves longas, quas nunc liburnas vocant, mille quingentas; et alias ad cibaria militum deportanda mille; auri quoque et argenti grande pondus, ita ut de Egypto per singulos annos quatuordecim milia octingenta argenti talenta acciperet, et totidem frumenti artabas, que quidem mensura tres modios et tertiam modii partem habet; quinquies et decies centena milia, et reliqua huiusmodi.

36 Et tamen ex hac sola et unica sacre Scripture interpretatione, cuius ipse duntaxat auctor extitisse perhibetur, plus glorie quam ex ceteris omnibus preclarissimis eius gestis assecutus est. Nunc ad eam, de qua supradiximus, Hieronymi et Augustini circa huiusmodi interpretationem opinionem parumper accedamus. Augustinus quippe predictam Eusebii Cesariensis sententiam pluribus

Jerome and Augustine, two luminaries of the Christian religion, thought about this famous Septuagint translation, I will report a little later, but first, to illustrate his reputation, I would like to draw attention briefly to several aspects of Ptolemy Philadelphus that were, as it were, intentionally omitted.

For Jerome in his *Commentary on Daniel*, in speaking about Ptol- 34
emy, says the following:

> This is Ptolemy Philadelphus, the second king of Egypt, son of Ptolemy the elder, under whom the Seventy translators are said to have translated the Holy Scripture into the Greek tongue at Alexandria. He sent to Jerusalem for Eleazar the High Priest many vessels as gifts for the temple in order that he might store away in his wondrous library the translation of the Holy Scripture that had been ordered by him and then completed. Demetrius of Phaleron was in charge of this library, a Greek orator and philosopher, and Philadelphus is said to have been so powerful that he sur-
> passed his father Ptolemy. The histories narrate that he had 35
> 200,000 infantry, 20,000 cavalry, 2,000 chariots, 400 elephants which he was the first to bring from Ethiopia, 1,500 long ships which they now call Liburnian galleys, and another thousand for carrying the soldiers' provisions; also a great amount of gold and silver, such that he received from Egypt each year 14,800 talents of silver and as many bushels of grain. This measure has 3 and 1/3 pecks; 15 times 100,000 etc.[15]

Nevertheless, he achieved more glory from this unique transla- 36
tion of the sacred Scripture, of which he is considered to be the sole sponsor, than from all his other extraordinary deeds. Now let us, as I mentioned above, briefly examine the opinion of Jerome and Augustine about this translation. Augustine is indeed believed to have followed the aforementioned opinion of Eusebius of

librorum suorum locis ac presertim decimo octavo *De civitate Dei* secutus fuisse creditur ubi verba hec ponit, que explanande veritatis ac maioris declarationis gratia hoc loco inserere curavi. Inquit enim:

37 Cum fuerint et alii interpretes, qui ex hebraica lingua in grecam sacra illa eloquia transtulerunt, sicut Aquila, Simacus et Theodotion; sicut etiam illa est interpretatio, cuius auctor non apparet et ob hoc sine nomine interpretis quinta editio nuncupatur; hanc tamen, que Septuaginta est, sic recipit Ecclesia, eaque utuntur greci populi christiani, quorum plerique utrum alia sit aliqua ignorant. Ex hac Septuaginta interpretatione etiam in latinam linguam interpretatum est, quod et Ecclesie latine tenent; quamvis non defuerit temporibus nostris presbyter Hieronymus, homo doctissimus et omnium trium linguarum peritus, qui non ex Greco, sed ex Hebreo in Latinum eloquium easdem Scripturas converterit.

38 Sed eius tam litteratum laborem quamvis Iudei fateantur esse veracem, ac Septuaginta interpretes in multis errasse contendant, tamen Ecclesie Christi tot hominum auctoritati ab Eleazaro pontifice ad hoc tantum opus electorum neminem iudicant preferendum, quia etsi non in eis unus apparuisset Spiritus sine dubitatione divinus, sed inter se se verba interpretationis sue Septuaginta doctorum more hominum contulissent et, quod placuisset omnibus, hoc maneret, nullus eis unus interpres debuit anteponi. Quisquis profecto alius illarum Scripturarum ex Hebrea in quamlibet aliam linguam interpres est verax, aut congruit illis Septuaginta interpretibus, aut si non congruere videtur, altitudo prophetica ibi esse credenda est.

Caesarea at many points in his writings and especially in the eighteenth book of the *City of God,* where he writes the following. I have taken care to introduce this passage here for the sake of explaining the truth and for greater clarity. He says:

> Although there were also other translators who had translated those sacred words from Hebrew into Greek, like Aquila, Symmachus, and Theodotion, and the translation whose author is unclear and for that reason is called the fifth edition without the name of a translator; nevertheless, the Church has endorsed the Septuagint translation. The Christian Greek peoples also use it, many of whom are unaware that there is any other translation. A translation was also made from the Septuagint into the Latin language which the Latin Churches use, even though in our times we have had the presbyter Jerome, a very learned man and trained in all three languages, who translated the same Scriptures not from Greek but from Hebrew into Latin. 37
>
> But although the Jews admit that his learned labor is accurate and they maintain that the Seventy Translators made many errors, nevertheless the Churches of Christ judge that no one ought to be preferred to the authority of so many men chosen by Eleazar the priest for so great an endeavor. Even if one clearly divine Spirit had not appeared among them, but the seventy learned men had compared the words of their translation among themselves, as men will do, and what pleased all remained, no one translator ought to be preferred to them. Certainly if any other translator of these Scriptures from Hebrew into any other given language is faithful to the original, either he agrees with the Seventy translators, or if he seems not to, then one must believe in the presence of prophetic exaltation. 38

39 Spiritus enim, qui in prophetis erat, quando illa dixerunt, idem ipse erat etiam in Septuaginta viris, quando illa interpretati sunt: qui profecto auctoritate divina et aliud dicere potuit tanquam propheta ille utrunque dixisset, quia utrunque idem Spiritus diceret et hoc ipsum aliter, ut si non eadem verba, idem tamen sensus bene intelligentibus dilucesceret et aliquid pretermittere et aliquid addere, ut etiam hinc ostenderetur non humanam fuisse in illo opere servitutem, quam verbis dicebat interpres, sed divinam potius potestatem, que mentem replebat et erigebat interpretis.

40 Non nulli codices grecos interpretationis Septuaginta ex hebreis codicibus emendandos curarunt; nec tamen ausi sunt detrahere, quod Hebrei non habebant et Septuaginta posuerunt, sed tantummodo addiderunt, que in Hebreis inventa, apud Septuaginta non erant, eaque signis quibusdam in stellarum modum factis ad capita eorundem versuum notaverunt, que signa *asteriscos* vocant. Illa vero que non habent Hebrei, habent autem Septuaginta, similiter ad capita versuum iacentibus virgulis, sicut scribuntur *unciae,* signaverunt.

41 Et multi codices has notas habentes usquequaque diffusi sunt et Latini. Que autem non pretermissa nec addita, sed aliter dicta sunt sive alium sensum faciant etiam ipsum non abhorrentem, sive alio modo eundem sensum explicare monstrentur, sive utrisque codicibus inspectis nequeunt reperiri. Si ergo, ut oportet, nihil aliud intueamur in Scripturis illis nisi quid per homines dixerit Dei Spiritus, quicquid est in hebreis codicibus et non est apud interpretes Septuaginta,

For the same Spirit who was among the prophets when they spoke these words was also among the Seventy when they translated them. Certainly the Spirit was also able to say something else with divine authority, as if the prophet concerned had said both things, because the same Spirit said both and indicated the same thing in another way. So that if the words are not the same, nevertheless the same sense would become clear to those who fully understand that he could omit one thing and add something else. In this way it is revealed that there was no human drudgery in that work which the translator indicated with his words, but rather a divine power, which replenished and elevated the mind of the translator. 39

Several have taken care that the Greek volumes of the translation of the Seventy be corrected based on the Hebrew volumes. However, they have not dared to remove what the Hebrew volumes did not have and what the Seventy included, but they have only added what was found in the Hebrew volumes but was not included in the Septuagint, and they marked these inclusions with some symbols made in the shape of stars at the beginning of these same verses. They call these signs asterisks. Likewise they marked those verses that the Hebrew volumes do not have, but the Septuagint includes, at the beginning of the verses with horizontal strokes just as unciae are indicated. 40

Many volumes that have these indications, including Latin ones, have continually spread far and wide. As for things that have not been omitted or added but are said in a different way or yield a different sense not differing from the original: these cannot be determined except by inspecting both books.[16] If, then, as we ought, we look at nothing in the Scriptures other than what the Spirit of God has said through men, whatever is in the Hebrew volumes and not in 41

noluit ea per istos, sed per illos prophetas Dei Spiritus di-
42 cere. Quicquid vero est apud Septuaginta, in hebreis autem codicibus non est, per istos ea maluit quam per illos idem Spiritus dicere, sic ostendens utrosque prophetas. Isto enim modo alia per Esaiam, alia per Hieremiam, alia per alium aliumque prophetam vel aliter per hunc ac per illum dixit, ut voluit, unus atque idem Spiritus, sed ut illi precederent prophetando quia sicut in illis vera et concordantia dicentibus unus patris Spiritus fuit, sic et in istis non secum conferentibus et tamen tanquam uno ore cuncta interpretantibus idem Spiritus unus apparuisset.

43 Atque cum hec ipse dixisset, singulare quoddam et admirabile de Iona propheta exemplum his verbis in medium adduxit:

> Sed ait aliquis: 'Quomodo sciam quid Ionas propheta dixerit Ninivitis, utrum: *Triduum Ninive evertetur;* an: *Quadraginta dies?*' Quis non viderit non potuisse utrunque dici a propheta, qui missus fuerat terrere comminatione imminentis excidii civitatem? Cui si tertio die fuerat futurus interitus, non utique quadragesimo die; si autem quadragesimo, non utique tertio. Si igitur a me queritur, quid horum Ionas dixerit, hoc puto potius quod legitur in Hebreo: *Quadraginta dies, et Ni-*
> 44 *nive evertetur.* Septuaginta quippe longe posterius interpretati aliud dicere potuerunt, quod tamen ad rem pertineret et in unum eundemque sensum, quamvis sub altera significatione, concurreret, admoneretque lectorem auctoritate utraque non spreta ab historia se se attollere ad ea requirenda, propter

the Seventy Translators, the Spirit of God was unwilling to
say through them, but through those prophets. Whatever is 42
in the Seventy but is not in the Hebrew volumes, the same Spirit preferred to say through the former, rather than the latter, thus showing both to be prophets. For in this way one and the same Spirit has spoken some things through Isaiah, other things through Jeremiah, and other things through one prophet or another, saying one thing through this prophet and something else through another, as he wished, but it did so that they should excel as prophets, because just as the one Spirit of the Father was in the prophets saying true and consistent things, thus also the same one Spirit had appeared among those translators who did not compare their works and nevertheless translated everything as though with one mouth.[17]

When he had said these things, he cited this unique and mar- 43
velous example concerning Jonah the prophet:

But someone says: "How do I know what the prophet Jonah said to the people of Nineveh? Was it *In three days Nineveh will be overthrown* or *In forty days?*" Who does not see that the prophet, who had been sent to terrify the city with the threat of imminent destruction, could not have said both? If this city was to be destroyed on the third day, certainly it would not be destroyed on the fortieth; and if it was going to be destroyed on the fortieth, it certainly would not be destroyed on the third. If therefore I investigate which of these Jonah said, I think it was what was written in the Hebrew, i.e.,
Forty days, and Nineveh will be destroyed. For the Seventy, trans- 44
lating much later, could say something else, which nevertheless related to the subject and concurred in the same sense, although with a different detail. This warned the reader not to spurn the authority of either text and to lift himself above

que significanda historia ipsa conscripta est. Gesta sunt quippe illa in Ninive civitate, sed aliquid etiam significaverunt, quod modum illius civitatis excedat; sicut est gestum, quod ipse Propheta in ventre ceti triduo fuit, et tamen aliud significavit in profundum inferni triduo futurum, qui Dominus est omnium Prophetarum. Quapropter si per illam civitatem recte accipitur Ecclesia gentium prophetice figurata, eversa scilicet per penitentiam, ut qualis fuerat iam non esset; hoc quoniam per Christum factum est in Ecclesia gentium, cuius illa in Ninive figuram gerebat, sive per quadraginta dies sive per triduum idem ipse significatus est Christus; per quadraginta scilicet, quia tot dies peregit cum discipulis suis post resurrectionem et ascendit in celum; per triduum vero, quia die tertio resurrexit; tanquam lectorem nihil aliud quam historie rerum gestarum inherere cupientem, de somno excitaverint Septuaginta interpretes; iidemque Prophete ad perscrutandam altitudinem prophetie et quonam modo dixerint: 'In quadraginta diebus' Christum quere, in quo et triduum potueris invenire; illud in ascensione, hoc in eius resurrectione reperies. Propter quod utroque numero significari convenientissime potuit, quorum unum per Ionam prophetam, alterum per Septuaginta interpretum prophetiam, unus tamen atque idem Spiritus dixit.

history in order to investigate those things which history itself is written to disclose. Certainly these things happened in
the city of Nineveh, but they indicate something that ex-
tends beyond the limit of that city. It happened that the
prophet was in the belly of the whale for three days, and
nevertheless it indicated something else would be in the
depths of the underworld for three days, namely, He who is
the Lord of all prophets. Therefore if the Church of the 45
Gentiles is rightly understood to have been figured propheti-
cally by that city of Nineveh, which was destroyed by way of
penitence, in order for it no longer to be what it had been;
and since this was done by Christ in the Church of the Gentiles, the Church is figured in Nineveh, whether Christ
Himself is signified by forty days or three days: if "forty
days," no doubt because he spent so many days with the
disciples after the resurrection and then ascended to heaven,
but if "three days" because on the third day he rose again. It
is as though the Seventy translators roused from sleep a
reader who desires nothing other than to cling to the history
of the events, and likewise as though the prophets roused
the reader to explore the heights of prophecy and, as it were,
said: "In forty days" seek Christ, in whom you will also be
able to find the "three days": you will find one of them in the
ascension, the other in his resurrection. On account of this it
could be most appropriately communicated by either number, one number through the prophet Jonah, and another
number through the prophecy of the Seventy Translators.
Nevertheless, one and the same Spirit said both.[18]

46 Quibus quidem, ut supra recitavimus, ad verbum explicatis:

> Longitudinem—inquit—fugio, cum non hec per multa demonstrem, in quibus ab Hebraica veritate putantur Septuaginta interpretes discordare et bene intellecti videntur esse concordes. Unde etiam ego pro meo modulo vestigia sequens Apostolorum, qui et ipsi ex utrisque, id est ex Hebreis et Septuaginta, testimonia prophetica posuerunt, utraque auctoritate utendum putavi, quoniam utraque una atque divina est.

47 A quibus quidem, Eusebio scilicet et Augustino, etsi qui alii
fuerunt qui de hac re ita sentirent, ut diximus, Hieronymus usque
adeo dissensisse videtur, ut id tanquam incertum quiddam ac fal-
sum pluribus librorum suorum locis plane et aperte refellere et
48 confutare profiteatur. Nam quodam loco,

> Nescio—inquit—quis primus auctor Septuaginta cellulas Alexandrie mendacio suo extruxit quibus divisi eadem scriptitarent, cum Aristeus, eiusdem Ptholemei yperapistes, et multo post tempore Iosephus nihil tale retulerint, sed in una basilica congregatos, contulisse scribant, non prophetasse. Aliud est enim vatem, aliud est esse interpretem. Ibi Spiritus ventura predicit; hic eruditio et verborum copia ea, que intelligit, transfert. Nisi forte putandus est Tullius *Economicum* Xenophontis, et Platonis *Protagoram*, et Demosthenis *Pro Ctesiphonte* orationem afflatus rhetorico spiritu protulisse.

After he had explained these things as I have reported word for word, he said: 46

> I avoid going into this in great detail since I am not making my point with many examples, where the Seventy Translators are thought to diverge from the original Hebrew and if properly understood are seen to be in agreement. And so I also follow, as best as I can, in the footsteps of the Apostles, who also referred to prophecies from both, that is, the Hebrew and the Septuagint. I have thought that both should be used as authoritative, since each is one and divine.[19]

As I said, Jerome disagrees with them, namely Eusebius and Augustine, and if there were any others who agreed with them about this matter, to such a degree that he states clearly and explicitly in many places in his works that he disputes this account as unfounded and false. For in one place he says, 47
48

> I do not know who was the first to fabricate the story of the seventy cells in Alexandria among which they were distributed and then wrote the same things. Aristeas, the retainer of this same Ptolemy, and Josephus much later reported no such thing, but they write that [the Seventy] were gathered in one building and that they made comparisons but did not prophesy. For it is one thing to be a prophet and another thing to be a translator. In the first case the Spirit predicts what will happen; in the other case, the translator's erudition and vocabulary translate what he understands. Unless perchance Cicero should be thought to have brought forth the *Oeconomicus* of Xenophon, the *Protagoras* of Plato, and the *For Ctesiphon* of Demosthenes by having been breathed upon by the spirit of oratory. Or the Holy Spirit wove testimonia

Aut aliter de eisdem libris per Septuaginta interpretes, aliter per Apostolos Spiritus sanctus testimonia texuit, ut quod illi tacuerunt, hi scriptum esse mentiti sunt.

49 Multa huiusmodi de industria pretereo nimiam longitudinem
veritus. Huiusmodi igitur Septuaginta interpretum traductio, quo-
modocunque et qualitercunque, sive seorsum et separatim, sive simul ac coniunctim celebrata fuerit, tanto tamen in honore tanto-
que pretio primitus habita est, ut paucis post annis totam pene
50 Greciam occupaverit. Neque id temere et absque iustis causis
evenisse creditur, cum quia ea tempestate unica et sola ferebatur,
tum etiam quia solemniter admodum facta fuerat. Ad hec accedebat et Ptholemei potentissimi regis precipua et singularis dignitas
et maxima quoque atque admirabilis illorum interpretum auctoritas, que illis temporibus celeberrima habebatur; quorum nomina
litteris non immerito mandari debuerunt, quod utrum de omnibus
51 factum fuerit legisse non memini. Apud Eusebium enim in libro
De historia ecclesiastica ita scribitur: 'Aristobolus unus e Septuaginta
senioribus fuit, qui a Pontificibus ad Ptholemeum regem interpre-
tande divine legis gratia missi fuerant.' Ceterum apud Iosephum
omnium interpretum nomina in Eleazari ad Ptholemeum epistola
expressa fuisse legimus, que et ab eo et ab Eusebio pretermissa et
oblivioni tradita et admiramur et non sine aliquali molestia tolle-
ramus, cum res perpetuis litterarum monumentis digna et priscis
annalibus memoranda esset.

52 Iosephus enim XII *Antiquitatum* inter cetera verba hec ponit:
'Mihi vero non necessarium visum est Septuaginta seniorum ab
Eleazaro missorum nomina declarare, licet intimata sub epistola
fuissent'; et paulo post inter interpretandum simul contulisse et in

concerning the same books in one way through the Seventy Translators, in another way through the Apostles, so that the Apostles lied that what the translators left unsaid had been written.[20]

I intentionally pass over many examples of this kind for fear of 49
rambling on. Therefore the translation of the Seventy Translators (however and in whatever manner it became known, either as something achieved separately and apart or at the same time and together) was so dearly honored and esteemed that within a few
years it pervaded almost all of Greece. Nor is this believed to have 50
happened by accident or without good reason, both because at that time it was considered unique, but also because it had been created so solemnly. Moreover, there was the special and extraordinary dignity of the most powerful king Ptolemy and the exceptional and wondrous authority of those translators that was very well known in those times. Their names justly deserved to be committed to writing; I do not remember reading whether that
was done for all of them. For Eusebius in his *Church History* writes 51
the following: "Aristobulus was one of the Seventy elders who had been sent by the priests to King Ptolemy for the sake of translating the divine law."[21] But in Josephus we read that the names of all the translators had been expressed in a letter of Eleazar to Ptolemy. I am astonished by the fact that the names were omitted by him and by Eusebius and that they were condemned to oblivion.[22] I am annoyed at this, since this was something that should have been preserved in writing forever and should have been commemorated in the ancient annals.

Josephus has this to say in book twelve of the *Jewish Antiquities:* 52
"It does not seem necessary to me to set out the names of the Seventy Elders sent by Eleazar, although the names had been indicated in the letter."[23] A little later he declares that they conferred together while translating and that they began and finished the

Septuaginta diebus inceptam interpretationem consumasse testatur. In quibus duntaxat duobus ab ipso Eusebio discrepasse ac
dissensisse constat cum in ceteris omnibus maxime convenire
53 videantur. Nec post adventum Christi illa eorum tanta et tam
magna auctoritas aliqua ex parte diminuta, quin immo vel potius
adaucta fuisse videtur, cum Evangelistas et Apostolos ea traductione in allegationibus suis non nunquam usos fuisse manifestum
sit; atque his de causis per multa tempora sola in maxima quadam
estimatione perseveravit, donec aliqui alii interpretes accesserunt,
qui quidem cum in predicta seniorum traductione multa superaddita, non nulla omissa pleraque aliter traducta conspicarentur,
quarundam aliarum novarum translationum labores variis temporibus assumpserunt.

54 Eorum primus fuit quidam nomine Aquila Ponticus, qui quin-
gentis circiter annis post Septuaginta illos seniores sub Helio
Adriano maxime floruit. Hic cum a principio traduxisset, unica
illa sua interpretatione non contentus, secundam quandam aggres-
sus est traductionem, quam et perfecit et absolvit. Triginta postea
annorum quoque curriculis, Commodi imperatoris temporibus
accessit alter interpres Ephesius Theodotion. Helio deinde Pertinaci Severoque imperitantibus, Simacus tertius in medium appa-
55 ruit. Ac septem postea annis, Antonio Caracalla imperante, alia,
quinta scilicet, editio Hierico reperta est, que quidem sine certo
auctore inventa perhibetur. Quinta et Communis et Vulgata editio
variis nominibus a diversis scriptoribus nuncupatur. Non multis
post annis sexta etiam editio sine certo pariter auctore comperta
est. Brevi deinde post sub Alexandro, Mamee filio, claruit Orige-
nes, qui predictas inter se adeo diversas interpretationes cernens,
illam videlicet Septuaginta diligenter accurateque emendavit, universum opus suis asteri⟨s⟩cis obelisque, id est stellis verubusque
distinguens.

translation in seventy days. In only these two areas do they disagree with and differ from Eusebius, although in all other areas
they seem to agree in the highest degree. Nor after the arrival of 53
Christ did their extraordinary and immense authority diminish in any way. Instead, it seems to have grown even stronger, since it is clear that the Evangelists and Apostles often used this translation in their dispatches. As a result, this translation alone continued to be held in the greatest respect over many years, until other translators emerged who undertook the labors of new translations at various times when it was clear that many things had been added in the translation of the elders, many things omitted, and a number of things differently translated.[24]

The first of these was Aquila of Pontus, who was active under 54
Aelius Hadrian approximately five hundred years after the Seventy Elders. Although he had translated from the beginning, he was not content with his unique translation, so he undertook and completed a second translation. Thirty years later while Commodus was Emperor, a second translator was added, Theodotion of Ephesus. Then when Aelius Pertinax and Severus were emperors,
Symmachus emerged as a third translator. Seven years after this, 55
while Antonius Caracalla was emperor, another edition, namely the fifth, was found at Jericho. It is said to have been discovered without an author indicated. It is called the fifth version, common, or Vulgate, with various names by different writers. Not many years after this a sixth edition was discovered, also without a clear author. It was unclear who had translated this one as well. A little later in the time of Alexander, son of Mamea, Origen was a man of distinction. He perceived that the aforementioned translations differed one from the other. So he corrected the Septuagint, attentively and precisely, marking his whole work with asterisks and obeli, that is, with stars and swords.[25]

56 Atque omnes de Hebreo in grecum idioma Hieronymi nostri
temporibus extabant. Quas cum inter se plurimum discrepare ex
accurata lectione vicissitudinariaque omnium invicem comparatione plane aperteque et luce, ut dicitur, meridiana clarius et sole
ipso illustrius cognosceret atque omnes et singulas quasque ab
hebraica veritate plurimum dissentire non dubitaret, laborem nove
ab integro traductionis assumpsit atque inchoavit, inchoatumque
57 mirabiliter ac divinitus absolvit. Quod opus ita magnanimiter ag-
gressus, in ea in qua nunc legitur integritate per multos annos
magnis cum diurnis laboribus maximisque lucubrationibus perfecit, partim ut Iudeis Christianis hominibus divinarum Scripturarum veterum falsitatem obicientibus responderet silentiumque
posthac indiceret, partim etiam ut tantam ac tam multiplicem diversarum traductionum varietatem auferret. De qua quidem translatione pauca quedam nequaquam a nostro proposito aliena
deinceps breviter referemus, si prius eius vitam et mores parumper
attigerimus, ut qualis quantusque fuerit hic solus universalis cunctarum sacrarum Scripturarum veterum et novarum interpres,
probe intelligere ac vere cognoscere valeamus.

58 Hieronymus igitur, patre natus Eusebio, ex opido Stridonis
oriundus, quod a Gothis eversum Dalmatie quondam Pannonie-
que confinium fuit, hic ubi in patria prima litterarum elementa
percepit, adolescentie sue tempore discendi gratia Romam, ubi ea
tempestate bonarum artium studia apprime florebant, se contulisse perhibetur et dicitur, atque ibi Donati cuiusdam, excellentis-
simi grammatici, primo discipulus fuit. Paucis post annis sub
Victorino, insigni rhetore, in arte oratoria admodum eruditus est,
atque inter acquirendum has duas peregregias ac libero dignas
grammatice atque rhetorice disciplinas singularem quandam greca-
59 rum litterarum cognitionem adeptus est. Non multo post ibidem
presbyter ordinatus, i⟨m⟩menso quodam ac pene incredibili dis-
cendarum sacrarum Scripturarum amore flagrabat. Quocirca ad

All of these, translated from the Hebrew into Greek, were extant in the time of our Jerome.[26] When, after careful reading and repeated comparison among them all, he realized that they varied greatly and this, as they say, became more obvious than the midday light and more conspicuous than the sun itself; and when he did not doubt that each and every one of them was greatly at variance with the Hebrew original, he began the task of a new translation from scratch, and miraculously and with divine aid he finished what he started. He tackled this project manfully and brought it to term, with the completeness in which it is now read, over many years with enormous labors by day and night. His aim was partly to reply to Jews who taunted Christians with the inaccuracy of the ancient divine Scriptures and reduce them to silence, partly to eliminate so great and manifold a variety of diverse renderings.[27] About this translation I will briefly say a few words relevant to our discussion, but first I will touch briefly on Jerome's life and character so that we can properly understand and truly know the quality and greatness of this unique and universal translator of all the sacred Scriptures, both old and new. 56

57

Jerome was the son of Eusebius and came from Strido which, having been conquered by the Goths, was once at the border of Dalmatia and Pannonia.[28] When he had first learned grammar there, on becoming a young man, he is said to have traveled to Rome to further his education since that was where the liberal arts were particularly flourishing at that time. At first he was the student of a certain Donatus, an exceptional teacher of grammar. After a few years as a student of Victorinus, a famous rhetorician, he was fully educated in the art of oratory. While acquiring this training in two very distinguished areas worthy of a gentleman—grammar and rhetoric—he obtained a fine knowledge of Greek letters. Shortly after being ordained a presbyter in the same place, he was burning with a great and almost unbelievable passion for learning the sacred Scriptures. So in pursuit of education, he went 58

59

Gregorium Nazianzenum virum per ea tempora divinarum litterarum ceterorum omnium prestantissimum, discendi causa Constan-
tinopolim usque contendit. Ubi aliquot annos in ea disciplina diligenter accurateque perseveravit mirabiliterque profecit. Romam
inde reversus ac singulari quadam grece latineque lingue erudi-
tione admodum armatus, ad cognoscendum hebreas litteras ani-
60 mum mentemque convertit. Earum quidem accuratam cognitionem non modo utilem, sed etiam necessariam ad perfectam et
absolutam sacrarum Scripturarum, quarum, ut diximus, amore
exardescebat, intelligentiam in primis fore arbitrabatur.

Idque ut ita putaret, duabus precipue rationibus probabiliter
adducebatur. Prima erat quedam troporum ac metaphorarum co-
pia, quibus ea lingua vel maxime abundabat, ubi non nulla ingentia
divinarum rerum mysteria interdum abstrusa latere videbantur,
que quidem in alienam linguam cum tanta ac tam propria illarum
61 sententiarum expressione transferri non poterant. Ad hanc unam
altera accedebat, que illum peritissimum ac santissimum virum
multo vehementius angere urgereque debebat. Diverse enim et
Septuaginta, ut priorem illam, si qua alia fuit, omittamus, et
Aquile et Simachi et Theodotionis et quinte et sexte editionis et
Origenee, ut ita dixerim, emendationis interpretationes hinc inde
pro varietate locorum diversimode ferebantur. Que quidem ita inter se distabant ac sic ab invicem dissidebant, ut in plerisque pene
62 contrarie viderentur. Hanc igitur sanctarum Litterarum inter se
discrepantiam et quasi contrarietatem, quemadmodum christia-
num religiosum et sanctum virum in primis decere videbatur, diligenter et accurate conspicatus, pro virili sua tolerare non potuit.
Unde eam auferre cupiens, non modo utile, sed etiam et necessarium fore existimavit, si, per novam quandam et integram de
hebreo in latinum eloquium traductionem, omnis sacrarum Scripturarum, quecunque ex diversis traductionibus oriretur ambigui-
tas, penitus et omnino et usquequaque tolleretur.

all the way to Constantinople to Gregory of Nazianzus who at that time was the most knowledgeable expert about divine letters and all other matters. For several years he continued training there diligently and carefully, and he made marvelous progress. He then returned to Rome armed with this impressive learning in Greek and Latin and dedicated his heart and soul to learning Hebrew.
He thought that a precise understanding of this language would 60
not only be useful but even necessary for a perfect and complete understanding of the sacred Scriptures, for the knowledge of which he had, as I said, a passionate desire.

He was probably led to think this by the following two considerations. First, this language abounds in a great stock of tropes and metaphors, where some profound mysteries concerning divine things sometimes seemed hidden and concealed. These indeed could not be translated into another language while maintaining
the weighty and proper articulation of those ideas. In addition to 61
this, there was another factor that must have troubled and exerted pressure upon that skilled and holy man. For the various translations, both the Septuagint—to omit the earlier one, if indeed any existed—and those of Aquila and Symmachus and Theodotion and the fifth and sixth editions along with what might be called Origen's emendation were produced in different ways in a number of different places. Because of these distances they so differed from each other that in many places they appeared almost to contradict
one another. Therefore, after taking careful and diligent note of 62
these differences or even contradictions in the holy letters, for his part, as was fitting for a devout and holy Christian, he was unable to endure them any longer. Desiring to erase these differences, he thought that it would be not only useful but even necessary, if, through a new and complete translation from Hebrew into Latin, every ambiguity of the Holy Scriptures which arose from the different translations could be entirely and completely removed.

63 Atque his duabus, ut diximus, causis adductus, ad cognitionem lingue hebree ceteris posthabitis sese convertit. In qua quidem perdiscenda tanta diligentia tantaque cura ac tantis lucubrationibus per multos annos usus fuit, ut licet eius lingue notitia admodum difficillima haberetur et esset, nihilominus magna ex parte cognovit; et ad tollendam predictarum interpretationum diversitatem novam hanc, qua omnes ecclesie latine utuntur, non solum totius veteris ex Hebreo, sed etiam novi ex Greco Testamenti tra-
64 ductionem ab integro inchoavit absolvitque. Quod idcirco preter duas commemoratas causas etiam fecisse videtur, ut illorum temporum et posterorum suorum Hebreis, manifestam quandam divinarum Scripturarum falsitatem ob tot et tam diversas interpretationes christianis hominibus obicientibus, magnanimiter simul ac verissime responderet. Hoc quidem tam arduum ac tam difficile et tam asperum traductionis sue opus usque adeo christiano generi presertim latinis hominibus utile, usque adeo necessarium, usque adeo denique ad consecutionem humane salutis saluberrimum non iniuria fuisse arbitror, ut nihil unquam a creatione orbis usque ad hec nostra tempora ab uno solo auctore scriptum fuisse credam,
65 quod cunctis christianis latinisque populis tantopere profuisse videatur.

Nec tamen id, cuius gratia ad interpretandum adductus fuerat, assecutus est. Hebrei nanque post hanc ultimam, de qua loquimur, divinorum librorum interpretationem de falsitate Scripturarum nostrarum adversus Christianos quotidie insultare ac latrare non desinunt; at vero si sui iuris essent, ita ut ea dicere ac facere liceret quecunque vellent, profecto maledictis nostrarum Scripturarum et execrationibus non contenti, cuncta nostratia lacerarent
66 ignique damnarent. Primo nanque maiores suos imitati atque ideo adversus Christianos infensi, omnes passim uno ordine odio

So, as I have said, led by these two causes, he committed him- 63
self to learning Hebrew and postponed his other projects. Over
many years he worked late into the evening, demonstrating so
much diligence and care in learning this language, that he learned
it to a great extent, even though it was considered and was a very
difficult language to master. In order to get rid of the variety of the
aforementioned translations, he began and completed a fresh
translation not only of the entire Old Testament from Hebrew,
but also of the New Testament from Greek, which all the Latin
churches use. In addition to the two reasons already mentioned, 64
he seems also to have done this in order to respond manfully and
truthfully to the Hebrews of those and later times who taunted
Christians with the manifest unreliability of the divine Scriptures
because there were so many and such diverging translations. I believe with justification that this difficult and labor-intensive translation was so useful to Christians, especially Latin Christians, and
also so necessary and so beneficial for achieving human salvation,
that from the creation of the world up to our times nothing has
ever written by one single author that is seen to have benefited all 65
Christian and Latin peoples so much.

However, he did not achieve the very thing for the sake of
which he had been led to translate. For after this last translation of
the divine books, about which I am speaking, the Hebrews do not
cease to bark at and scoff daily at the Christians on grounds of the
spuriousness of our Scriptures. But truly if they were free of any
constraint, so that they were permitted to do and say whatever
they wished, not content with reviling and cursing our Scriptures,
they would ravage all our possessions and condemn them to the
flames. For in the first place, imitating their ancestors and there- 66
fore hostile to Christians, they hated everyone, serially, everywhere.

habent. Nobis deinde in sacris litteris vel maxime invident, quoniam nos eam sacrarum Scripturarum copiam, quibus solis ipsi vel
maxime gloriari solebant, cum cetere gentes illas apprime contem-
nerent, tum grecis interpretationibus tum etiam hac presertim lin-
67 gua latina ab illis arripuimus ac nobismet ipsis vendicavimus. Ad
hec accedit quod nulli Hebreorum vel certe admodum pauci ullam
vel grecarum vel latinarum litterarum cognitionem post Philonem
ac Iosephum, duos illos nobiles celebresque Iudeos hebree simul ac
grece lingue peritissimos, habuisse videntur; cuius quidem notitia
illustrati, ea que aut in grecis aut in latinis interpretationibus de-
pravata aut corrupta recteve traducta fuerant, diiudicare possent.
68 Unde factum est ut ex hac ipsa alienarum litterarum ignoratione
non modo ea que recte ac etiam illa que perperam, si qua fuissent,
in christianis traductionibus contenta, intelligere nequirent, sed
propriam quoque et vernaculam linguam perfecte cognoscere cal-
lereque non possent. Fieri enim non potest ut una lingua, presertim regulis canonibusque et normis instituta, sine aliquali vel
modica saltem alienorum excellentium idiomatum cognitione ad
unguem percipi perfecteque cognosci possit et valeat, ceu in latina
lingua manifestissime apparet, quam grecarum litterarum penitus expertes probe nancisci ac sibi ipsis omnino vendicare non
69 possunt. Quapropter neque de erratis, si qua forte sunt, neque
etiam de rectis, cum neque sua optime intelligant neque aliena vel
parumper cognoscant, prorsus iudicare nequeunt. Vera est enim
illa celebrata Aristotelis sententia, quam primo *Ethicorum* his verbis
expressit: 'Unusquisque bene iudicat que cognoscit,' et reliqua.
Ex qua quidem oppositum non immerito inferri posse videtur,
cum contrariorum contraria sint consequentia, ut scilicet quaruncunque rerum ignari homines habeantur, earum ipsarum boni
iudices esse non possint.

Secondly, they envied us particularly in regard to Sacred Letters, since with Greek and especially this Latin translation, while other nations spurned them, we have taken from them and claimed for ourselves that abundance of Sacred Scriptures on which alone they were especially wont to pride themselves . Moreover, no He- 67
brews, or at least very few, seem to have had any knowledge of Greek or Latin letters after Philo and Josephus, two illustrious Jews and distinguished experts in Hebrew and Greek. By the light of this knowledge, they would be able to distinguish what had been either spoiled or disfigured or correctly translated in either the Greek or Latin translations. So it came about that from this 68
very ignorance of foreign languages they were not only unable to understand whether the elements contained in the Christian translations were correct or, if there were any such, incorrect, but they even lacked understanding and expertise in their own native language. For it is not possible that any language, especially one organized on the basis of rules, canons, and norms, can be understood exactly and known perfectly without at least some acquaintance with other outstanding languages, such as is clearly the case with Latin, which those who are profoundly ignorant of Greek literature are unable properly to grasp and claim entirely for themselves. Therefore, they are entirely unable to make judgments 69
about errors, if there happen to be any, or about correct translations, since they neither perfectly understand their own language nor do they know any others even superficially. Aristotle's famous saying at the beginning of his *Ethics* is true: "Every person judges well what he knows."[29] From this it seems that the opposite can be reasonably inferred, since the consequents of contraries are contrary, namely that men cannot be good judges of the things of which they are ignorant.

70 Suis ergo duntaxat contenti nec aliena querentes, iandiu peregrinis linguis caruere, et propriam quoque ac vernaculam perperam intellexere. Quocirca et poetis et historicis et oratoribus et mathematicis et dialecticis et physicis et moralibus ac metaphysicis privati, certa quadam omnium liberalium artium cognitione penitus ac omnino caruisse videntur. Proinde in crassa ac supina cunctarum rerum ignoratione diutius versati, quasi immunde sues in
71 ceno moribundi iacent. Atque per hunc modum in eorum perfidia velut in sepulchro vivi sepelliuntur ac tante et tam crasse eorum ignorantie et consequentis et inveterate perfidie cause fuisse videntur illi qui primi traditionum suarum inventores extiterunt. Nam cum acritate ingenii plurimum valerent, Mosaycam legem, maxime post adventum Christi—quo quidem tempore predictarum traditionum scriptores vel compilatores potius floruerunt—tandem aliquando ad nihilum recisuram intelligebant, si eorum posteri primo peregrina et aliena per celebratas Grecorum et Latinorum disciplinas percipere ac sibi vendicare potuissent, si deinde hebraicarum litterarum caracteres ac documenta alibi quam in sacris codicibus discere intelligereque valerent.

72 Quod facile evenisset, nisi et primum constitutis asperis adversus quoscunque temerarios transgressores penis ac suppliciis traditionibus suis severe admodum cavissent, et secundum quoque ordinationes puntorum suorum, que loco grecarum vel latinarum vocalium apud eos habentur, ita instituissent, ut in sacris duntaxat codicibus commemorata punta, hoc est vocales sine quibus ullatenus legi ac nequaquam ulla lectio fieri formarique potest,
73 tantummodo reperiantur. Ex quo factum est ut quicunque hebreas litteras noverunt, cum alibi quam in sacris libris ob carentiam puntorum legere non potuerunt, divinarum Scripturarum saltem scioli

Content with their own affairs only and incurious about others, 70
they have lacked foreign languages for a long time, and understood even their own native language poorly. Unexposed to poetry, history, oratory, mathematics, dialectics, physics, ethics, and metaphysics, they seem to have completely and profoundly lacked secure knowledge of all the liberal arts. So, wallowing for too long in a stolid and lazy ignorance of all things, they lie in filth like foul,
dying pigs. In this way they are buried alive in their faithlessness 71
as though in a tomb. Those who are responsible for such deep-seated ignorance and the resultant longstanding faithlessness seem to have been those who were the first authors of their traditions. For although these authors were very able through their keenness of wit, they understood that the law of Moses, especially after the advent of Christ — the very time that these writers or rather compilers of the aforementioned traditions flourished — would eventually be reduced to nothing, had their descendants, first of all, been able to learn about foreign cultures through the celebrated learning of the Greeks and Latins, had they been able to claim them for themselves, and had they, consequently, had the ability to learn and understand the letters and proofs of Hebrew literature elsewhere than in the sacred volumes.

This might easily have happened if they had not, first, very 72
strictly protected their traditions through stiff penalties and punishments against those who rashly broke the rules and secondly, if they had not established a system of points, which in their language took the place of Greek or Latin vowels, in such a way that these points, that is, vowels, without which words can be read in any way whatsoever and by no means can any reading occur, were
found only in the sacred books. The result is that whoever knows 73
Hebrew letters is both considered and in fact is somewhat knowledgeable about the divine Scriptures, since they are unable to read

habeantur et sint. Quapropter cum ex crassa quadam cunctarum rerum ignorantia, tum etiam quia ab infantia et cunabulis sacris litteris, quemadmodum diximus, imbuti et per diversas etates postea progressi erant, falsam Scripturam nostram et im-
74 piam fidem arbitrantur. Unde in sua perfidia quotidie obstinatius obdurare videntur, quanquam plura et quidem magna miracula crebro ad astructionem catolice fidei in dies quondam evenisse intellexerint, ac etiam quotidie coram apparere intueantur. Que profecto, nisi mentis oculos clausos obseratosque et, ut expressius dixerim, cecutientes haberent, nimirum quotidianam perfidie sue abolitionem ac certam quandam fidei nostre confirmationem luce, ut dicitur, meridiana clarius soleque ipso illustrius conspicarentur.

75 Cum igitur Hieronymus tantam diversorum interpretum varietatem primo animadverteret, unde divina sacri eloquii auctoritas in mentibus christianorum hominum aliquatenus debilitari infringique posse videbatur, atque deinde tam perversam ac tam pertinacem hebrea de falsitate sacrarum Scripturarum tam grecarum quam latinarum opinionem intelligeret; utrunque per novam quandam totius Veteris Testamenti traductionem omnino tollere
76 abolereque constituit. Quocirca laborem nove interpretationis assumpsit, eamque per hunc modum magnanimiter assumptam mirabiliter absolvit divinitusque perfecit. Proinde tantam diversorum interpretum multiplicitatem, alterum duorum propositorum assecutus, quasi penitus abolevisse videtur, quod nulla alia preterquam Septuaginta interpretatio apud Grecos, qua sola omnes illi populi adhuc uti videntur, nec apud Latinos usquam reperiatur. Alterum vero de abolitione iudaice adversus nos eorum opinionis cum ob crassam quandam utriusque et grece et latine lingue ignorantiam,

anything else but the sacred books because of the lack of points.
Therefore both because of their vast ignorance of all things, and
also because they have been imbued from infancy and the cradle
with the sacred letters, as I said, and have continued on afterward
as they become older, they think that our scripture is false and our
faith impious. So they seem each day to grow more stubborn in 74
their own faithlessness, though they have understood that many
miracles — and great ones — have occurred frequently, thus daily
strengthening the Catholic faith, and even though they see them
appearing on a daily basis right in front of them. If the eyes of
their mind were not closed and barred and, to speak more clearly,
blind, without doubt they would see the daily destruction of their
faithlessness and the assured confirmation of our faith more clearly
than the midday light, as the saying goes, and more brightly than
the sun itself.

When Jerome, then, first noticed this great variety of different 75
translations, as a result of which the divine authority of sacred eloquence might be weakened and compromised to some degree in
the minds of Christians, and he also understood the perverse and
stubborn opinion that the Greek and Latin translations of the
Sacred Scriptures had been badly translated from Hebrew, he decided utterly to remove and eliminate both problems through a
new translation of the entire Old Testament. So he took on the 76
labor of a new translation, and having taken it up in this way with
a lofty spirit, he wondrously brought it to an end and perfected it
with divine aid. Accordingly he seems to have almost completely
obliterated that extraordinary number of different translations,
thus achieving one of his goals, since no other translation save
the Septuagint is ever found among the Greeks — which all
those peoples are seen to be using still — or among the Latins. He
was not able to accomplish his other goal of destroying the Jewish opinion against us because of their obstinate ignorance of
both Greek and Latin and because of their deep-seated hatred of

tum etiam ob inveteratam in Christianos omnes simultatem, sua
vehementi et pertinaci obstinatione conditam, assequi non potuit,
licet quantum in eo fuerit, id ipsum sibi vendicare nanciscique
77 conaretur. Et tamen pro maiori Sacre Scripture dignitate hanc
suam interpretationem verborum ornamentis parumper exornare
curavit et voluit. Unde ab hebraica veritate, cum aliter eam ipsam
illustrare non posset, interdum recedere coactus est. Sed ceteris
omnibus universe traductionis sue inpresentiarum pretermissis, ad
interpretationem Psalterii, cuius huiusmodi quinque librorum additamenta huic nostre traductioni non iniuria subiunximus, paulis-
per accedamus.

78 Psalterium, quemadmodum ceteros omnes totius Veteris Testamenti codices, a Septuagint — hec enim opinio communior esse
videtur — ex hebreo in grecum eloquium conversum traditur, licet
non defuerint alii et quidem eruditi viri qui ab illis mosaicam duntaxat legem traductam fuisse arbitrantur; ab Aquila deinde, a
Theodotione, a Simaco, a quinta deinceps, a sexta denique edi-
tione ex hebreo in grecum idioma traductum extitisse confirmant.
79 Sed cunctis aliis traductionibus abolitis, sola Septuaginta seniorum utpote ceteris omnibus prestantior remansit; atque adhuc
apud Grecos extare vigereque non dubitatur. Quam quidem Hieronymus cum temporibus suis iam ita prevaluisse videret, ut uni-
versos totius pene catolice Ecclesie campos antea preoccupasset,
eam ipsam de greco quam de hebreo in latinum sermonem convertere maluit, ne paulo post primitive Ecclesie incunabula nova quedam ac suspitiosa introducere videretur, presertim cum illa vetera
huiusmodi essent, ut ob frequentiam diuturni usus ordinaria et
80 quotidiana apparerent. Sed cum non multo post illa ipsa de greco
in latinum conversa ab hebraica veritate plurimum discrepare distareque calumniarentur, commemorati Sophronii precibus et obse-
crationibus motus, rursus aliam de hebreo in latinum sermonem

Christians, seasoned with their strong-willed stubbornness, although to the best of his ability he tried to claim and secure this
accomplishment for himself. Nevertheless, for a brief period he 77
also wished and took pains to adorn his translation with verbal ornaments, in keeping with the dignity of the sacred Scripture, and for this reason he departed from time to time from the true Hebrew sense, being otherwise unable to adorn it. But leaving aside all the other aspects of his complete translation for the moment, let us turn for a little while to his translation of the Psalter, to our own translation of which I have rightly appended these five additional books.[30]

Traditionally, it is said that the Psalter was translated by the 78
Seventy from Hebrew into Greek, just like all the other volumes of the complete Old Testament—this seems to be the more common belief—but there are other men—and quite learned ones—who think that the Mosaic law alone had been translated by the Seventy.[31] They maintain that [the Psalter] was then translated by Aquila, by Theodotion, by Symmachus, next by the fifth edition,
then finally by the sixth from Hebrew into Greek. But after all the 79
other translations fell away, only the translation of the Seventy elders remained, clearly more preeminent than all the others. There is still no question that it is extant and thriving among the Greeks today. Indeed, when Jerome realized that this translation was so pervasive in his day that it had earlier won over almost the entire Catholic Church, he preferred to translate from the Greek into Latin rather than from the Hebrew. After the recent infancy of the ancient Church, he did not want to appear to be introducing some new and suspicious elements, especially since the old version was
one that appeared normal and usual through daily use. But when 80
not much later they slanderously charged that this translation from Greek into Latin was very much different from the original Hebrew, moved by the prayers and entreaties of Sophronius, he began and completed another translation from Hebrew into Latin.

inchoavit atque absolvit, cuius titulus est *Psalterium secundum Hieronymum de hebraica veritate*. Quod ipse in *Prefatione ad* predictum *Sophronium* his verbis plane aperteque ostendit.

81 Que idcirco hoc loco ponere curavimus, ut communis pene omnium tam doctorum quam indoctorum hominum, qui aliter putant, opinio de falsitate convincatur: tum ex certa et expressa rei veritate cum pleraque huius translationis partim per additamenta, partim per omissiones, partim denique per alienas conversiones ab hebraica veritate plurimum dissidere videantur; tum etiam ex propria et indubitata predicti Hieronymi attestatione, qui in hac ipsa ad preallegatum Sophronium prefatione, quodam loco, verba hec ponit:

> 82 Quia nuper cum Hebreo disputans, quedam pro Domino Salvatore de Psalmis testimonia protulisti volensque ille te illudere, per sermones pene singulos asserebat, non ita haberi in hebreo ut tu de Septuaginta interpretibus opponebas; studiosissime postulasti ut post Aquilam et Simacum et Theodotionem latino sermone transferrem. Aiebas enim te magis interpretum varietate turbari et amore quo laberis, vel translatione, vel iudicio meo esse contentum. Unde impulsus a te, cui et que non possum, debeo, rursus me obtrectatorum latratibus tradidi, maluique te vires meas quam voluntatem in amicitia querere,

83 ut supra in primo libro ad aliud propositum recitasse meminimus, et reliqua huiusmodi ad manifestam quandam et expressam huius communis falseque opinionis confutationem latissime prosecutus est. Patet ergo ex his que dicta et explicata sunt, duas ipsius Psalterii esse et quidem celeberrimas Hieronymi interpretationes: alteram scilicet de greco quam Septuaginta duorum fuisse constat,

Its title is *The Psalter according to Jerome from the Hebrew Original*. He reveals this clearly with these words in the preface to the aforementioned Sophronius.

I have taken care to reproduce these words here so that the common opinion of almost all learned and unlettered men who think otherwise can be shown to be wrong: first, the truth of the matter shows that much of this translation of the Seventy is seen to disagree greatly with the Hebrew original, partly through additions, partly through omissions, and partly through unsuitable translations; and secondly there is the undoubted evidence of Jerome, who in the Preface itself to Sophronius at one point says the following: 81

> You were recently arguing with a Jew, and you offered some evidence about the Lord Savior from the Psalms. Your interlocutor wished to ridicule you and claimed that in almost every instance what you adduced from the Seventy Translators was different in the Hebrew text. Because of this you most eagerly demanded that I translate the text into Latin, as the next in line after Aquila, Symmachus, and Theodotion. For you said that you were more confused by the variety of translators and that, by the love by which you are falling into error,[32] you were content with either my translation or my judgment. When, compelled by you, to whom I owe more than I can ever repay, I handed myself over again to the barking of my detractors, and I preferred you to find my strength lacking rather than my willing friendship,[33] 82

as I mentioned above in book one in reference to another point,[34] 83
and he followed up extensively with other points to clearly refute the common and false opinion. Therefore it is clear from what has been said and explained that there were two very well known translations of the Psalter by Jerome: one based on the Greek translation of the Seventy-Two, and the other based on Hebrew

84 alteram de hebreo in latinum sermonem; licet tertia vulgo circunferatur quam Gallicanam dicunt et apud quosdam in usu habetur, sed unde prodierit quisve auctor fuerit, a plerisque ignoratur et presertim ab illis qui id qualecunque sit, a Hieronymo emanasse contendunt et hoc idem sese scire profitentur, haud intelligentes hanc ipsam Psalterii interpretationem nisi bifariam, alteram e greco, alteram vero ex hebreo in latinum eloquium traductionem presertim ab eodem interprete probabiliter fieri non potuisse, nisi iam non unam, sed duas Psalterii interpretationes ab eo (instar Aquile, quem primam et secundam totius veteris Testamenti traductionem, ut paulo superius commemoravimus, edidisse tradunt), factas fuisse allegarent.

85 Quod mihi pluribus de causis non fit verisimile. Primo enim una et quidem integra et fida translatio et ad intelligentiam et ad salutem nostram sufficere videbatur. Hieronymus deinde etsi ita res se haberet, huius duplicis Psalterii interpretationis sue, ceu in aliis eius operibus memoratu dignis semper facere consueverat, alicubi certam quandam et expressam mentionem habuisset. At hec de primo a nobis proposito hactenus dixisse sufficiat.

86 Nunc ad secundum de differentiis utriusque Psalterii deinceps accedamus. Quantum inter se distent he due celeberrime Psalterii iam crebro commemorate interpretationes (tertia illa Gallicana penitus omissa, cum certum eius auctorem ignoremus, nec Hieronymi opus per ea que superius dicta sunt, iure existimemus), vix excogitari, nedum dici explicarique potest. Cunctis quippe predictarum interpretationum differentiis diversitatibusque diligentissime enumeratis accuratissimeque, ut ita dixerim, recensitis, sex circiter milia numero (mirabile et incredibile dictu) comperiuntur.
87 Quas quidem si omnes in hunc secundum librum singillatim congereremus, quemadmodum seorsum et separatim alibi annotasse meminimus, profecto totum volumen in nimiam quandam longitudinem prolixitatemque extenderetur ac propterea Maiestati tue

and translated into Latin; although a third is in wide circulation 84
which they call the Gallicana and which is used by some, but where it came from and who its author is, is not known to many and in particular to those who maintain and assert as a fact that whatever this translation is, it came from Jerome. They do not understand that this translation of the Psalter could not with any probability have been the work of the same translator unless in two parts, one translation into Latin from the Greek, the other from the Hebrew, unless they were now claiming that he had made not one but two translations of the Psalter (like Aquila, who, as I mentioned above and as tradition holds, published a first and then a second translation of the entire Old Testament).

But I do not think that this is likely for several reasons. In the 85
first place, one whole and faithful translation seems sufficient for our understanding and salvation. Secondly, Jerome, if this were the case, would have made clear mention of his translation of this double Psalter elsewhere, just as he had always been accustomed to do in his other works that deserved mention. Let these words suffice for our first proposition.

Let us now turn to the second proposition concerning the dif- 86
ferences of each Psalter. How much these two translations of the Psalter that we have so often mentioned differ from each other can scarcely be imagined, let alone said or explained (leaving aside that third translation, the Gallicana, since I do not know its author, and I think that it is not Jerome's work on the grounds mentioned above, and rightly so). When all the differences and divergences of the two aforementioned translations have been carefully and accurately enumerated and, so to speak, inventoried, around 6000 of
them — as incredible as that is — are found. If I were to gather 87
these individually into this second book, just as I have recorded them elsewhere individually, certainly the entire volume would grow excessively long and detailed, and on that account, reading it would cause Your Majesty boredom and disgust. Since I

inter legendum fastidium nauseamque afferret. Quod nos fugere
atque evitare vel maxime cupientes, pleraque de industria omisi-
88 mus. Aliqua vero et quidem maiora et graviora ex maxima turba et
ingentissima silva per singulos quinque libros excerpsimus atque
diligenter et accurate hoc tertio quod subsequitur volumine, anno-
tabimus, presertim cum hoc secundum iam ad convenientem magnitudinem creverit.

EXPLICIT LIBER SECVNDVS

particularly wish to avoid doing this, I have purposely omitted
many examples. I have excerpted the greater and more important 88
examples from a great throng and huge forest of them that I have divided into five separate books, and I will diligently and accurately record them in this third book that follows, especially since this second one has now grown to an appropriate size.

END OF THE SECOND BOOK

LIBER TERTIVS

1 Quoniam de multis ac magnis duarum celeberrimarum totius Psalterii interpretationum differentiis ac diversitatibus hoc tertio libro disserere ac tractare constituimus, ut res ipsa planius et apertius cognoscatur, singulari quodam ac precipuo ordine inter disserendum procedemus. In unaquaque enim seria gravique traductione tres duntaxat errores esse reperirique possunt. Nam aut error per aliqua additamenta aut per omissiones aut per alienas interpretationes fieri provenireque potest. A superadditis ergo primo inchoantes, proposito ordine de quibusdam gravioribus breviter prosequemur.

⟨*I. De superadditis*⟩

2 In primo quippe Psalmo superadditum invenimus 'Non sic,' secundo replicatum. In eodem etiam 'Et erit tanquam pulvis, quem proicit ventus a facie terre,' superfluum est 'a facie terre.'

In II 'Postula a me et dabo tibi,' superadditum 'tibi' reperies, quamvis leve quiddam et frivolum videatur. In eodem 'Apprehendite disciplinam, et ne pereatis de via iusta,' supervacuum est 'iusta.'

In III 'Non est salus in Deo eius,' superadditur 'eius.' In eodem 'Tu autem Domine, susceptor meus es,' superadditum est 'es.' In eodem 'quoniam tu percussisti omnes adversantes mihi sine causa,' supervacuum est 'sine causa.'

In IV 'que dicitis in cordibus vestris,' 'que' superfluum est. In eodem 'A fructu frumenti, vini et olei,' supervacuum est 'olei.'

In V 'quoniam irritaverunt te, Domine,' supervacuum est 'Domine.'

BOOK THREE

Since in this third book we have decided to discuss and investigate 1
the many significant differences and divergences of the two most famous translations of the complete Psalter, in order to plainly and clearly understand this matter, our discussion will proceed in a particular order. For in each serious and significant translation, only three errors can exist and be discovered. For an error can occur or appear either through additions or through omissions or through unsuitable translations. Therefore we will start first with additions and then we will continue concisely in our planned order to more serious errors.

I. Concerning additions

In the first Psalm we find that "Not thus" is added and repeated 2
in another place. In the same Psalm also, "And he will be like dust, which the wind casts forth from the face of the earth," "from the face of the earth" is superfluous.

In 2, "Demand from me, and I will give to you," you will discover that "to you" has been added, although it seems a minor and insignificant issue. In the same Psalm, "Acquire knowledge, and lest you perish on the just path," "just" is additional.

In 3, "There is no safety in his God," "his" is added. In the same Psalm, "You however, O Lord, are my ally," "you are" is added. In the same Psalm, "since you have struck all those who are against me for no reason," "for no reason" is additional.

In 4, "which you say in your own hearts," "which" is superfluous. In the same Psalm, "from the harvest of corn, wine, and oil," "oil" is additional.

In 5, "since they have provoked you, O Lord," "O Lord" is superfluous.

In VI nihil abundat.

3 In VII 'et gloriam meam in pulverem deducat,' 'meam' non habetur in hebreo. In eodem 'Iustum adiutorium meum a Domino,' 'Iustum' superadditur. In eodem 'Deus, iudex iustus et fortis et patiens, nunquid irascetur per singulos dies?' omnia hec 'et fortis et patiens, nunquid' superaddita cernuntur.

In VIII nihil superadditur.

In IX 'et civitates eorum destruxisti,' 'eorum' superest.

In X 'Dixit enim in corde suo,' 'enim' superfluum est. In eodem 'Cuius maledictione os eius plenum est,' 'Cuius' supervacuum est. In eodem 'in occultis ut interficiat innocentem,' abundat 'ut.' In eodem 'Dixit enim in corde suo,' 'enim' superadditur. In eodem 'ut tradas eos in manus tuas,' vacat 'eos.' In eodem 'ut non apponat ultra magnificare se homo super terram,' 'Ut' et 'se' supersunt.

4 In XI 'iustus autem quid fecit?' 'autem' superfluum est. In eodem 'Oculi eius in pauperem respiciunt,' 'in pauperem' supervacuum est.

In XII 'Disperdet Dominus universa labia dolosa,' 'universa' superest. In eodem 'ponam in salutari suo, fiducialiter agam in eo,' 'fiducialiter' superadditur.

In XIII 'qui bona tribuit mihi, et psallam nomini Domini altissimi,' totum hoc 'et psallam nomini Domini altissimi' affluit.

5 In XIIII 'non est usque ad unum,' vacat 'est.' In eodem cuncta que secuntur (mirabile dictu!) superflua sunt, sed longe mirabilius videbitur, cum a Paulo Apostolo in Epistola ad Romanos hec eadem, allegata fuisse cognoverimus:

Sepulchrum patens guttur eorum,
linguis suis dolose agebant,

There is nothing extra in 6.

In 7, "and let him drive my glory into dust," "my" is not found in 3
the Hebrew. In the same Psalm, "My just support from God," "just" is added. In the same Psalm, "God, a judge just, strong, and patient, will he not be angry every single day?" all of "strong, and patient, not," is perceived to be added.

There is nothing added in 8.

In 9, "and you have destroyed their cities," "their" is additional.

In 10, "For he spoke in his heart," "for" is superfluous. In the same Psalm, "With a curse for whom his mouth is full," "for whom" is additional. In the same Psalm, "so that he can kill the innocent in hiding," "so that" is extra. In the same Psalm, "For he spoke in his heart," "For" is added. In the same Psalm, "that you deliver them into your hands," "them" is missing. In the same Psalm, "so that a man may not presume to glorify himself on earth," "so that" and "himself" are superfluous.

In 11, "however what did the just man do," "however" is super- 4
fluous. In the same Psalm, "His eyes look at the poor man," "at the poor man" is superfluous.

In 12, "The Lord will destroy all the cunning lips," "all" is superfluous. In the same Psalm, "I will place him in safety, I will deal faithfully with him," "faithfully" is added.

In 13, "who gave good things to me, and a psalm to the name of the highest Lord," all of "and a psalm to the name of the highest Lord," is added.

In 14, "there is not even one," "is" is additional. In the same 5
Psalm, all the text that follows is superfluous, amazing as that is, but it will seem even more amazing because we know that these same words were cited by the Apostle Paul in his Epistle to the Romans:

Their throat is an open sepulcher,
They behave deceivingly with their tongues,

venenum aspidis sub labiis eorum
quorum os maledictione et amaritudine plenum est,
veloces pedes eorum ad effundendum sanguinem.
Contritio et infelicitas in viis eorum,
et viam pacis non cognoverunt:
Non est timor Dei ante oculos eorum (Ad Rom., 3, 13–18).

In eodem 'qui devorant plebem meam sicut escam panis,' 'sicut escam' superadditur. In eodem 'illic trepidaverunt timore, ubi non erat timor,' superfluum est 'ubi non erat timor.' In eodem 'exultabit Iacob, et letabitur Israel,' 'et' superfluum est.

6 In XV 'aut quis requiescet in monte sancto tuo?' 'Aut' supervacuum est. In eodem 'qui pecuniam suam non dedit ad usuram,' 'Qui' superest.

In XVI 'tu es qui restitues hereditatem meam mihi,' 'es qui,' 'mihi,' ista superflua sunt. In eodem 'etenim hereditas mea preclara est mihi,' 'mea' superfluum est. In eodem 'insuper et usque ad noctem increpuerunt me renes mei,' 'et' superadditur.

In XVII 'Probasti cor meum et visitasti nocte,' 'et' superfluum est. In eodem 'Ego autem in iustitia apparebo in conspectu tuo,' 'autem' supervacuum est.

7 In XVIII 'Et exaudivit de templo sancto suo vocem meam,' 'Et' ac 'sancto' superflua sunt. In eodem 'et commota sunt, quoniam iratus est eis,' 'Et' superfluum est. In eodem 'Et posuit tenebras latibulum suum,' supervacuum est 'Et.' In eodem 'eloquia Domini igne examinata,' 'igne' abundat. In eodem 'et disciplina tua correxit me in finem, et disciplina tua ipsa me docebit in finem,' 'ipsa' superfluum est. In eodem 'liberator meus de inimicis meis iracundis,' vacat 'iracundis.'

The venom of the asp is under their lips,
Their mouths are filled with cursing and bitterness,
Their feet are swift to shed blood.
Grief and misfortune lie in their path,
And they do not know the path of peace:
There is no fear of God before their eyes. (Rom. 3.13–18)

In the same Psalm, "who devour my people like a serving of bread," "like a serving" is added. In the same Psalm, "there they trembled in fear, where there was no fear," "where there was no fear" is superfluous. In the same Psalm, "Jacob will rejoice, and Israel will be joyful," "and" is superfluous.

In 15, "or who will rest on your sacred mountain," "or" is super- 6
fluous. In the same Psalm, "who did not give his money for usury," "who" is added.

In 16, "you are the one who will restore my inheritance to me," "you are the one who" and "to me" are superfluous. In the same Psalm, "for my inheritance is magnificent," "my" is superfluous. In the same Psalm, "moreover up even until the night my kidneys rebuked me," "even" is added.

In 17, "You have tested my heart and you have visited me at night," "and" is superfluous. In the same Psalm, "However, I will appear before you in justice," "However" is superfluous.

In 18, "And he heard my voice from his holy temple," "And" and 7
"holy" are superfluous. In the same Psalm, "and they were shaken, since he is angry with them," "and" is superfluous. In the same Psalm, "And he made darkness his hiding place," "And" is superfluous. In the same Psalm, "the words of God have been tested in fire," "in fire" is additional. In the same Psalm, "and your teaching corrected me to the end, and your very teaching will teach me to the end," "very" is superfluous. In the same Psalm, "my liberator from my angry enemies," "angry" is superfluous.

In XVIII 'Et erunt ut complaceant eloquia oris mei,' 'Et' abundat.

8 In XX 'Tribuat tibi secundum cor tuum, et omne consilium tuum confirmet,' 'omne' superadditur. In eodem 'Domine, salvum fac regem, et exaudi nos,' supervacuum est 'et.'

In XXI 'et voluntate labiorum eius non fraudasti eum,' superadditur 'eum.' In eodem 'Quoniam dabis eum in benedictionem in seculum seculi,' superfluum est 'in seculum seculi.' In eodem 'Quoniam declinaverunt in te mala, cogitaverunt consilia que non potuerunt stabilire,' abundat 'stabilire.'

In XXII 'Deus, Deus meus, respice in me,' superadditur 'respice in me.' In eodem 'Quoniam circundederunt me canes multi,' superfluum est 'multi.' In eodem 'Dinumeraverunt omnia ossa mea, ipsi vero consideraverunt me et despexerunt me,' supervacua sunt 'vero' et primum 'me.' In eodem 'et de manu canis unicam meam,' abundat 'et.' In eodem 'et, cum clamarem ad eum, exaudivit me,' abundat 'me.' In eodem 'et semen meum serviet ipsi,' 'meum' supervacuum est.

In XXIII nihil abundat.

9 In XXIIII 'neque iuravit in dolo proximo suo,' superfluum est 'proximo suo.' In eodem 'Hic accipiet benedictionem a Domino,' superadditur 'Hic.'

In duobus subsequentibus nihil abundat.

In XXVII 'Quoniam abscondit me in tabernaculo suo,' supervacuum est 'suo.' In eodem 'Exaudi, Domine, vocem meam, qua clamavi ad te,' superadduntur et 'qua' et 'ad te.'

In XXVIII 'Exaudi, Domine, vocem deprecationis mee, dum oro ad te,' abundat 'Domine.' In eodem 'et cum operantibus iniquitatem ne perdas me,' superfluum est 'ne perdas me.'

10 In XXVIIII 'Afferte Domino, filii Dei, afferte Domino filios arietum,' totum hoc 'Afferte Domino, filii Dei,' supervacuum est. In eodem 'et commovebit Dominus desertum Cades,' 'Et' superfluum est.

In 19, "And the words of my mouth will greatly please," "And" is extra.

In 20, "May he bestow on you according to your heart, and may 8
he strengthen your every intention," "every" is added. In the same Psalm, "Lord, make the king safe, and hear us," "and" is additional.

In 21, "and you have not beguiled him of the desire of his lips," "him" is added. In the same Psalm, "Since you will bless him forever," "forever" is superfluous. In the same Psalm, "Since they directed evils toward you, they devised plans which they were unable to fulfill," "to fulfill" is extra.

In 22, "God, my God, look upon me," "look upon me" is added. In the same Psalm, "Since many dogs surrounded me," "many" is superfluous. In the same Psalm, "They have counted all my bones, truly they themselves have examined me and despised me," "truly" and the first "me" are additional. In the same Psalm, "and my beloved from the hand of the dog," "and" is extra. In the same Psalm, "and, when I cried to him, he heard me," "me" is extra. In the same Psalm, "and my seed will serve him," "my" is additional.

There is nothing extra in 23.

In 24, "nor has sworn deceitfully against his neighbor," "against 9
his neighbor" is superfluous. In the same Psalm, "This man will receive a blessing from the Lord," "This man" is added.

In the following two Psalms there is nothing extra.

In 27, "Since he has hidden me in his tent," "his" is superfluous. In the same Psalm, "Hear, O Lord, my voice, by which I called to you," "by which" and "to you" are added.

In 28, "Hear, O Lord, the words of my appeal, while I pray to you," "O Lord" is extra. In the same Psalm, "and do not destroy me with those working iniquity," "do not destroy me," is superfluous.

In 29, "Give to the Lord, sons of God, give to the Lord the sons 10
of rams," all of "Give to the Lord, sons of God" is superfluous. In the same Psalm, "and the Lord will shake the desert of Kadesh," "and" is superfluous.

In XXX 'avertisti faciem tuam a me,' abundat 'a me.' In eodem 'Ut cantet tibi gloria mea,' vacat 'mea.'

In XXXI 'Erubescant impii et deducantur in infernum,' abundat 'et.' In eodem 'Quam magna multitudo dulcedinis tue, Domine,' affluit 'Domine.' In eodem 'Diligite Dominum, omnes sancti eius, quoniam . . . ,' superfluum est 'quoniam.'

11 In XXXII 'Dixi: Confitebor adversus me [in] iustitiam meam Domino,' abundat 'adversus me.' In eodem 'Tu es refugium meum a tribulatione que circundedit me,' superfluum est 'que circundedit me.'

In XXXIII 'Cantate ei canticum novum, bene psallite ei in vociferatione,' secundum 'ei' supervacuum est. In eodem 'Dominus dissipat consilia gentium, reprobat autem cogitationes populorum,' superfluum est 'autem.' In eodem 'Consilium autem Domini in eternum manet,' abundat 'autem.' In eodem 'gigas non salvabitur in multitudine virtutis sue,' abundat 'sue.'

12 In XXXIIII 'Timete Dominum, omnes sancti eius,' superfluum est 'omnes.' In eodem 'Clamaverunt iusti, et Dominus exaudivit eos,' superabundant 'iusti' et 'eos.' In eodem 'Custodit Dominus omnia ossa eorum,' supervacuum est 'Dominus.'

In XXXV 'Quoniam mihi quidem pacifice loquebantur,' 'mihi' et 'quidem' superflua sunt. In eodem 'Et lingua mea meditabitur iustitiam tuam,' abundat 'Et.'

In XXXVI 'Iniquitatem locutus est in cubili suo, astitit omni vie non bone,' superfluum est 'omni.' In eodem 'Malitiam autem non odivit,' supervacuum est 'autem.'

13 In XXXVII 'iniusti punientur, et semen impiorum peribit,' superfluum est 'Iniusti punientur.' In eodem 'Iusti autem hereditabunt terram,' supervacuum est 'autem.' In eodem 'Lex Dei eius in corde ipsius, et non supplantabuntur gressus eius,' superfluum est

In 30, "you have turned your face from me," "from me" is extra. In the same Psalm, "so that my glory may sing to you," "my" is additional.

In 31, "Let the ungodly be ashamed and let them be led into the grave," "and" is extra. In the same Psalm, "How great is the abundance of your sweetness, O Lord," "O Lord" is additional. In the same Psalm, "Love the Lord, all you his saints, since . . . ," "since" is superfluous.

In 32, "I said: I will confess against myself my wrongdoing to 11
the Lord," "against myself" is extra. In the same Psalm, "You are my refuge from the hardship which has surrounded me," "which has surrounded me" is superfluous.

In 33, "Sing a new song for him, play well for him with a loud sound," the second "for him" is superfluous. In the same Psalm, "The Lord scatters the plans of the gentiles and rejects the designs of the peoples," "and" is superfluous. In the same Psalm, "However, the plan of the Lord remains forever," "However" is extra. In the same Psalm, "a giant will not be saved by the abundance of his strength," "his" is extra.

In 34, "Fear the Lord, all his saints," "all" is superfluous. In the 12
same Psalm, "The just shouted, and the Lord heard them," "just" and "them" are extra. In the same Psalm, "The Lord guards all their bones," "The Lord" is superfluous.

In 35, "Since indeed they spoke peacefully to me," "indeed" and "to me" are superfluous. In the same Psalm, "And my tongue will sing your righteousness," "And" is extra.

In 36, "He spoke wickedness in his bed, he stood at every way that is not good," "every" is superfluous. In the same Psalm, "However, he did not hate malice," "However" is superfluous.

In 37, "the unjust will be punished, and the seed of the ungodly 13
will perish," "the unjust will be punished" is superfluous. In the same Psalm, "However, the just will inherit the earth," "However" is superfluous. In the same Psalm, "The law of his God is in his

'et.' In eodem 'Dominus autem non derelinquet eum in manibus eius,' supervacuum est 'autem.' In eodem 'Et transivi, et ecce non erat; et quesivi eum et non est inventus locus eius,' superfluum est 'locus eius.'

In XXXVIII 'Miser factus sum et curvatus,' supervacuum est 'et.' In eodem 'Inimici autem mei vivunt et conturbati sunt super me,' abundat 'super me.' In eodem 'Intende in adiutorium meum, Domine Deus salutis mee,' superfluum est 'Deus.'

14 In XXXVIIII 'thesaurizat et ignorat cui congregabit ea,' abundat 'ea.' In eodem 'que est expectatio mea? Nonne Dominus? Et substantia mea apud te est,' superaddita sunt 'Nonne,' 'substantia mea.' In eodem 'Remitte mihi ut refrigerer priusquam abeam et amplius non ero,' abundat 'amplius.'

In XL 'Sacrificium et oblationem noluisti, aures autem perfecisti mihi,' vacat 'autem.' In eodem 'Ferant confestim confusionem suam,' superfluum est 'confestim.'

In XLI 'Beatus qui intelligit super egenum et pauperem,' abundat 'egenum.' In eodem 'egrediebatur foras et loquebatur in id ipsum,' superabundat 'in id ipsum.'

15 In XLII, qui est primus secundi libri, 'quoniam transibo in locum tabernaculi admirabilis,' supervacua sunt 'tabernaculi admirabilis.' In eodem 'Quare tristis es, anima mea, et quare conturbas me?' abundat secundum 'quare.'

In XLIII nihil superest.

In XLIIII 'Tu es ipse, rex meus et Deus meus,' supervacua sunt 'et' ac 'meus' secundum. In eodem 'et in nomine tuo aspernemus insurgentes in nos,' vacat 'et.' In eodem 'Nunc autem repulisti et confudisti nos,' abundat 'autem.' In eodem 'Avertisti nos retrorsum post inimicos nostros,' abundat 'nostros.'

heart, and his steps will not be tripped up," "and" is superfluous. In the same Psalm, "However, the Lord will not abandon him in his hands," "However" is superfluous. In the same Psalm, "And I crossed, and behold, he was not there; and I sought him and his place was not found," "his place" is superfluous.

In 38, "I became wretched and bent," "and" is superfluous. In the same Psalm, "However, my enemies live and are confounded over me," "over me" is extra. In the same Psalm, "Come to my aid, O Lord God of my salvation," "God" is superfluous.

In 39, "he stores up treasures and does not know for whom he 14
gathers them," "them" is extra. In the same Psalm, "What am I waiting for? Is it not the Lord? And my wealth resides with you," "Is it not" and "my wealth" are added. In the same Psalm, "Grant me that I be refreshed before I depart and do not exist any longer," "any longer" is extra.

In 40, "You refused sacrifice and offerings, however you opened my ears," "however" is additional. In the same Psalm, "Let them immediately be confounded," "immediately" is superfluous.

In 41, "Blessed is he who thinks about the needy and the poor," "needy" is extra. In the same Psalm, "he went forth and talked about it," "about it" is extra.

In 42, which is the first Psalm of the second book, "since I will 15
cross into the place of the wonderful tabernacle," "wonderful tabernacle" is superfluous. In the same Psalm, "Why are you sad, my soul, and why do you disquiet me," the second "why" is superfluous.

Nothing is superfluous in 43.

In 44, "You yourself are my king and my God," "and" and the second "my" are superfluous. In the same Psalm, "And in your name we will spurn those rising against us," "And" is superfluous. In the same Psalm, "Now however you have driven us back and confounded us," "however" is extra. In the same Psalm, "You have made us turn back in the face of our enemies," "our" is extra.

In XLV 'Spetiosus forma pre filiis hominum,' superest 'forma.'

16 In XLVI 'Deus noster refugium et virtus, adiutor in tribulatio-
nibus que invenerunt nos nimis,' superaddita sunt 'que' et 'nos.' In eodem 'Sonuerunt, et turbate sunt aque,' vacat 'et.' In eodem 'Conturbate sunt gentes, et conturbata sunt regna,' abundat 'et.' In eodem 'Venite et videte opera Domini, que posuit prodigia super terram,' vacat 'et.' In eodem 'et scuta comburet igni,' abundat 'Et.' In eodem 'Vacate et videte quoniam ego sum Deus: exaltabor in gentibus, exaltabor in terra,' abundat secundum 'et.'

In XLVII nihil superest.

In XLVIII 'Quoniam ecce reges terre congregati sunt, et convenerunt in unum,' superfluum est 'terre.' In eodem 'Ponite corda vestra in virtute eius et distribuite domos eius,' vacat 'et.'

17 In XLVIIII 'Quique terrigene et filii hominum, simul in unum
dives et pauper,' abundat 'in unum.' In eodem 'Frater non redimet: redimet homo: et non dabit Deo placationem suam,' vacat 'et.' In eodem 'Et sepulchrum eorum domus illorum,' abundat 'et.' In eodem 'vocaverunt nomina sua in terris suis,' vacat 'suis.' In eodem 'Et homo, cum in honore esset, non intellexit: comparatus est iumentis insipientibus, et similis factus est illis,' affluunt 'insipientibus' atque 'et.'

In L 'Im⟨m⟩ola Deo sacrificium laudis,' vacat 'sacrificium.' In eodem 'Et invoca me in die tribulationis: et eruam,' vacat secundum 'et.' In eodem 'et adversus filium matris tue ponebas scandalum,' affluit 'Et.' In eodem 'Hec fecisti, et tacui: existimasti inique quod ero tui similis,' abundat 'inique.'

In 45, "Splendid in appearance compared to the sons of men," "in appearance" is superfluous.

In 46, "Our God is a refuge and strength, a support during 16
tribulations which heavily beset us," "which" and "us" are added. In the same Psalm, "They have resounded, and the waters are troubled," "and" is additional. In the same Psalm, "The people are confounded, and the kingdoms are confounded," "and" is extra. In the same Psalm, "Come and see the works of the Lord, which he has placed as omens upon the earth," "and" is additional. In the same Psalm, "and he will burn shields with fire," "and" is extra. In the same Psalm, "Be at leisure and see that I am God: I will be exalted among the gentiles, I will be exalted on the land," the second "and" is extra.[1]

Nothing is superfluous in 47.

In 48, "For look, the kings of the earth have assembled, and have gathered together," "of the earth" is superfluous. In the same Psalm, "Entrust your life to her strength, and divide her homes," "and" is additional.

In 49, "All earthborn men and sons of men, both rich and poor 17
together," "together" is extra. In the same Psalm, "brother will not redeem: man will not redeem: and he will not pacify God," "and" is superfluous. In the same Psalm, "And their tomb is their home," "And" is extra. In the same Psalm, "they called their names in their own lands," "their own" is superfluous. In the same Psalm, "And man, when he was in honor, did not understand: he is like the dumb beasts, and he has been made like them," "dumb" and "and" are superfluous.

In 50, "Make a sacrifice of praise to God," "sacrifice" is additional. In the same Psalm, "And call me in the day of tribulation: and I will rescue," the second "and" is superfluous. In the same Psalm, "and you slandered the son of your own mother," "and" is superfluous. In the same Psalm, "You did this, and I was quiet: you thought unjustly that I will be like you," "unjustly" is extra.

18 In LI 'Miserere mei, Deus, secundum magnam misericordiam tuam,' superest 'magnam.' In eodem 'et secundum multitudinem miserationum tuarum,' superfluum est 'et.' In eodem 'ut iustificeris in sermonibus tuis, et vincas cum iudicaris,' vacat 'et.' In eodem 'Ecce enim in iniquitatibus conceptus sum,' abundat 'enim.' In eodem 'Ecce enim veritatem dilexisti,' superest 'enim.' In eodem 'Asperges me, Domine, isopo, et mundabor,' vacat 'Domine.' In eodem 'Auditui meo dabis gaudium et letitiam, et exultabunt ossa humilitate,' abundat secundum 'et.' In eodem 'Quoniam, si voluisses sacrificium, dedissem,' vacat 'si.' In eodem 'Benigne fac, Domine, in bona voluntate tua Syon,' superest 'Domine.' In eodem 'tunc imponam super altare tuum vitulos,' superfluum est 'tunc.'

In LII 'Videbunt iusti et timebunt, et super eum ridebunt et dicent,' vacat 'et dicent.'

19 In LIII 'Corrupti sunt et abominabiles facti sunt iniquitatibus suis,' superabundat 'suis.' In eodem 'ut videas si est intelligens aut requirens Deum,' vacat 'aut.' In eodem 'Nonne sciunt omnes qui operantur iniquitatem?' abundat 'omnes.' In eodem 'qui devorant plebem meam, ut cibum panis,' vacat 'ut cibum.'

In LIIII 'Ecce enim Deus adiuvat me, et Dominus susceptor est anime mee,' affluit 'enim' atque 'et.' In eodem 'Averte mala inimicis meis, et in veritate tua disperde illos,' abundat 'et.' In eodem 'Voluntarie sacrificabo et confitebor nomini tuo, quoniam bonum est,' vacant 'et' atque 'est.' In eodem 'et super inimicos meos despexit oculus meus,' abundat 'super.'

20 In LV 'Quoniam, si inimicus meus maledixisset mihi, sustinuissem utique,' affluunt 'si' et 'utique.' In eodem 'et, si is qui oderat me

In 51, "Pity me, O God, according to your great mercy," "great" 18
is superfluous. In the same Psalm, "and according to the multitude of your mercies," "and" is superfluous. In the same Psalm, "so that you may be justified when you speak, and so that you may prevail when you are judged," "and" is superfluous. In the same Psalm, "For behold, I was conceived in iniquity," "For" is extra. In the same Psalm, "For behold, you valued the truth," "For" is superfluous. In the same Psalm, "You will sprinkle me, O Lord, with hyssop, and I will be clean," "O Lord" is additional. In the same Psalm, "You will give joy and happiness to me as I listen, and my bones will rejoice in humility," the second "and" is extra. In the same Psalm, "Since, if you had wanted a sacrifice, I would have given it," "if" is additional. In the same Psalm, "Treat Zion well, O Lord, with your goodwill," "O Lord" is superfluous. In the same Psalm, "then I will place bullocks on your altar," "then" is superfluous.

In 52, "The just will see and will fear, and they will laugh over him and will say," "and will say" is additional.

In 53, "They have been corrupted and made abhorrent because 19
of their sins," "their" is extra. In the same Psalm, "so that you may see if he understands or seeks God," "or" is superfluous. In the same Psalm, "Do not all know who works iniquity," "all" is extra. In the same Psalm, "who devour my people like a ration of bread," "like a ration" is superfluous.

In 54, "For behold, God helps me, and God lifts up my soul," "For" and "and" are superfluous. In the same Psalm, "Direct evils against my enemies, and destroy them in your truth," "and" is extra. In the same Psalm, "I will willingly sacrifice and I will confess to your name, since it is good," "and" and "is" are additional. In the same Psalm, "and my eye looked down upon over my enemies," "upon" is extra.

In 55, "Since, if my enemy had slandered me, I would certainly 20
have tolerated it," "if" and "certainly" are additional. In the same

super me magna locutus fuisset, abscondissem me forsitan ab eo,' vacat 'et, si is' ac 'forsitan.' In eodem 'Ego autem ad Dominum clamavi, et Dominus salvavit me,' superest 'autem.' In eodem 'et non dabit in eternum fluctuationem iusto,' vacat 'Et.' In eodem 'ego autem sperabo in te, Domine,' superest 'Domine.'

In LVI 'Ab altitudine Dei timebo, ego vero in te sperabo,' vacat 'Ab altitudine' et 'vero.' In eodem 'Inhabitabunt et abscondent,' superest 'et.' In eodem 'posuisti lachrymas meas in conspectu tuo, sicut et in promissione tua, Domine,' affluunt 'sicut' et 'Domine.'

21 In LVII 'et eripiet animam meam de medio catulorum leonum,' vacat 'Et eripiet.' In eodem 'Laqueum paraverunt pedibus meis et incurvaverunt animam meam,' abundat 'et.' In eodem 'Exaltare super celos, Deus, et super omnem terram gloria tua,' superest 'est.'

In LVIII nihil affluit.

22 In LVIIII 'Deus ostendit mihi super inimicos meos,' abundat 'super.' In eodem 'quia factus es susceptor meus, et refugium meum,' vacat 'meum.' In eodem 'Adiutor meus, tibi psallam, quia Deus susceptor meus, Deus meus, misericordia mea,' affluit secundum 'meus.'

In LX 'Deus, reppulisti nos et destruxisti nos, iratus es et miseratus es nobis,' duo 'et' superflua sunt. In eodem 'Commovisti terram et conturbasti eam,' vacat 'et.'

In LXI nihil superest.

In LXII 'Nonne Deo subiecta erit anima mea? ab ipso enim salutare meum,' abundat 'enim.'

In LXIII 'Rex vero letabitur in Deo; et laudabuntur,' vacat 'et.'

Psalm, "and, if he who hated me had vaunted over me, I would perhaps have hidden myself from him," "and, if he" and "perhaps" are superfluous. In the same Psalm, "I however called to the Lord, and the Lord saved me," "however" is superfluous. In the same Psalm, "and he will not allow the just to waver forever," "and" is superfluous. In the same Psalm, "I however will hope in you, O Lord," "O Lord" is superfluous.

In 56, "I will fear by reason of the majesty of God, but I will trust in you," "by reason of the majesty" and "but" are additional. In the same Psalm, "They will dwell there and hide themselves," "and" is superfluous. In the same Psalm, "You put my tears in your sight, just as also in your promise, O Lord," "just as" and "O Lord" are superfluous.

In 57, "and he will wrest my soul from the midst of the lions' 21
whelps," "and he will wrest" is superfluous. In the same Psalm, "They prepared a snare for my feet and they bent my soul," "and" is extra. In the same Psalm, "Be exalted above the heavens, O God, and your glory over all the earth," "and" is superfluous.

There is nothing superfluous in 58.

In 59, "God shows me above my enemies," "above" is extra. In 22
the same Psalm, "because you became my defense, and my refuge," "my" is additional.[2] In the same Psalm, "My helper, I will sing to you, because God is my defense, my God, my mercy," the second "my" is superfluous.

In 60, "O God, you drove us back and destroyed us, you were angry, and you pitied us," each "and" is superfluous. In the same Psalm, "You moved the earth and you confounded it," "and" is additional.

Nothing is superfluous in 61.

In 62, "Will my soul not be subjected to God? For my salvation is from him," "For" is extra.

In 63, "But the king will rejoice in God; and they will be praised," "and" is superfluous.

In LXIIII nihil superest.

23 In LXV 'Te decet hymnus, Deus, in Syon, et tibi reddetur vo-
tum in Hierusalem,' vacat 'in Hierusalem.' In eodem 'Visitasti terram et inhabitasti eam,' abundat 'eam.'

In LXVI 'Dicite Deo: Quam terribilia sunt opera tua, Domine!' superfluum est 'Domine.' In eodem 'Quoniam probasti nos, Deus, igne nos examinasti quemadmodum examinatur argentum,' vacat 'igne.'

In LXVII 'Deus misereatur nostri et benedicat nobis, illuminet vultum suum super nos; miserere nostri,' abundat 'Miserere nostri.'

24 In LXVIII 'sicut fluit cera a facie ignis, sic pereant peccatores a
facie Dei,' superest 'sic.' In eodem 'et exultate in conspectu eius. Turbabuntur a facie eius,' affluit 'turbabuntur a facie eius.' In eodem 'terra mota est, etenim celi distillaverunt a facie Dei,' abundat 'enim.' In eodem 'infirmata est: tu vero perfecisti eam,' vacat 'vero.' In eodem 'Dum discernit celestis reges super eam, nive dealbabuntur in Salmon,' superfluum est 'nive.' In eodem 'Psallite Deo, qui ascendit super celum celi ad orientem,' supervacuum est 'Psallite Deo.'

In LXVIIII 'Salvum me fac, Deus, quoniam intraverunt aque usque ad animam meam,' vacat 'meam.'

In LXX 'Confundantur et revereantur simul qui querunt animam meam,' abundat 'simul.'

25 In LXXI 'Esto mihi in Deum protectorem, et in locum muni-
tum, tu salvum me facies,' vacat 'in Deum protectorem.' In eodem 'quoniam firmamentum meum et refugium meum es tu,' abundat primum 'meum.' In eodem 'Confundantur et deficiant detrahentes anime mee,' vacat 'et.'

Nothing is superfluous in 64.

In 65, "Praise becomes you, God, in Sion, and the vow will be 23
rendered to you in Jerusalem," "in Jerusalem" is additional. In the same Psalm, "You visited the earth and you dwelled in it," "it" is extra.

In 66, "say to God: how terrible are your works, O Lord," "O Lord" is superfluous. In the same Psalm, "Since you have tested us, O God, you have examined us in fire just as silver is tested," "fire" is additional.

In 67, "May God pity us and bless us, and may he shine his countenance upon us; pity us," "pity us" is extra.[3]

In 68, "just as wax melts in the presence of fire, so may sinners 24
perish in the presence of God," "so" is superfluous. In the same Psalm, "and exult in his presence. They will be confounded before him," "They will be confounded before him" is additional. In the same Psalm, "the earth shook, for it rained in the heavens in the presence of God," "for" is extra. In the same Psalm, "it was weak, but you fulfilled it," "but" is additional. In the same Psalm, "While God divides kings over it, they will be whitened by snow in Salmon," "by snow" is superfluous. In the same Psalm, "Sing to God, who rises above the heaven of heaven to the east," "Sing to God," is superfluous.

In 69, "Save me, O God, since the waters have entered all the way into my soul," "my" is additional.

In 70, "Let them be confounded and at the same time afraid who seek my life," "at the same time" is extra.

In 71, "May you be my protector, O God, and you will save me 25
in a fortified place," "protector, O God" is additional. In the same Psalm, "since you are my strength and my refuge," the first "my" is extra. In the same Psalm, "Let those robbing me of my life be confounded and overwhelmed," "and" is additional.

In LXXII 'et permanebit cum sole et ante lunam in generatione generationum,' superest 'et.' In eodem 'Et benedicentur in ipso omnes tribus terre,' abundat 'terre.'

26 In LXXIII (Et est primus tertii libri) 'Et dixerunt: Quomodo scit Deus, et si est scientia in excelso,' superest 'si.' In eodem 'Quid enim mihi est in celo? et a te quid volui super terram?' 'enim' et secundum 'quid' superflua sunt. In eodem 'ut annuntiem omnes predicationes tuas in portis filie Syon,' affluit 'in portis filie Syon.'

In duobus subsequentibus Psalmis nihil supervacaneum est.

In LXXVI 'Turbati sunt omnes insipientes corde,' superfluum est 'omnes.'

In LXXVII 'In die tribulationis mee Deum exquisivi; manibus meis nocte contra eum, et non sum deceptus,' abundat 'contra eum.' In eodem 'Cogitavi dies antiquos, et annos eternos in mente habui,' superflua sunt hec omnia 'et' atque 'in mente habui.' In eodem 'Deus, in sancto via tua: quis Deus magnus sicut Deus noster?' vacat 'noster.' In eodem 'vox tonitrui tui in rota; illuxerunt corruscationes tue orbi terre,' abundat 'tue.'

27 In LXXVIII 'Quanta audivimus et cognovimus ea,' vacat 'ea.' In eodem 'Sicut posuit in Egypto signa sua et prodigia eius in campo Taneos,' superfluum est 'et prodigia eius.' In eodem 'et iumenta eorum in eorum morte conclusit,' abundat 'Et.' In eodem 'Et percussit omne primogenitum in terra Egypti, primitias laborum eorum,' vacat 'eorum.'

In LXXVIIII 'Ne forte dicant in gentibus: Ubi est Deus eorum? et innotescat in nationibus coram oculis nostris,' abundat 'Et.'

In LXXX nihil superest.

In 72, "and he will remain with the sun and before the moon for generations on end," "and" is superfluous. In the same Psalm, "all the tribes of the world will be blessed in him," "of the world" is additional.

In 73 (and this is the first psalm of the third book), "And they 26
said: How does God know, and if there is knowledge in the Most High," "if" is additional. In the same Psalm, "For what is there for me in heaven? And what did I want from you on earth?" "for" and the second "what" are superfluous. In the same Psalm, "so that I can sing all your praises in the ports of your daughter Sion," "in the ports of your daughter Sion" is superfluous.

In the following two Psalms nothing is superfluous.

In 76, "All those foolish in their hearts have been confounded," "All" is superfluous.

In 77, "On the day of my tribulation I sought God with my hands at night toward him, and I was not deceived," "toward him" is extra. In the same Psalm, "I reflected on the days of old, and I pondered the eternal years," "and" and "I pondered" are both superfluous. In the same Psalm, "God, your way is holy: which God is as great as our God?" "our" is additional. In the same Psalm, "the voice of your thunder was on the wheel: your lightening flashed on the world," "your" is extra.[4]

In 78, "All the things which we have heard and known them," 27
"them" is additional. In the same Psalm, "thus he placed his signs in Egypt and his wonders in the plain of Zoan," "and his wonders" is superfluous. In the same Psalm, "and he encompassed their cattle in their death," "and" is extra. In the same Psalm, "And he struck every firstborn in Egypt, the firstfruits of their labors," "their" is additional.

In 79, "Lest perchance they say among the gentiles: Where is their God? and let him be known among the peoples before our eyes," "and" is extra.

There is nothing superfluous in 80.

In LXXXI 'Ego enim sum Dominus Deus tuus,' abundat 'enim.'

In LXXXII nihil superest.

In LXXXIII 'Qui dixerunt: Hereditate possideamus sanctuarii Dei,' abundat 'hereditatem.'

28 In LXXXIIII 'Quia misericordiam et veritatem diligit Deus,' superfluum est 'diligit.'

In LXXXV 'Misericordia et veritas obviaverunt sibi,' vacat 'sibi.'

In LXXXVI 'Iudica me, Domine, in viam tuam, et ingrediar,' superest 'et.'

In LXXXVII nihil abundat.

29 In LXXXVIII 'Intret in conspectu tuo oratio mea, inclina ad me aurem tuam ad precem meam,' superfluum est 'ad me.' In eodem 'Pauper sum ego in laboribus a iuventute mea; exaltatus autem,' vacat 'mea' atque 'autem.' In eodem 'In me transierunt ire tue, et terrores tui conturbaverunt me,' vacat 'et.'

In LXXXVIIII 'et exaltavi electum de plebe mea,' abundat 'mea' atque 'Et.'

In LXXXX, qui est primus quarti libri, 'Mane sicut herba transeat; mane floreat et transeat; vespere decidat, induret, et arescat,' superflua sunt hec 'sicut herba' et secundum 'mane' atque 'induret.' In eodem 'Quoniam omnes dies nostri defecerunt, et in ira tua defecimus: anni tui sicut aranea meditabuntur,' supervacua sunt 'aranea' et 'meditabuntur.' In eodem 'Quis novit potestatem ire tue, et pre timore tuo iram tuam dinumerare?' superfluum est 'dinumerare.'

30 In XCI 'ad te autem non appropinquabit,' vacat 'autem.' In eodem 'Quoniam tu es, Domine, spes mea,' abundat 'es.'

In XCII 'Quia delectasti me, Domine, in factura tua, et in operibus manuum tuarum exultabo,' vacat 'et.'

In XCIII nihil abundat.

In 81, "For I am the Lord your God," "For" is extra.

There is nothing superfluous in 82.

In 83, "Who said: let us possess the inheritance of the sanctuary of God," "inheritance" is extra.

In 84, "Because God loves mercy and truth," "loves" is superflu- 28
ous.

In 85, "Mercy and truth have met themselves," "themselves" is additional.

In 86, "Judge me, O Lord, in your way, and I will walk," "and" is superfluous.

Nothing is superfluous in 87.

In 88, "Let my words enter your presence, incline your ear to 29
me to my prayer," "to me" is superfluous. In the same Psalm, "I am poor, in distress since my youth; but I am exalted," "my" and "but" are additional. In the same Psalm, "Your angers passed into me, and your terrors have confounded me," "and" is additional.

In 89, "and I have exalted the one chosen from my people," "my" and "and" are extra.

In 90, which is the first Psalm of the fourth book, "Just as grass grows in the morning; it flourishes in the morning and grows; in the evening it fails, hardens, and dries," "Just as grass," the second "in the morning" and "hardens" are superfluous. In the same Psalm, "Since all our days have disappeared, and we have disappeared in your anger: your years will plan like a spider," "will plan" and "spider" are superfluous. In the same Psalm, "Who knows the power of your anger and to reckon your anger according to the fear you inspire," "to reckon" is superfluous.

In 91, "however, it will not approach you," "however" is superflu- 30
ous. In the same Psalm, "Since you, O Lord, are my hope," "you . . . are" is extra.

In 92, "Because you have delighted me, O Lord, by your work, and I will exalt in the works of your hands," "and" is superfluous.

There is nothing superfluous in 93.

In XCIIII 'Effabuntur et loquentur,' affluit 'et.'

In XCV 'Preoccupemus faciem eius in confessione, et in psalmis iubilemus ei,' vacat 'et.' In eodem 'quoniam ipsius est mare,' abundat 'quoniam.' In eodem 'Quadraginta annis offensus fui generationi illi,' vacat 'illi.'

31 In XCVI 'Cantate Domino et benedicite nomini eius,' affluit 'et.' In eodem 'dicite in gentibus, quia Dominus regnavit, etenim correxit orbem,' superflua sunt 'quia' ac 'enim.'

In XCVII 'Confundantur omnes qui adorant sculptilia, qui gloriantur in simulachris suis,' abundat 'suis.'

In XCVIII 'in tubis ductilibus et voce tube cornue,' superfluum est 'ductilibus.'

In XCVIIII 'Et in columna nubis loquebatur ad eos,' vacat 'Et.'

In C nihil abundat.

32 In CI 'Et intelligam in via immaculata: quando venies ad me?' abundat 'Et.'

In CII 'Quia edificavit Dominus Syon et videbitur in gloria sua,' vacat 'et.' In eodem 'et sicut opertorium mutabis eos, et mutabuntur,' abundat 'Et.' In eodem 'tu autem idem ipse es,' superest 'idem ipse.'

In CIII nihil vacat.

In CIIII 'Qui emittis fontes in convallibus, inter medium montium pertransibunt aque,' superfluum est 'aque.' In eodem 'Saturabuntur ligna campi, et cedri Libani quas plantavit,' vacat 'et.' In eodem 'Avertente autem te faciem turbabuntur,' abundat 'autem.' In eodem 'Emictes spiritum tuum, et creabuntur,' vacat 'et.' In eodem

In 94, "they will speak out and talk," "and" is superfluous.

In 95, "Let us come into his presence in acknowledgment and celebrate him with psalms," "and" is superfluous. In the same Psalm, "Since the sea is his," "Since" is extra. In the same Psalm, "For forty years I was displeased with that generation," "that" is additional.

In 96, "Sing to the Lord and bless his name," "and" is additional. 31
In the same Psalm, "say among the nations, that the Lord has reigned, for he restored the world," "because" and "for" are superfluous.

In 97, "Let all be confounded who worship statues, who glory in their own idols," "their own" is extra.

In 98, "with malleable trumpets and the sound of the cornet," "malleable" is superfluous.

In 99, "And he spoke to them in the column of a cloud," "And" is additional.

There is nothing superfluous in 100.

In 101, "And I will understand in the perfect way: when will you 32
come to me?" "And" is extra.

In 102, "Because God built Sion and he will be seen in his glory," "and" is additional. In the same Psalm, "and you will change them like a covering, and they will be changed," "and" is extra. In the same Psalm, "however you yourself are the same," "yourself . . . the same," is superfluous.

Nothing is superfluous in 103.

In 104, "You who send forth the streams in the valleys, the waters will pass between the mountains," "the waters" is superfluous. In the same Psalm, "The trees of the field will be full and the cedars of Lebanon which he planted," "and" is additional. In the same Psalm, "However, when you avert your face, they will be confounded," "However" is extra. In the same Psalm, "You will

'Iocundum sit ei eloquium meum; ego vero delectabor in Domino,' superest 'vero.'

33 In CV 'annuntiate inter gentes studia eius et opera,' superabundant 'studia eius' ac 'et.' In eodem 'Cantate ei et psallite,' vacat 'et.' In eodem 'Et vocavit famem super terram et omne firmamentum panis contrivit,' secundum 'et' superfluum est. In eodem 'Dixit, et venit cynomia et [s]cinifes in omnibus finibus eorum,' abundat 'et.' In eodem 'Et commedit omne fenum et commedit omnem fructum terre eorum,' superest 'omnem.' In eodem 'Expandit nubem in protectionem eorum et ignem, ut luceret eis per noctem,' vacat 'eis.' In eodem 'Et eduxit populum suum et electos suos in letitia,' supervacuum est 'et.'

In CVI 'Aperta est terra et deglutivit Dathan, et operuit super congregationes Abiron,' affluit 'super.' In eodem 'Et fecerunt vitulum in Oreb,' abundat 'Et.' In eodem 'et dicit omnis populus: Fiat, fiat,' vacat alterum 'Fiat.'

34 In CVII, qui est primus quinti libri, 'Et clamaverunt ad Dominum cum tribularentur, et de necessitatibus eorum eripuit eos,' superest secundum 'et.' In eodem 'Et eduxit eos de tenebris,' abundat 'Et.' In eodem 'Et statuit procellam eorum in auram,' superfluum est 'Et.' In eodem 'Effusa est contentio; et errare fecit eos in invio et non in via,' vacat primum 'et.'

In CVIII 'Paratum cor meum, Deus, paratum cor meum,' secundum 'Paratum cor meum' affluit.

In CVIIII nihil superest.

In CX 'Iuravit Dominus, et non penitebit eum,' vacat 'eum.'

send forth your breath and they will be created," "and" is additional. In the same Psalm, "May my speech be pleasing to him; but I will delight in the Lord," "but" is superfluous.

In 105, "announce among the peoples his kindness and works," 33
"his kindness" and "and" are superfluous. In the same Psalm, "Sing to him, and sing psalms to him," "and" is additional. In the same Psalm, "And he called for famine on the earth and he destroyed the whole supply of bread," the second "and" is superfluous. In the same Psalm, "He spoke, and dog-flies came and insects in all their lands," "and" is extra. In the same Psalm, "And he ate up all the hay and he ate up every fruit of their land," "every" is superfluous. In the same Psalm, "He spread a cloud to protect them and fire so that there would be light for them throughout the night," "for them" is additional. In the same Psalm, "And he brought forth his people and his chosen with joy," "and" is superfluous.

In 106, "The earth opened and swallowed Dathan and covered over the people of Abiram," "over" is superfluous. In the same Psalm, "And they made a calf in Horeb," "And" is additional. In the same Psalm, "and all the people say: let it happen, let it happen," the second "let it happen" is additional.

In 107, which is the first Psalm of the fifth book, "And they 34
shouted to the Lord when they were confounded, and he rescued them from their troubles," the second "and" is superfluous. In the same Psalm, "And he led them out from darkness," "And" is additional. In the same Psalm, "And he changed their storm into a breeze," "And" is superfluous. In the same Psalm, "He spread strife; and he made them wander in the wilderness and not on a path," the first "and" is additional.

In 108, "My heart is ready, O God, my heart is ready," the second "my heart is ready" is additional.

Nothing is additional in 109.

In 110, "The Lord has sworn and he will not repent," "he" is additional.

In CXI 'Confitebor tibi, Domine, in toto corde meo,' abundat 'tibi.'

In duobus subsequentibus nihil affluit.

35 In CXIIII 'Quid est tibi, mare, quod fugisti? et tu, Iordanis, quia conversus es retrorsum?' superflua sunt hec 'Et tu,' 'quia.' In eodem 'Qui convertit petram in stagna aquarum et rupem in fontes aquarum,' vacat 'et.'

In CXV 'Num mortui laudabunt te, Domine,' abundant 'te.' In eodem 'Sed nos, qui vivimus, benedicimus Domino ex hoc nunc,' vacat 'hoc.'

In CXVI 'Credidi, propter quod locutus sum; ego autem humiliatus sum nimis,' abundat 'autem.'

In CXVII nihil superest.

36 In CXVIII 'Omnes gentes circuierunt me, et in nomine Domini,' superfluum est 'et.' In eodem 'Dextera Domini fecit virtutem, dextera Domini exaltavit me, dextera Domini fecit virtutem,' superabundant hec omnia 'dextera Domini fecit virtutem' in principio posita.

In CXVIIII 'Utinam dirigantur vie mee ad custodiendas iustificationes tuas!' vacat 'Utinam.' In eodem 'sederunt principes et adversum me loquebantur; servus autem tuus exercebatur in iustificationibus tuis,' superest 'autem.' In eodem 'Superbi inique agebant usque quaque, a lege autem tua ⟨non⟩ declinavi,' abundat 'autem.' In eodem 'Funes peccatorum circumplexi sunt me, et legem tuam non sum oblitus,' vacat 'et.' In eodem 'Coagulatum est sicut lac cor meum; ego vero legem tuam meditatus sum,' supervacuum est 'vero.' In eodem 'ego autem exercebor in mandatis tuis,' abundat 'autem.' In eodem 'Defecit in salutare tuum anima mea, et in verbum tuum super speravi,' superest 'et.' In eodem 'Super omnes doctores meos intellexi, quia testimonia tua meditatio mea est,'

In 111, "I will confess to you, O Lord, with all my heart," "to you" is extra.

In the following two Psalms there is nothing additional.

In 114, "For what cause, sea, did you flee? And you, Jordan, that 35
you turned back?" "And you" and "that" are superfluous. In the same Psalm, "who turned a rock into pools of water and a cliff into fountains of water," "and" is additional.

In 115, "Will the dead praise you, O Lord," "you" is extra. In the same Psalm, "But we, who live, will bless the Lord from this now onward," "this" is additional.

In 116, "I believed, because I spoke; I however was too afflicted," "however" is extra.

Nothing is superfluous in 117.

In 118, "All the nations surrounded me, and in the name of the 36
Lord," "and" is superfluous. In the same Psalm, "the right hand of the Lord did bravely, the right hand of the Lord exalted me, the right hand of the Lord did bravely," the first phrase "the right hand of the Lord did bravely," is extra.

In 119, "Would that my ways were directed toward keeping your laws," "Would that" is superfluous. In the same Psalm, "Princes sat and spoke against me; however your servant was committed to your laws," "however" is additional. In the same Psalm, "The proud continuously behaved wickedly, however I did not turn away from your law," "however" is extra. In the same Psalm, "The bands of wicked men have encompassed me, and I have not forgotten your law," "and" is additional. In the same Psalm, "my heart is fat like milk; but I studied your law," "but" is additional. In the same Psalm, "I however will be committed to your commands," "however" is extra. In the same Psalm, "My heart failed for your salvation, and I trusted in your word," "and" is superfluous. In the same Psalm, "I understood beyond all my teachers, because your testimonies are my meditation," "are" is superfluous. In the same

vacat 'est.' In eodem 'In iudiciis tuis ⟨non⟩ declinavi, quia tu legem posuisti mihi,' supervacuum est 'legem.'

In quattuor subsequentibus Psalmis nihil superabundat.

37 In CXXIIII 'Nisi quia Dominus erat in nobis, dicat nunc Israel,' vacat 'quia.' In eodem iterum 'Nisi quia Dominus erat in nobis,' abundat 'quia.'

In CXXV 'Qui confidunt in Domino, sicut mons Syon: non commovebitur in eternum, qui habitat,' affluit 'Qui.' In eodem 'ex hoc nunc et usque in seculum,' vacat 'hoc.'

In quattuor subsequentibus Psalmis nihil superest.

38 In CXXX 'Quia apud te propitiatio est, et propter legem tuam sustinui te, Domine,' 'legem tuam' et 'te Domine' affluunt. In eodem 'speret Israel in Domino, ex hoc nunc et usque in seculum,' supervacuum est 'hoc.'

In duobus subsequentibus nihil abundat.

In CXXXIII 'Sicut unguentum in capite, ⟨quod descendit⟩ in barbam, barbam autem Aaron,' supervacuum est 'autem.'

In CXXXIIII 'Ecce nunc benedicite Dominum, omnes servi Domini; qui statis in domo Domini, in atriis domus Dei nostri,' omnia hec 'nunc,' 'in atriis domus Dei nostri' superabundant.

In tribus subsequentibus nihil supervacuum est.

In CXXXVIII 'et super iram inimicorum suorum,' vacat 'Et.'

In CXXXVIIII 'Si assumpsero pennas meas diluculo,' superest 'Si.' In eodem 'sicut tenebre eius, ita et lumen eius,' vacat utrunque 'eius.' In eodem 'et substantia mea in inferioribus terre,' superest 'Et.' In eodem 'Dinumerabo eos, et super harenam multiplicabuntur,' superfluum est 'et.'

Psalm, "I turned away in your judgments, because you gave the law to me," "the law" is superfluous.

There is nothing extra in the following four Psalms.

In 124, "Unless because the Lord was among us, now let Israel 37
speak," "because" is additional. In the same Psalm again, "Unless because the Lord was among us," "because" is additional.

In 125, "Who trust in the Lord, like mount Sion: he who inhabits it will not be moved forever, which abides," "Who" is additional. In the same Psalm, "from this now and forever more," "this" is additional.

There is nothing superfluous in the following four Psalms.

In 130, "Because forgiveness is with you, and because of your 38
law I upheld you, O Lord," "your law" and "you, O Lord" are additional. In the same Psalm, "May Israel trust in the Lord, from this now and forever more," "this" is superfluous.

There is nothing additional in the following two Psalms.

In 133, "Just like ointment on the head which falls on to the beard, the beard of Aaron, however," "however" is superfluous.

In 134, "Behold, now bless the Lord, all you servants of the Lord; you who stand in the house of the Lord, in the rooms of the house of our God," all of these, "now," "in the rooms of the house of our God," are extra.

There is nothing superfluous in the following three Psalms.

In 138, "and over the anger of their enemies," "and" is superfluous.

In 139, "If I take my wings in the morning," "If" is superfluous. In the same Psalm, "just like his darkness, so also is his light," each "his" is additional. In the same Psalm, "and my substance in the lowest parts of the earth," "and" is additional. In the same Psalm, "I will number them, and they will multiply beyond the sand," "and" is additional.

39 In CXL 'Custodi me, Domine, de manu peccatoris et ab hominibus iniquis eripe me,' superest 'et.' In eodem 'Domine Domine, virtus salutis mee, obumbrasti super caput meum in die belli,' abundat 'super.' In eodem 'Non tradas me, Domine, a desiderio meo peccatori,' superflua sunt 'a' et 'meo.' In eodem 'cogitaverunt contra me, ne derelinquas me, ne forte exaltentur,' vacat utrunque 'me' et 'contra.' In eodem 'Cognovi quia faciet Dominus iudicium inopis et vindictam pauperum,' abundat 'et.' In eodem 'Veruntamen iusti confitebuntur nomini tuo, et habitabunt recti cum vultu tuo,' superfluum est 'et.'

In CXLI 'Dirigatur oratio mea sicut incensum in conspectu tuo,' abundat 'sicut.' In eodem 'Pone, Domine, custodiam ori meo, et ostium circunstantie labiis meis,' vacant 'et' atque 'circustantie.' In eodem 'oleum autem peccatoris non impinguet caput meum,' supervacuum est 'autem.'

40 In CXLII 'Effundo in conspectu eius orationem meam, et tribulationem meam ante ipsum pronuntio,' vacat 'et.' In eodem 'In via hac qua ambulabam absconderunt superbi laqueum mihi,' abundat 'superbi.'

In CXLIII nihil superest.

In CXLIIII 'Benedictus Dominus Deus meus, qui docet manus meas ad prelium, et digitos meos ad bellum,' vacat 'et.' In eodem 'Domine, quid est homo, quod innotuisti ei? aut filius hominis, quod reputas eum?' abundat 'aut.' In eodem 'emitte manum tuam de alto, eripe me et libera me de aquis multis et de manu filiorum alienorum,' supervacuum est 'et.' In eodem 'Beatum dixerunt populum cui hec sunt,' superfluum est 'dixerunt.'

41 In CXLV 'Fidelis Dominus in omnibus verbis suis; et sanctus in omnibus operibus suis,' totus hic versus superabundat, cum nihil hebraice habeatur.

In 140, "Protect me, O Lord, from the hand of a sinner and 39
rescue me from wicked men," "and" is additional. In the same Psalm, "O Lord, O Lord, the strength of my salvation, you have covered over my head on the day of battle," "over" is extra. In the same Psalm, "Do not hand me over, O Lord, from my desire to a sinner," "from" and "my" are superfluous. In the same Psalm, "they plotted against me, do not abandon me lest perchance they be exalted," both "me" and "against" are superfluous. In the same Psalm, "I know that the Lord will provide judgment for the weak and protection for the poor," "and" is extra. In the same Psalm, "Nevertheless the just will confess to your name, and the righteous will live in your presence," "and" is additional.

In 141, "Let my prayer be placed before your presence like incense," "like" is extra. In the same Psalm, "Place, O Lord, a watch for my mouth and a guard door around my lips," "and" and "guard" are superfluous. In the same Psalm, "however, the oil of the wicked will not anoint my head," "however" is superfluous.

In 142, "I pour out my prayer in his presence, and I announce 40
my tribulations before him," "and" is additional. In the same Psalm, "On the path on which I walked the proud hid a snare for me," "the proud" is extra.

Nothing is superfluous in 143.

In 144, "Blessed is the Lord my God, who teaches my hands for battle and my fingers for war," "and" is additional. In the same Psalm, "O Lord, what is man that you have become known to him? or the son of man, that you think of him?" "or" is extra. In the same Psalm, "send your hand from on high, rescue me and save me from many waters and from the hand of strange children," "and" is superfluous. In the same Psalm, "They said the people are blessed who have these things," "they said" is superfluous.

In 145, "The Lord is faithful in all his words; and holy in all his 41
works," this entire verse is extra, since it does not appear in the Hebrew.

In CXLVI 'Exibit spiritus eius et revertetur in terram suam,' vacat 'et.'

In CXLVII 'qui numerat multitudinem stellarum et omnibus eis nomina vocat,' abundat 'Qui' atque 'et.' In eodem 'Magnus Dominus noster et magna virtus eius, et sapientie eius non est numerus,' abundat secundum 'et.' In eodem 'Suscipiens mansuetos Dominus, humilians autem peccatores usque ad terram,' vacat 'autem.' In eodem 'qui producit in montibus fenum et herbam servituti hominum,' totum hoc 'et herbam servituti hominum' superfluum est. In eodem 'Qui posuit fines tuos pacem et adipe frumenti satiat te,' vacat 'et.' In eodem 'Emittet verbum suum et liquefaciet ea, fluit spiritus eius et fluent aque,' abundat 'et.' In eodem 'Non fecit taliter omni nationi et iudicia sua non manifestavit eis,' supervacua sunt 'sua' et 'eis.'

42 In CXLVIII 'Laudate eum, sol et luna, laudate eum, omnes stelle et lumina,' vacat ultimum 'et.' In eodem 'Quia ipse dixit et facta sunt, ipse mandavit et creata sunt,' superabundant hec 'dixit, et facta sunt' et secundum 'ipse.'

In CXLVIIII 'Letetur Israel in eo qui fecit eum, et filii Sion exultent in rege suo,' vacat 'et.' In eodem 'Laudent nomen eius in choro et timpano, et psalterio psallant ei,' vacat 'et' primum. In eodem 'Quia beneplacitum est Domino, et exaltabit mansuetos in salutem,' abundat 'et.'

In CL nihil superest.

⟨II.⟩ *De omissis*

43 Cum de superadditis hactenus dixerimus, deinceps de omissis pauca dicamus.

In primo et in secundo nihil omittitur.

In 146, "His breath will go out and will return to his land," "and" is additional.

In 147, "who numbers the multitude of the stars and gives names to them all," "who" and "and" are extra. In the same Psalm, "Great is our Lord and his strength is great and there is no limit to his wisdom," the second "and" is extra. In the same Psalm, "The Lord lifting up the gentle, but humbling the wicked down to the earth," "but" is additional. In the same Psalm, "who brings forth hay in the mountains and grass for the use of men," all of "and grass for the use of men" is superfluous. In the same Psalm, "He established peace on your borders and satisfies you with the fat of corn," "and" is additional. In the same Psalm, "He will send forth his word and he will melt them, his breath flows and the waters will flow," "and" is extra. In the same Psalm, "He has not behaved this way with every nation and he has not shown his judgments to them," "his" and "to them" are superfluous.

In 148, "Praise him, sun and moon, praise him, all the stars and 42
lights," the last "and" is additional. In the same Psalm, "Because he spoke and they were made, he commanded and they were created," "he spoke and they were made" and the second "he" are extra.

In 149, "Let Israel be joyful in him who made it, and let the sons of Sion exult in their king," "and" is additional. In the same Psalm, "Let them praise his name with the dance and timbrel, and play for him with the harp," the first "and" is additional. In the same Psalm, "Because it was very pleasing to the Lord, and he will exalt the gentle to salvation," "and" is extra.

There is nothing superfluous in 150.

II. Concerning omissions

Having spoken so far about additions, let us next say a few 43
words about omissions.

Nothing is omitted in the first and second psalms.

In III 'Non est salus ipsi in Deo eius,' deficit 'semper' in fine. In eodem 'de monte sancto suo,' omittitur 'semper' ut ante. In eodem 'et super populum tuum benedictio tua,' deficit 'semper' ut supra.

In IIII 'in cubilibus vestris compungimini,' omittitur 'semper' ut superius.

In V nihil deest.

In VI 'quoniam infirmus sum,' deficit 'ego.'

In VII 'Consumetur nequitia peccatorum,' omittitur, post 'Consumetur,' 'queso.'

In VIII 'Minuisti eum paulo minus ab angelis,' deficit 'Et' in principio. In eodem 'gloria et honore,' deest 'Ac' ut ante.

44 In VIIII 'Quoniam fecisti,' omittitur in medio 'tu.' In eodem 'in operibus manuum suarum comprehensus est peccator,' deficit in fine 'susurratione continua.' In eodem 'sciant gentes quoniam homines sunt,' deest in antepenultima 'ipse,' et in fine 'semper.'

In undecim subsequentibus Psalmis nihil omittitur.

In XXI 'voluntate labiorum eius non fraudasti eum,' deficit in fine 'semper.'

In XXII 'Deus, Deus meus,' deest post primam dictionem alterum 'meus.' In eodem 'et nocte, et non ad insipientiam mihi,' omittitur 'erit' in antepenultima.

In six subsequentibus Psalmis nihil deficit.

In XXVIIII 'in templo eius omnes dicent gloriam,' ab initio deest 'Et.'

In duobus subsequentibus nihil pretermittitur.

45 In XXXII 'conversus sum in erumna mea, dum confringitur spina,' deest in fine 'semper.' In eodem 'et tu remisisti impietatem

In 3, "There is no safety for him in his God," "always" is missing at the end. In the same Psalm, "from his sacred mountain," "always" is omitted as before. In the same Psalm, "and your blessing over your people," "always" is missing, as above.

In 4, "you are goaded in your beds," "always" is omitted, as above.

There is nothing missing in 5.

In 6, "since I am weak," "myself" is missing.

In 7, "the wickedness of sinners will be destroyed," after "will be destroyed," "I pray" is missing.

In 8, "you made him a little less than the angels," "And" is missing at the beginning. In the same Psalm, "with glory and honor," "And" is missing, as before.

In 9, "Since you made," "yourself" is missing from the middle. 44
In the same Psalm, "the wicked man is caught by the works of his own hands," "by a continuous whisper" is missing at the end. In the same Psalm, "that the nations may know since they are men," "themselves" is missing from the third last spot, and "always" is missing at the end.

Nothing is missing in the following eleven Psalms.

In 21, "you did not deprive him of the desire of his lips," "always" is missing at the end.

In 22, "God, my God," another "my" is missing after the first word. In the same Psalm, "and at night, and not by my folly," "it will be" is missing from the third last spot.

Nothing is omitted in the six following Psalms.

In 29, "everyone will speak of his glory in his temple," "And" is missing from the beginning.

In the following two Psalms nothing is omitted.

In 32, "I am changed in my tribulation while my spine is bro- 45
ken," "always" is missing at the end. In the same Psalm, "and you forgave the impiety of my sin," "always" is missing at the end. In

peccati mei,' deficit in fine 'semper.' In eodem 'exultatio mea, erue me a circundantibus me,' deest in fine 'semper.'

In tribus subsequentibus nihil vacare conspicitur.

In XXXVI 'Et torrente voluptatis tue potabis eos,' in principio deficit 'De.'

In duobus subsequentibus nihil deesse videmus.

46 In XXXVIIII 'veruntamen universa vanitas,' deficit in fine 'semper.' In eodem 'Verumtamen conturbabitur omnis homo,' deest in fine 'semper.'

In XL nihil omittitur.

In XLI 'Benedictus Dominus, a seculo et usque in seculum. Fiat, fiat,' deficit 'et' ante ultimum 'Fiat.'

In XLII, qui est primus secundi libri, 'Sitivit anima mea ad Deum fontem vivum,' deficit, post 'Deum,' in replicatione alterum 'Deum.'

In XLIII 'confitebor tibi in cythara, Deus Deus meus,' deest in principio 'Et.'

In duobus subsequentibus nihil pretermittitur.

47 In XLVI 'Sonuerunt et conturbate sunt aque eorum, conturbati sunt montes in fortitudine eius,' deficit in fine 'semper.' In eodem 'Dominus virtutum nobiscum, susceptor noster Deus Iacob,' deest in fine 'semper.' In eodem 'Deus virtutum nobiscum, susceptor noster Deus Iacob,' deest in fine 'semper.'

In XLVII 'Elegit nobis hereditatem suam; spetiem Iacob quem dilexit,' vacat in fine 'semper.' In eodem 'Quoniam rex omnis terre Deus,' deficit 'est' in antepenultima.

In XLVIII nihil omittitur.

In XLVIIII 'Hec via illorum scandalum ipsis; et postea in ore suo complacebit,' deest in fine 'semper.' In eodem 'cum acceperit me,' deficit in fine 'semper.'

the same Psalm, "my exaltation, save me from those who surround me," "always" is missing at the end.

In the following three Psalms nothing appears to be missing.

In 36, "and you will make them drink the torrent of your pleasure," "From" is missing at the beginning.

We observe that nothing is missing in the following two Psalms.

In 39, "but complete vanity," "always" is missing at the end. In 46
the same Psalm, "But every man will be confounded," "always" is missing at the end.

Nothing is missing in 40.

In 41, "Blessed is the Lord, from eternity to eternity. May it be, may it be," "and" is missing before the last "may it be."

In 42, which is the first Psalm of the second book, "My soul thirsted for God, the living fountain," after "God" another "God" is repeated.

In 43, "I will confess to you on the harp, O God, my God," "And" is missing at the beginning.

Nothing is missing in the following two Psalms.

In 46, "Their waters sounded and were troubled, the mountains 47
were shaken by its force," "always" is missing at the end. In the same Psalm, "The Lord of our strengths is with us, our protector is the God of Jacob," "always" is missing at the end. In the same Psalm, "God of our strengths is with us, our protector is the God of Jacob," "always" is missing at the end.

In 47, "He chooses his own inheritance for us, the splendor of Jacob whom he loved," "always" is missing at the end. In the same Psalm, "Since the king of all the earth God," "is" is missing from the second last spot.

Nothing is omitted in 48.

In 49, "This path of theirs is folly for them; and afterward they will be pleased with their own audacity," "always" is missing at the end. In the same Psalm, "since he will accept me," "always" is missing at the end.

48 In L 'Deus, deorum Dominus, locutus est et vocavit terram ab ortu solis usque ad occasum,' deficit in fine 'suum.' In eodem 'Peccatori dixit Deus: Quare tu enarras iustitias meas?' deficit a principio 'Et.'

In LI 'Tibi soli peccavi et malum coram te feci,' deest alterum 'tibi' post 'soli.'

In LII 'et emigrabit te de tabernaculo tuo,' deficit a principio 'Confringet te.'

In duobus subsequentibus nihil omittitur.

In LV 'Ecce elongavi fugiens et mansi in solitudine,' deficit in fine 'semper.' In eodem 'Exaudiet Deus et humiliabit illos, qui est ante secula,' deest in fine 'semper.'

In LVI nihil omittitur.

49 In LVII 'Misit de celo et liberavit me, dedit in obprobrium conculcantes me,' deficit in fine 'semper.'

In duobus subsequentibus Psalmis nihil pretermittitur.

In LX 'Da nobis auxilium de tribulatione, quia vana salus hominis,' vacat 'est' in antepenultima.

In LXI nihil omittitur.

In LXII 'Ore suo benedicebant, et corde suo maledicebant,' deficit in principio 'In' et in fine 'semper.' In eodem 'Quia ipse Deus meus et salvator meus, adiutor meus: non emigrabo,' deficit 'robur meum' in antepenultima.

In LXIII 'Deus, Deus meus, ad te de luce vigilo,' in medio arithmetico deficit 'es tu.' In eodem 'Sitivit anima mea; quam multipliciter tibi caro mea,' deficit post principium 'ad te.' In eodem 'in terra deserta, in via inaquosa,' deficit in medio 'et.'

In LXIIII nihil omittitur.

In 50, "God, Lord of gods, spoke and he called the earth from the rising of the sun all the way to the setting," "its" is missing near the end. In the same Psalm, "God said to the wicked: why do you recount my laws?" "And" is missing from the beginning. 48

In 51, "I sinned for you alone and I did evil in your presence," another "for you" is missing after "alone."

In 52, "and he will take you away from your dwelling place," "he will destroy you" is missing from the beginning.

There is nothing missing in the following two Psalms.

In 55, "Behold, I fled a great distance and remained in the wilderness," "always" is missing at the end. In the same Psalm, "God will hear and will humble them, who is before the ages," "always" is missing at the end.

Nothing is missing in 56.

In 57, "He sent from heaven and saved me, he gave those tram- 49
pling upon me to disgrace," "always" is missing at the end.

There is nothing missing in the following two psalms.

In 60, "Give us help from tribulation, because the salvation of man vain," "is" is missing in the third last spot.[5]

Nothing is missing in 61.

In 62, "They blessed with their mouth, and cursed in their heart," "In" is missing at the beginning, and "always" at the end. In the same Psalm, "Because my God himself is my savior, my helper: I will not depart," "my strength" is lacking from the second last position.[6]

In 63, "O God, my God, early I am watchful for you," in the middle of the phrase "you are" is missing. In the same Psalm, "My soul thirsted; in how many ways was my flesh pulled to you," "to you" is missing after the beginning. In the same Psalm, "in a barren land, on a road with no water," "and" is missing in the middle.

Nothing is missing in 64.

50 In LXV 'Exaudi nos, Deus,' deficit in principio 'Veneranda cum iustitia.' In eodem 'Turbabuntur gentes,' deficit 'Et' in principio.

In LXVI 'offeram tibi oves cum hircis,' deest in fine 'semper.'

In LXVII 'Confiteantur tibi populi, Deus, confiteantur tibi populi omnes,' deficit in fine 'ipsi.' In eodem 'Letentur et exultent gentes, quoniam iudicas populos in equitate, et gentes in terra dirigis,' vacat in fine 'eas' et 'semper.'

In LXVIII 'Terra mota est, et celi distillaverunt a facie Dei Synai,' deficit ante ultimam 'hic est.' In eodem 'Benedictus Dominus quotidie! Prosperum iter faciet nobis Deus salutarium nostrorum,' deficit in fine 'semper.' In eodem 'Regna terre, cantate Deo, psallite Domino,' deest in fine 'semper.'

In duobus subsequentibus Psalmis nihil omittitur.

51 In LXXI 'Introibo in potentias Domini, Domine, memorabor iustitie tue solius,' deficit in fine 'tue.' In eodem 'Et usque in senectam et senium, Deus,' deest post principium 'etiam.'

In LXXII 'Benedictus Deus Israel, qui facit mirabilia solus,' deest in fine 'ipse.' In eodem 'et replebitur maiestate eius omnis terra. Fiat, fiat,' deficit ante ultimum 'Fiat,' 'et.'

In LXXIII, qui est primus tertii libri, 'In labore hominum non sunt,' vacat in fine 'ipsi.'

In LXXIIII nihil omittitur.

In LXXV 'Liquefacta est terra et omnes qui habitant in ea; ego confirmavi columnas eius,' deficit in fine 'semper.'

In 65, "Hear us, O God," "with venerable justice" is missing at the beginning. In the same Psalm, "The nations will be confounded," "And" is missing at the beginning. 50

In 66, "I will offer sheep with goats to you," "always" is missing at the end.

In 67, "Let the peoples confess to you, O God; let all peoples confess to you," "themselves" is missing at the end. In the same Psalm, "Let the nations be glad and rejoice, since you judge the peoples with justice, and rule the nations on the earth," "those" and "always" are missing at the end.

In 68, "The earth shook, and the skies dropped in the presence of the God of Sinai," "this is" is missing before the last word. In the same Psalm, "Blessed God everyday! The God of our salvation will make our journey favorable," "always" is missing at the end. In the same Psalm, "Kingdoms of the earth, sing to God, sing praises to the Lord," "always" is missing at the end.

Nothing is omitted in the following two Psalms.

In 71, "I will enter into the powers of the Lord, O Lord, I will remember your justice alone," "your" is missing at the end. In the same Psalm, "And all the way into old age and infirmity, O God," "even" is missing after the beginning. 51

In 72, "Blessed God of Israel, who alone makes miracles," "himself" is missing at the end. In the same Psalm, "and all the earth will be filled with his majesty. May it happen, may it happen," "May it happen" and "and" are missing at the end.

In 73, which is the first Psalm of the third book, "They do not suffer like other men," "themselves" is missing at the end.

Nothing is omitted in 74.

In 75, "The earth dissolved and everyone who lives in it: I supported its pillars," "always" is missing at the end.

In LXXVI 'Ibi confregit potentias arcus, scutum, gladium et bellum,' deest in fine 'semper.' In eodem 'Cum exurgeret in iudicium Deus, ut salvos faceret omnes mansuetos corde,' deficit in fine 'semper.'

52 In LXXVII 'Memor fui Dei et delectatus sum, et exercitatus sum et defecit spiritus meus,' deest in fine 'semper.' In eodem 'aut obliviscitur misereri Deus? aut continebit in ira sua miserationes suas,' deficit in fine 'semper.' In eodem 'Redemisti in brachio tuo populum tuum, filios Iacob et Ioseph,' deest in fine 'semper.'

In LXXVIII 'Aperiam in parabolis os meum, loquar propositiones ab initio,' post 'meum' deficit 'et.'

In LXXVIIII 'Adiuva nos, Deus salutaris noster, et propter gloriam nominis tui libera nos,' deficit, post 'propter,' 'causam.'

53 In LXXX 'Exterminavit eam, aper de silva, et singularis ferus depastus est,' vacat in fine 'eam.' In eodem 'Deus virtutum, convertere,' deficit 'queso' post 'converte.'

In LXXXI 'probavi te apud aquam contradictionis,' deest in fine 'semper.'

In LXXXII 'Usquequo iudicabitis iniquitatem et faciem peccatorum summitis,' deficit in fine 'semper.'

In LXXXIII 'Etenim Assur venit cum illis, facti sunt in adiutorium filiis Loth,' vacat in fine 'semper.'

In LXXXIIII 'Domine Deus virtutum, exaudi orationem meam, auribus percipe, Deus Iacob,' deficit in fine 'semper.' In eodem 'Quia misericordiam et veritatem diligit Deus,' deficit 'Dominus' ante 'Deus.'

In LXXXV 'Remisisti iniquitatem plebis tue, operuisti omnia peccata eorum,' deficit in fine 'semper.'

In LXXXVI nihil omittitur.

In 76, "There he broke the powers of the bow, the shield, sword, and war," "always" is missing at the end. In the same Psalm, "when God rose up to judgment to save every one gentle in heart," "always" is missing at the end.

In 77, "I remembered God and I was pleased, and I was agi- 52
tated and my spirit failed," "always" is missing at the end. In the same Psalm, "or does God forget to feel pity? Or will he withhold all his mercies in his anger," "always" is missing at the end. In the same Psalm, "You have redeemed your people with your arm, the sons of Jacob and Joseph," "always" is missing at the end.

In 78, "I will open my mouth in parables, I will speak of subjects from long ago," "and" is missing after "parables."

In 79, "Help us, O God of our salvation, and on account of the glory of your name free us," "the reason" is missing after "on account of."

In 80, "The wild boar from the wood destroyed it, and one by 53
one the wild animals consumed," "it" is missing at the end. In the same Psalm, "O God of strength, return," "I pray" is missing after "return."

In 81, "I tested you by the water of contradiction," "always" is missing at the end.

In 82, "How long will you judge wickedness and suffer the countenance of sinners," "always" is missing at the end.

In 83, "For Assur came with them, and they have become helpers for the sons of Lot," "always" is missing at the end.

In 84, "O Lord God of strength, hear my prayer; listen, O God of Jacob," "always" is missing at the end. In the same Psalm, "Because God loves mercy and truth," "Lord" is missing before "God."

In 85, "You have forgiven the wickedness of your people, you have concealed all of their sins," "always" is missing at the end.

Nothing is missing in 86.

54 In LXXXVII 'Gloriosa dicta sunt de te civitas Dei,' deest in fine 'semper.' In eodem 'Dominus narrabit in scripturis populorum et principum, horum qui fuerunt in ea,' deficit in fine 'semper.'

In LXXXVIII 'Super me confirmatus est furor tuus; induxisti super me,' deest in fine 'semper.'

In LXXXVIIII 'Usque in eternum preparabo semen tuum, et edificabo ⟨in⟩ generationem et generationem fidem tuam,' vacat in fine 'semper.' In eodem 'et sicut luna perfecta in eternum, et testis in celo fidelis,' deficit in fine 'semper.' In eodem 'Minorasti dies temporis eius, perfudisti eum confusione,' deest in fine 'semper.'

55 In LXXXX, qui est primus quarti libri, 'Priusquam montes fierent, aut formaretur terra et orbis, a seculo tu es Deus,' in antepenultima deficit 'usque in seculum.' In eodem 'et opera manuum nostrarum dirige,' deest in fine 'ipsum.'

In quatuor subsequentibus Psalmis nihil omittitur.

In XCV 'venite et adoremus et procidamus ante Dominum,' deficit in antepenultima 'ac genuflectamus.'

In tribus subsequentibus Psalmis nihil omittitur.

In XCVIIII 'Dominus in Syon magnus et excelsus,' deficit 'est' in fine.

In duobus subsequentibus Psalmis nihil pretermittitur.

In CII 'a facie indignationis tue,' deficit in principio 'Et.'

In sequenti Psalmo nihil deest.

56 In CIIII 'Omnia a te expectant, ut des eis escam in tempore,' in fine deficit 'suo.'

In duobus subsequentibus nihil pretermittitur.

In CVII, qui est primus quinti libri, et in septem aliis subsequentibus Psalmis nihil deficit.

In 87, "Glorious things have been said about you, city of God," 54
"always" is missing at the end. In the same Psalm, "The Lord will set forth in the writings of the peoples and the princes, those of them who were there," "always" is missing at the end.

In 88, "Your anger is asserted above me; you have led over me," "always" is missing at the end.

In 89, "I will prepare your seed for ever, and I will strengthen your faith from generation to generation," "always" is missing at the end. In the same Psalm, "and just as the moon perfected for ever, and a faithful witness in heaven," "always" is missing at the end. In the same Psalm, "You have shortened the days of his time, you have steeped him in disorder," "always" is missing at the end.

In 90, which is the first Psalm of the fourth book, "Before the 55
mountains were made, or the earth and the world were formed, you were God from eternity," "forever" is missing from the third last position. In the same Psalm, "and direct the works of our hands," "itself" is missing at the end.[7]

In the following four Psalms nothing is omitted.

In 95, "come and let us worship and lie prostrate before the Lord," "and let us kneel" is missing from the third position from the end.

In the following three Psalms nothing is omitted.

In 99, "The Lord great in Sion and exalted," "is" is missing in the third position.

In the following two Psalms nothing is omitted.

In 102, "in the presence of your fury," "And" is missing from the beginning.

In the following Psalm nothing is missing.

In 104, "They wait for everything from you, so that you may 56
give food to them in time," "their" is missing at the end.

In the following two Psalms nothing is omitted.

In 107, which is the first Psalm of the fifth book, and in the other seven following Psalms, nothing is missing.

In CXV 'Domus Aaron speravit in Domino; adiutor eorum est,' vacat in fine 'ipse.' In eodem 'Qui timent Dominum speraverunt in Domino; adiutor eorum et protector eorum est,' deficit, post penultimam, 'ipse.'

In CXVI 'Et nomen Domini invocavi: Domine, libera animam meam,' deficit 'queso' in medio post 'invocavi.'

In CXVII nihil omittitur.

In CXVIII 'Hec porta Domini, iusti intrabunt per eam,' post principium deficit 'est.'

57 In CXVIIII 'Fiat misericordia,' deest 'queso' post principium. In eodem 'Voluntaria oris mei et beneplacita fac, Domine,' post penultimam deficit 'queso.' In eodem 'Hereditate acquisivi et testimonia tua in eternum, quia exultatio cordis mei sunt,' post antepenultimam deficit 'ipsa.' In eodem 'Iustus Domine, et rectum iudicium tuum,' statim post principium deficit 'es.'

In duobus subsequentibus nihil omittitur.

In CXXII 'Propter fratres meos et proximos meos loquebar pacem de te,' in antepenultima deficit 'queso.'

In duobus subsequentibus Psalmis nihil deest.

58 In CXXV 'Benefac, Domine, bonis et rectis corde,' deficit in ⟨pen⟩ultima 'in' et in fine 'eorum.' In eodem 'declinantes autem in obligationes, adducet Dominus,' vacat in antepenultima 'suas' et in penultima 'eos.'

In CXXVI nihil deficit.

In CXXVII 'non confundetur, cum loquetur inimicis suis in porta,' vacat 'cum' ante 'inimicis.'

In quatuor subsequentibus Psalmis nihil pretermittitur.

In CXXXII 'si dedero somnum oculis meis, palpebris meis dormitationem,' deficit 'et' in antepenultima. In eodem 'et filie eorum usque in seculum sedebunt super sedem tuam,' post principium deest 'quoque.'

In 115, "The house of Aaron trusted in the Lord; he is their aid," "himself" is missing at the end. In the same Psalm, "Those who fear the Lord have trusted in the Lord; he is their helper and protector," "himself" is missing after "he."

In 116, "And I invoked the name of the Lord: O Lord, free my soul," "I pray" is missing from before "O Lord."

Nothing is missing in 117.

In 118, "This the door of the Lord, the just will enter through it," "is" is missing after the beginning.

In 119, "May mercy be done," "I pray" is missing after the begin- 57
ning. In the same Psalm, "Accept these voluntary and pleasing statements of my mouth, O Lord," after the second last position "I pray" is missing. In the same Psalm, "I have obtained by inheritance even your testimonies for ever, because they are the joy of my heart," "themselves" is missing at the end. In the same Psalm, "You just, O Lord, and your judgment correct," immediately after the beginning "are" is missing.

In the following two Psalms nothing is missing.

In 122, "On account of my brothers and my family I declared peace with you," in the third last position "I pray" is missing.

In the following two Psalms nothing is missing.

In 125, "Do good, O Lord, for those who are good and upright 58
in heart," "in" is missing after "upright" and "their" before "heart." In the same Psalm, "Those refusing, however, the Lord will lead to obligations," "their own" is missing after "to," and "them" is after "lead."

Nothing is missing in 126.

In 127, "He will not be disconcerted, when he speaks to his enemies at the gate," "with" is missing before "his enemies."

In the four following Psalms nothing is missing.

In 132, "if I give sleep to my eyes, slumber to my eyelids," "and" is missing in the third last position.[8] In the same Psalm, "and their daughters will sit upon your throne for ever," "also" is missing after the beginning.

59 In CXXXIII 'Ecce quam bonum et quam iocundum habitare fratres in unum,' vacat 'etiam' in penultima.

In duobus subsequentibus Psalmis nihil omittitur.

In CXXXVI 'Qui facit mirabilia magna solus,' deficit in fine 'ipse.'

In duobus subsequentibus nihil deest.

In CXXXVIIII 'Imperfectum meum viderunt oculi mei, et in libro tuo omnes scribentur,' vacat ante ultimam 'ipsi.'

60 In CXL 'Acuerunt linguas suas sicut serpentes; venenum aspidum sub labiis eorum,' deficit in fine 'semper.'

In duobus subsequentibus nihil omittitur.

In CXLIII 'Expandi manus meas ad te; anima ⟨mea⟩ sicut terra sine aqua tibi,' vacat in fine 'semper.'

In CXLIIII 'Quorum filii sicut novelle plantationes in iuventute sua,' post principium deficit 'nostri.'

In tribus subsequentibus Psalmis nihil omittitur.

In CXLVIII 'Iuvenes et virgines, senes cum iunioribus,' post 'et,' deest 'etiam.'

In CXLVIIII nihil deficit.

61 In CL 'omnis spiritus laudet Dominum,' vacat in fine 'laudate Dominum.'

Sed ne forte huius tertii voluminis magnitudo ultra accomodatum convenientemque modum extenderetur, de duobus duntaxat a nobis antea propositis in hoc loco hactenus disseruisse sufficiat. Tertium vero de alienis interpretationibus una cum differentibus cunctorum Psalmorum titulis quarto, qui subsequitur libro, non iniuria reservavimus.

EXPLICIT LIBER TERTIVS

In 133, "Behold, how good and how delightful that brothers live 59
together," "also" is missing in the second last position.

In the following two Psalms nothing is missing.

In 136, "Who alone makes great miracles," "himself" is missing at the end.

In the following two Psalms nothing is missing.

In 139, "My eyes have seen my incompleteness, and they will all be written in your book," "themselves" is missing before the final position.

In 140, "They sharpened their tongues just like serpents; the 60
venom of asps under their lips," "always" is missing at the end.

In the following two Psalms nothing is missing.

In 143, "I open my arms to you; my soul is to you just as a land without water," "always" is missing at the end.

In 144, "Whose children just as new plants in their youth," "our" is missing after the beginning.

In the following three Psalms nothing is missing.

In 148, "Young men and young women; old men with younger," after "and" "even" is missing.

Nothing is missing in 149.

In 150, "may every breath praise the Lord," "praise the Lord" is 61
missing at the end.

But in order to avoid expanding the size of this third book beyond a suitable and appropriate scale, let it suffice to have discussed only two of the points we proposed earlier. We have appropriately postponed the third topic about unsuitable translations together with the different titles of all the psalms for the fourth book, which follows.

END OF BOOK THREE

LIBER QVARTVS

1 Si ordo noster, gloriosissime Princeps, exigere et postulare videtur ut hoc quarto libro de alienis interpretationibus una cum differentibus omnium Psalmorum titulis deinceps agamus, cum de iis que a Septuaginta senioribus partim superaddita, partim vero pretermissa inter interpretandum fuisse cernantur, tertio ad sufficientiam disseruisse meminerimus, a primo Psalmo incipientes, ea que aliene traducta sunt seriatim prosequemur.

⟨*I. De alienis interpretationibus*⟩

2 ⟨In I:⟩ 'in cathedra pestilentie,' *in sede derisorum;* in eodem: 'meditabitur,' *ratiocinabitur;* in eodem: 'neque peccatores in concilio iustorum,' *neque peccatores in congregatione iustorum.*

In II: 'Ego autem constitutus sum rex ab eo,' *At ego constitui regem meum;* in eodem: 'super Syon montem sanctum eius,' *super Syon montem sanctum meum;* in eodem: 'Reges eos in virga ferrea,' *Confringes eos in virga ferrea;* in eodem: 'et tanquam vas figuli confringes eos,' *tanquam vas figuli disperges eos;* in eodem: 'Apprendite disciplinam,' *Osculamini filium.*

In III: 'Ego dormivi et soporatus sum,' *Ego iacui et obdormivi;* in eodem: 'quoniam tu percussisti omnes adversantes mihi sine causa,' *Quoniam tu percussisti omnes inimicos meos in maxillam.*

3 In IIII: 'Filii hominum, usquequo gravi corde? ut quid diligitis vanitatem, et queritis mendacium semper?' *Filii hominis usquequo honorem meum ad ignominiam diligetis inaniter, queretis mendacium semper?*

In V: 'dirige in conspectu tuo,' *dirige ante me;* in eodem: 'cor eorum vanum est,' *viscera eorum dolosa;* in eodem: 'linguis suis dolose

BOOK FOUR

Most glorious Prince, since we sufficiently examined in the third book partly what the Seventy Elders added to and partly what they left out of their translation, our plan for this fourth book seems to require and demand that we next discuss unsuitable translations together with the different titles of all the Psalms. We will start with the first Psalm and then proceed in order through what has been inappropriately translated. 1

I. On unsuitable translations

In 1: "in the chair of pestilence," *in the seat of the mockers;* in the same Psalm: "he will think," *he will reason;* in the same Psalm: "nor sinners in the assembly of the just," *nor sinners in the congregation of the just.* 2

In 2: "I however was established king by him," *But I established my king;* in the same Psalm: "upon his holy hill of Zion," *upon my holy hill of Zion;* in the same Psalm: "You will rule them with an iron rod," *You will shatter them with an iron rod;* in the same Psalm: "and you will shatter them like a potter's vessel," *you will scatter them like a potter's vessel;* in the same Psalm: "Hold fast learning," *Kiss the son.*

In 3: "I slept and was deep in sleep," *I lay down and slept;* in the same Psalm: "since you struck all those opposing me without reason," *Since you struck all of my enemies on the jaw.*

In 4: "Sons of men, how long with a heavy heart? Why do you 3
prize vanity, and do you search for falsehood always," *Sons of men, how long will you vainly choose my glory for shame, will you seek for falsehood always?*

In 5: "arrange in your presence," *arrange before me;* in the same Psalm: "their heart is empty," *their inner parts are deceitful;* in the

agebant,' *Lingue eorum blandientur;* in eodem: 'Domine, ut scuto bone voluntatis tue coronasti nos,' *Domine, ut scuto benignitatis coronabis eum.*

In VI nihil alienum est.

In VII: 'Domine Deus meus, si feci istud, si est iniquitas in manibus meis,' *Domine Deus meus, si feci istud an est iniquitas in manibus meis?* in eodem: 'Iustum adiutorium meum a Domino, clipeus meus in Deo:' nam 'iustus' potius quam 'iustum' refertur ad versum superiorem, ubi dicit 'Deus,' supple postea 'iustus.'

In VIII nihil alieni est.

In VIIII: 'constitue, Domine, legislatorem super eos,' *Constitue, Domine, timorem eis.*

4 In X: 'Despicis in oportunitatibus, in tribulatione?' *Absconderis in temporibus angustie;* in eodem: 'auferentur iudicia tua a facie eius,' *excelsa iudicia tua contra eum;* in eodem: 'et cadet, cum dominatus fuerit pauperum,' *Et concidet viribus suis mendicos;* in eodem: 'Non requiret,' *Non requires.*

In XI: 'Transmigra in montem sicut passer,' *Vagamini ad montes vestros* ⟨sicut⟩ *aves;* in eodem: 'Quoniam que perfecisti destruxerunt,' *Quoniam retia dispergentur.*

In XII: 'ponam in salutari suo, fiducialiter agam in eo,' *ponam in salutari, loquetur ei;* in eodem: 'secundum altitudinem tuam multiplicasti filios hominum,' *quando exaltatur contentio filiorum hominum.*

In XIII nihil alieni est.

5 In XIIII: 'Corrupti sunt et abominabiles facti sunt in studiis suis,' *Corruperunt et labefactaverunt opera;* in eodem: 'Omnes declinaverunt, simul inutiles facti sunt,' *Omnes abiere, simul convenere.*

same Psalm: "they were behaving deceitfully with their tongues," *their tongues will flatter;* in the same Psalm: "O Lord, you crowned us as with a shield of goodwill," *O Lord, you will crown him as with a shield of kindness.*

There is nothing unsuitable in 6.

In 7: "O Lord, my God, if I have done this, if there is wickedness in my hands," *O Lord, my God, if I have done this or is there wickedness in my hands;* in the same Psalm: "My just support from the Lord, my shield in God:" for "just" belongs to the verse above; where it says "God" in the verse above, supply "just" after it.

There is nothing unsuitable in 8.

In 9: "establish, O Lord, a lawmaker over them," *O Lord, strike terror in them.*

In 10: "Do you look down in prosperity, in adversity?" *You will* 4
hide in times of trouble; in the same Psalm: "your judgments will be
taken away from his presence," *your exalted judgments against him;* in
the same Psalm: "he will fall when he dominates the poor man,"
and he will destroy the poor with his strength; in the same Psalm: "He
will not demand," *You will not demand.*

In 11: "Travel to the mountain like a sparrow," *Wander to your mountains like birds;* in the same Psalm: "Since they have destroyed what you completed," *since the nets will be spread.*

In 12: "I will place him in safety, I will behave faithfully to him," *I will place him in safety, he will speak to him;* in the same Psalm: "according to your height you have increased the children of men," *when strife is increased among the children of men.*

There is nothing unsuitable in 13.

In 14: "They are corrupt and have become loathsome in their 5
desires," *They have spoiled and weakened their works;* in the same
Psalm: "They all turned aside, at the same time they have become
useless," *They all departed, they gathered together.*

In XV: 'Ad nihilum deductus est in conspectu eius malignus,' *Vilis in conspectu suo et abominatus;* in eodem: 'Qui iurat proximo suo et non decipit,' *Qui iurat ad perpetrandum, non permutabit.*

In XVI: 'quoniam bonorum meorum non eges,' *bona mea non sunt super te;* in eodem: 'tu es qui restituis hereditatem meam mihi,' *Tu sustinebis sortem meam;* in eodem: 'Funes ceciderunt mihi in preclaris,' *Partes ceciderunt mihi in suavitatibus.*

In XVII nihil alieni est.

In XVIII: 'et odientes me disperdidisti,' *et, insimulatores meos, disperdam eos;* in eodem: 'filii alieni inveterati sunt et claudicaverunt,' *filii alieni inveterascent a claustris suis.*

In XVIIII: 'In omnem terram exivit sonus eorum,' *In universam terram egredietur regula.*

In duobus subsequentibus Psalmis nihil alienum inest.

6 In XXII: 'Longe a salute mea verba delictorum meorum,' *Longe a salutari meo verba mugitus mei;* in eodem: 'et nocte, et non ad insipientiam mihi,' *In nocte nec erit silentium mihi;* in eodem: 'Tu autem, Domine, ne elongaveris auxilium tuum,' *At tu, domine, ne elongeris robur meum;* in eodem: 'de cornibus unicornium humilitatem meam,' *Et de cornibus unicornium exaudisti me.*

In XXIII nihil alienum reperitur.

In XXIIII: 'Attollite portas, principes, vestras,' *Attollite, porte, capita vestra.* Et paulo inferius, in replicatione eiusdem versus, similiter.

In XXV nulla est aliena interpretatio.

In XXVI: 'Lavabo inter innocentes manus meas,' *Lavabo in puritate manus meas.*

In XXVII: 'in die malorum, protexit me,' *in die mala abscondet me;* in eodem: 'et mentita est iniquitas sibi,' *et insusurratores iniquitatis.*

In XXVIII nihil alienatur.

In 15: "In his eyes a spiteful person is disdained," *In his eyes he is vile and detested;* in the same Psalm: "He who swears to his relation and does not deceive," *He who swears to commit crime will not change.*

In 16: "Since you do not need my goods," *my goods are not above you;* in the same Psalm: "You are the one who restores my inheritance to me," *You will sustain my lot;* in the same Psalm: "Cords have fallen to me remarkably," *Portions have fallen to me favorably.*

There is nothing unsuitable in 17.

In 18: "and you have destroyed those who hate me," *and, as for my adversaries, I will ruin them;* in the same Psalm: "Strangers' children have grown old and gone lame," *Strangers' children are entrenched in their defenses.*

In 19: "Their voice has gone out through all the earth," *their rule will proceed throughout the whole earth.*

There is nothing unsuitable in the following two Psalms.

In 22: "The words of my transgressions far from my safety," *the* 6
words of my roaring far from my safety; in the same Psalm: "and by night, and not for my folly," *nor will there be silence for me at night;* in the same Psalm: "You, however, O Lord, do not keep your help far away," *But you, O Lord, do not keep my strength far off;* in the same Psalm: "my lowliness from the horns of unicorns," *And you heard me from the horns of unicorns.*

Nothing unsuitable is found in 23.

In 24: "Lift up your gates, O Princes," *Lift up, O gates, your heads.* And likewise a little further down, in the repetition of the same verse.

There is no unsuitable translation in 25.

In 26: "I will wash my hands among the innocents," *I will wash my hands in purity.*

In 27: "on the day of troubles he protected me," *on the day of trouble he will hide me;* in the same Psalm: "and their wickedness lied," *and the whisperers of wickedness.*

Nothing is unsuitable in 28.

7 In XXVIIII: 'et dilectus quemadmodum filius unicornium,' *et Sirion tanquam filius unicornium.*

In XXX nihil alieni est.

In XXXI: 'infirmata est in paupertate virtus mea,' *offendit pre culpa virtus mea;* in eodem: 'quoniam mirificavit mihi misericordiam tuam in civitate munita,' *in civitate obsessa,* in reliquis similiter; in eodem: 'Ego autem dixi in excessu mentis mee,' *At ego dixi in festinatione mea;* in eodem: 'Diligite Dominum, omnes sancti eius, quoniam veritatem requiret Dominus,' *Diligite Dominum, omnes sancti sui! Fideles custodit Dominus.*

In XXXII: 'qui non approximent ad te,' *ne approximent ad te.*

In XXXIII: 'Diligit misericordiam et iudicium, misericordia Domini plena est terra,' *Diligit iustitiam et iudicium, misericordia Domini implevit terram.*

8 In XXXIIII: 'In Domino laudabitur anima mea,' *In Domino laudabit anima mea;* in eodem: 'Accedite ad eum et illuminanimi, et facies vestre non confundentur,' *Viderunt et illustrati sunt et facies eorum non confundentur;* in eodem: 'Divites eguerunt et esurierunt,' *Leunculi eguerunt et esurierunt.*

In XXXV nihil aliene interpretationis est.

In XXXVI: 'Dixit iniustus, ut [non] delinquat in semet ipso,' *Verbum delicti ad peccatorem intra cor meum.*

In XXXVII: 'Custodi innocentiam et vide equitatem, quoniam sunt reliquie homini pacifico,' *Observa, o integer, et considera, o recte, quoniam finis hominis est pax.*

In XXXVIII: 'miser factus sum et curvatus sum usque in finem,' *distortus sum, curvatus sum usque ad summum.*

In XXXVIIII nihil alieni est.

In XXXX: 'et non respexit in vanitates et insanias falsas,' *nec convertit se ad potentes adiutores falsitatis.*

In XXXXI nihil in interpretatione alienum est.

In 29: "and loved just like the son of unicorns," *and Sirion like the* 7
son of unicorns.

There is nothing unsuitable in 30.

In 31: "my strength was weakened by poverty," *my strength fails because of my fault;* in the same Psalm: "since he has magnified your mercy for me in a defended city," *in a besieged city,* with no change for the rest; in the same Psalm: "I however spoke in a digression of my mind," *But I spoke in my haste;* in the same Psalm: "Love the Lord, all you his saints, since the Lord will demand truth," *Love the Lord, all you his saints! The Lord guards the faithful.*

In 32: "they who do not approach you," *lest they approach you.*

In 33: "He loves mercy and judgment, the earth is filled with the mercy of the Lord," *He loves justice and judgment, the mercy of the Lord has filled the earth.*

In 34: "My soul will be praised in the Lord," *My soul will praise* 8
in the Lord; in the same Psalm: "Approach him and be illuminated, and your faces will not be disturbed," *They saw and were illuminated and their faces will not be disturbed;* in the same Psalm: "The rich were in need and were hungry," *The lions were in need and were hungry.*

There is no unsuitable translation in 35.

In 36: "The unjust spoke so that he might [not] fail in himself," *The word of the wrongdoer's offense is within my heart.*

In 37: "Guard innocence and regard justice, since they are the remains for the man of peace," *Heed, O upright man, and consider, O righteous man, since the goal for man is peace.*

In 38: "I became wretched and I am greatly bowed down," *I am twisted and extremely bowed down.*

There is nothing unsuitable in 39.

In 40: "He did not regard vanities and senseless frenzies," *nor did he turn to the powerful aides of deception.*

In 41 there is nothing unsuitable in the translation.

9 In XXXXII, qui est primus secundi libri: 'quoniam transibo in congregationem,' *sperabo usque ad domum Dei;* in eodem: 'in voce exultationis et iubilationis, sonus epulantis,' *in voce exultationis et laudationis cetus tripudians;* in eodem: 'Abyssus abyssum invocat in voce cataractarum tuarum,' *Abyssus abyssum invocat in voce aqueductuum tuorum;* in eodem: 'omnia excelsa tua et fluctus tui super me transierunt,' *Omnis unda tua et fluctus tui super me transierunt.*

In XXXXIII: 'Quare tristis es, anima mea, et quare conturbas me?' *Quare affligeris, anima mea, et quare eiulas super me?*

In XXXXIIII: 'et non fuit multitudo in commutationibus eorum,' *et non multiplicasti in obolis.*

10 In XXXXV: 'Intende, prospere procede et regna propter veritatem et mansuetudinem et iustitiam, et deducet te mirabiliter dextera tua,' *Et spetie tua proficiscere, equita super causam veritatis et humilitatem iustitie, et ostendet tibi venerabilia dextera tua.*

In tribus subsequentibus Psalmis nihil aliene interpretationis reperitur.

In XXXXVIIII: 'quoniam terrigene et filii hominum,' *insuper filii hominum filiique virorum.*

In L nihil aliene traductionis est.

In LI: 'lavabis me, et super nivem dealbabor,' *lavabis me, et supra:* hoc est plusquam *nix,* et non *super nivem dealbabor.*

In LII: 'Quid gloriaris in malitia, qui potens es iniquitate? Tota die,' *Quid gloriaris in malitia, qui potens es misericordia Dei? Quolibet die.*

In duobus subsequentibus Psalmis nihil alieni in traductione est.

11 In LV: 'Divisi sunt ab ira vultus eius, et appropinquabit cor illi⟨us⟩,' *Lubrice fuerunt pinguedines oris sui, et bella cordis sui;* in eodem:

In 42, which is the first Psalm of the second book: "Since I will 9
cross to the congregation," *I will trust all the way to the house of God;* in the same Psalm: "in the voice of joy and exaltation, the sound of a feaster," *in the voice of joy and praise, a dancing assembly;* in the same Psalm: "The deep calls to the deep with the voice of your cataracts," *The deep calls to the deep with the voice of your aqueducts;* in the same Psalm: "Everything above is yours and your waves have passed over me," *All your waves and your floods passed over me.*

In 43: "Why are you sad, my soul, and why do you trouble me?" *Why are you afflicted, my soul, and why do you lament over me?*

In 44: "and there was no great amount in their exchanges," *and you did not increase in obols.*

In 45: "Endeavor, advance in good fortune, and rule according 10
to truth, kindness, and justice, and your right hand will lead you admirably," *Proceed in your splendor, ride for the cause of truth and for the humbleness of justice, and your right hand will show you venerable deeds.*

In the following three Psalms no unsuitable translation is found.

In 49: "since the earthborn men and the children of mankind," *in addition, the children of mankind and the children of men.*

There is no unsuitable translation in 50.

In 51: "You will wash me, and I will be whiter than snow," *you will wash me, and beyond*: this is more than *snow* and not *I will be whiter than snow.*

In 52: "Why do you boast of malice, you who are powerful through wickedness? The entire day," *Why do you boast of wickedness, you who are powerful in God's mercy? Each day.*

In the following two Psalms there is no unsuitable translation.

In 55: "They were divided by the anger of his expression, and 11
his heart will draw near," *The fatness of his mouth was slippery, and the wars of his heart;* in the same Psalm: "Your speeches are softer than

'Molliti sunt sermones tui super oleum, et ipsi sunt iacula,' *Mollita sunt verba sua super oleum, et ipsa sunt iacula.*

In LVI: 'Miserere mei, Deus, quoniam conculcavit me homo,' *Miserere mei, Deus, quia absorbet me homo;* in eodem: 'In Deo laudabo sermones meos,' *In Deo laudabo sermones eius;* in eodem: 'Posuisti lachrymas meas in conspectu, sicut et in promissione tua, Domine,' *Tu pones lachrymam meam in utre tuo, iam in recitatione tua.*

In LVII: 'et in umbra alarum tuarum sperabo donec transeat iniquitas,' *Donec transeant erumne,* in reliquis similiter; in eodem: 'Exaltare super celos, Deus, et super omnem terram gloria tua,' *Exalta super celos, Deus, super universam terram gloriam tuam.*

In LVIII: 'Sicut cera, que fluit, auferetur, supercecidit ignis, et non viderunt solem,' *Quemadmodum lumaca illico abibit, abortivi mulieris, qui non viderunt solem.*

12 In LVIIII: 'Convertentur ad vesperam et famem patientur ut canes, circuibunt civitatem,' *Convertentur ad vesperam, ululabunt ut canes, circuibunt civitatem;* in eodem: 'disperge illos in virtute tua et depone eos, protector meus Domine,' *protector noster,* in reliquis prioribus similiter.

In LX: 'Deus, reppulisti nos et destruxisti nos, iratus es et miseratus es nobis. Deus oblitus est nostri,' *Disperxisti, excanduisti, redire nos facies;* in eodem: 'Ostendisti populo tuo dura, potasti nos vino compunctionis,' *Potasti nos vino veneficii,* in reliquis similiter; in eodem: 'ut liberentur dilecti tui: salvum fac dextera tua et exaudi me,' *ut liberentur dilecti tui, salvet dextera tua, et exaudiet me;* in eodem: 'Iuda rex meus, Moab olla spei mee,' *Iuda scriba meus, Moab olla lavacri mei;* in eodem: 'mihi alienigene subditi sunt,' *super me, Philistei, belligerate.*

13 In LXI nihil alieni in interpretatione est.

oil, and they are darts," *His words are softer than oil, and they are darts.*

In 56: "Pity me, O God, since a man has trampled upon me," *Pity me, O God, because a man overwhelms me;* in the same Psalm: "In God I will praise my words," *In God I will praise his words;* in the same Psalm: "You put my tears on view, just as also in your promise, O Lord," *You will put my tears in your flask, now in your record.*

In 57: "and I will trust in the shadow of your wings until the wickedness passes," *Until hardships should pass* and no change for the rest; in the same Psalm: "Be raised above the heavens, O God, and above all the earth in your glory," *Raise your glory above the heavens, O God, above all the earth.*

In 58: "Just as wax, which flows, will be carried away, fire has fallen, and they have not seen the sun," *As the slug will depart there, the prematurely born of woman, who have not seen the sun.*

In 59: "They will return at evening and will endure hunger like 12
dogs, they will go about the city," *They will return at evening, they will howl like dogs, they will go about the city;* in the same Psalm: "scatter them with your strength and get rid of them, O Lord my protector," *our protector* with no change for the earlier words.

In 60: "O God, you drove us back and you destroyed us, you were angry and you took pity on us. God forgot us," *You scattered us, you grew angry, you will make us return;* in the same Psalm: "You have shown difficult things to your people, you gave us the wine of compunction to drink," *You gave us the wine of poison to drink,* with no change for the rest; in the same Psalm: "So that your beloved ones may be freed: save me with your right hand and hear me," *so that your beloved ones may be freed, may your right hand save them, and it will hear me;* in the same Psalm: "Judah is my king, Moab is the pot of my hope," *Judah is my scribe, Moab is my wash pot;* in the same Psalm: "foreigners are subject to me," *Philistines, wage war for me.*

There is no unsuitable translation in 61. 13

In LXII: 'Nonne Deo subiecta erit anima mea?' *Profecto ad Deum est expectatio anime mee;* in eodem: 'Nonne ipse est Deus meus et salutaris meus?' *Profecto ipse est fortitudo mea et salutare meum;* in eodem: 'Veruntamen pretium meum cogitaverunt repellere: cucurri in siti,' *Profecto ob sublimitatem suam consultabunt ad repellendum, volent mendacium;* in eodem: 'Sperate in eo, omnis congregatio populi,' *Sperate in eo in omni tempore;* in eodem: 'Veruntamen vani filii hominum, mendaces filii hominum in stateris,' *Profecto vanitas filii hominum, falsitas filii virorum in lancibus.*

In LXIII: 'in terra deserta, in via inaquosa,' *in terra sicca et defessa sine aquis.*

14 In LXIIII: 'Scrutati sunt iniquitatem, defecerunt scrutantes scrutinio,' *Scrutabuntur iniquitates, perfecerunt scrutinium scrutantium;* in eodem: 'et exaltabitur Deus. Sagitte parvulorum facte sunt plage eorum,' *Et sagittavit eos Deus sagittam, subito erunt plage eorum.*

In LXV: 'Te decet, Deus, hymnus in Syon, et tibi reddetur votum in Hierusalem,' *Tibi silentium laus Deo in Syon, et tibi perficietur votum;* in eodem: 'Exaudi orationem meam,' *Qui exaudis orationem meam;* in eodem: 'Verba iniquitatum prevaluerunt super nos,' *Verba iniquitatum prevaluerunt supra me;* in eodem: 'Qui conturbas profundum maris, sonum fluctuum eius,' *Turbabuntur gentes, sedans fremitum marium, fremitum fluctuum eorum;* in eodem: 'Visitasti terram et inebriasti eam, multiplicasti locupletare eam,' *Visitasti terram et rorasti ac multitudine locupletasti eam;* in eodem: 'Benedices corone anni benignitatis tue,' *Coronasti annum benignitatis tue;* in eodem: 'et campi tui replebuntur ubertate,' *et colles tui stillabunt adipem;* in eodem: 'Induti sicut arietes ovium, et valles abundabunt frumento;

In 62: "Will my soul not be subject to God?" *The longing of my soul is truly toward God*; in the same Psalm: "Is he not my God and my salvation," *Truly he is my strength and my salvation*; in the same Psalm: "However, they thought to reject my price: I ran in thirst," *Truly because of his height they will take counsel to repel him, they will desire a lie*; in the same Psalm: "Trust in him, every gathering of people," *Trust in him for all time*; in the same Psalm: "However, the vain children of men, the lying children of men are in the balance," *Truly the vanity of the son of men, the falsity of the son of men is on the scales.*

In 63: "in a deserted land, on a waterless road," *in a dry land and barren without water.*

In 64: "They examined wickedness, while examining they failed 14
scrutiny," *They will examine wickedness, they completed an examination of the examiners*; in the same Psalm: "and God will be exalted. The arrows of petty men have become their wounds," *And God shot at them with an arrow, suddenly they will have wounds."*

In 65: "A hymn is fitting for you, O God, in Sion, and the vow will be rendered to you in Jerusalem," *Silence is your praise in Sion, O God, and the vow will be completed for you*; in the same Psalm: "Hear my prayer," *You who hear my prayer*; in the same Psalm: "The words of wickedness have prevailed over us," *The words of wickedness have prevailed over me*; in the same Psalm: "You who disturb the depth of the sea, the sound of its waves," *the peoples will be troubled, calming the roar of the seas, the roar of their waves*; in the same Psalm: "You visited the earth and drenched it, you enlarged it to make it rich," *You visited the earth and bedewed it, and you made it rich with a great multitude*; in the same Psalm: "You will praise the crown of the year of your bounty," *You crowned the year of your bounty*; in the same Psalm: "and your fields will be filled with abundance," *and your hills will drip fat*; in the same Psalm: "dressed just like the rams of sheep, and the valleys will abound with grain; for they will speak praise,"

etenim hymnum dicent,' *Induantur prata ovibus, et valles cooperiantur frumento: et exultabunt et cantabunt.*

15 In LXVI: 'Imposuisti homines super capita nostra,' *Induxisti homines ad capita nostra;* in eodem: 'et eduxisti nos in refrigerium,' *et eduxisti nos in saturitatem.*

In LXVII nihil aliene interpretationis est.

In LXVIII: 'Deus, qui habitare facit unius moris in domo, qui
educit vinctos in fortitudine,' *Deus, qui habitare facit solitarios in*
domo, qui extrahit vinctos in cathenis; in eodem: 'similiter eos qui exas-
perant, qui habitant in sepulchris,' *tantum rebelles habitant in aridi-*
tate; in eodem: 'infirmata est: tu vero perfecisti eam,' *et defessa est, tu*
vero preparasti eam; in eodem: 'Rex virtutum dilecti, dilecti et spectati domus dividere spolia,' *Reges exercituum vagabuntur et vagabun-*
tur; et habitator domus dividet predam; in eodem: 'Currus Dei [in]
decem milibus multiplex, milia letantium; Dominus in eis in Synai
⟨in⟩ sancto,' *Currus Dei in decem milibus militum angelorum: Dominus*
in se ipsis Synai in sanctuario; in eodem: 'Prevenerunt principes con-
iuncti sunt psallentibus, in medio iuvencularum tympanistarum,'
Prevenerunt cantores, postea pulsatores, inter puellas tympanizantes; in
16 eodem: 'Ubi Beniamin adolescentulus in mentis excessu,' *Ubi Be-*
niamin parvulus dominabitur eis; in eodem: 'dissipa gentes que bella
volunt,' *Dissipavit populos qui bella volunt;* in eodem: 'Psallite Deo,
qui ascendit super celum celi ad orientem,' *Ei, qui ascendit in celos,*
celos ab initio; in eodem: 'Mirabilis Deus in sanctis tuis; Deus Israel
ipse dabit virtutem,' *Venerabilis Deus in sanctis tuis,* et reliqua similiter.

Let the meadows be clothed with sheep, and the valleys be covered with grain; and they will exult and sing.

In 66: "You placed men over our heads," *You led men to our heads;* 15
in the same Psalm: "And you led us into a place of rest," *and you led us into richness.*

There is no unsuitable translation in 67.

In 68: "God, who makes them live in one kind of home, who by his strength leads them bound," *God, who makes the lonely live in a home, who frees those bound in chains;* in the same Psalm: "Likewise those who provoke, who live in sepulchers," *only the rebels live in dryness;* in the same Psalm: "And it was weak: but you completed it," *and it was weary, but you prepared it;* in the same Psalm: "The king of strengths of the beloved, and the house of the beloved and honored divide the spoils," *The kings of the armies will wander and wander, and the inhabitant of the house will divide the plunder;* in the same Psalm: "The chariots of God are many thousands, thousands of those rejoicing; the Lord is among them in Sinai in his holy place," *The chariots of God are among the ten thousand angel-soldiers: the Lord is among them in his sanctuary at Sinai;* in the same Psalm: "The princes together with those singing praise came first, in the midst of the young women playing the timbrel," *The singers came first, afterward the drummers, among the girls playing the timbrel;* in
the same Psalm: "Where the young Benjamin in the distraction of 16
his mind," *Where little Benjamin will rule them;* in the same Psalm: "scatter the nations which desire wars," *He scattered the peoples who desire wars;* in the same Psalm: "Sing to God, who rises above the heaven of heaven to the east," *To him who ascends to the heavens, the heavens in the beginning;* in the same Psalm: "God, you are marvelous in your holy places; the God of Israel himself will give strength," *God, you are venerable in your holy places,* with no changes for the rest.

In LXVIIII: 'Fiat mensa eorum coram ipsis in laqueum et in retributionem et in scandalum,' *Et consolationes et offendiculum;* in reliquis similiter se habet usque ad 'retributionem' et 'scandalum.'

In LXX: 'avertantur statim erubescentes, qui dicunt mihi: Euge, euge!' *Convertantur in finem verecundie sue,* et reliqua huiusmodi.

In LXXI: 'quoniam non cognovi litteraturam,' *quoniam non cognovi comparationem.*

In LXXII: 'Et permanebit cum sole et ante lunam in generatione generationum,' *Timebunt te cum sole et ante lunam in generatione generationum;* in eodem: 'Ascendit velut pluvia in vellus,' *Descendent sicut pluvie super herbam;* in eodem: 'et replebitur maiestate eius omnis terra. Fiat, fiat,' *Et implevit gloria sua universam terram. Amen et amen.*

17 In LXXIII, qui est primus tertii libri: 'Ideo convertetur populus meus hic, et dies pleni invenientur in eis,' *Idcirco convertetur populus eius hic, et aque plene surgentur in eis;* in eodem: 'Ecce ipsi peccatores et abundantes,' *In seculo obtinuerunt divitias;* in eodem: 'Et dixi: Ergo sine causa iustificavi cor meum et lavi inter innocentes manus meas,' *Tantum vane mandavi cor meum et lavi in munditia palmas meas;* in eodem: 'Si[c] dicebam: Narrabo sic, ecce nationem filiorum tuorum reprobavi,' *Si dixi: Enarrabo, ecce quemadmodum generationem filiorum tuorum reprobavi;* in eodem: 'Veruntamen propter dolos posuisti; deiecisti eos dum allevarentur,' *Tantum in lubrica pones eos; deiecisti eos ad desolationes;* in eodem: 'subito defecerunt; perierunt propter iniquitatem suam,' *perierunt ob infortunia,* in reliquis prioribus similiter; in eodem: 'Quia inflamatum est cor meum, et renes mei commutati sunt,' *Quia exasperatum est cor meum, et renes meos*

In 69: "Let their table become a snare before them and retribution and an offense," *And consolations and a stumbling block,* and the rest is the same up to "retribution" and "offense."

In 70: "Let them immediately be turned away in shame who say to me: Hurray, hurray!" *Let them be turned back to the limit of their shame,* with no changes for the rest.

In 71: "since I did not know the writing," *since I do not know the total.*

In 72: "And it will remain with the sun and before the time of the moon through all generations," *They will fear you with the sun and before the moon through all generations;* in the same Psalm: "He rises like rain on wool," *They will fall just like showers of rain on the grass;* in the same Psalm: "and the whole earth will be filled with his majesty. Let it be done, let it be done," *And he filled the whole earth with his glory. Amen and amen.*

In 73, which is the first Psalm of the third book: "Therefore 17
this my people will return, and full days will be found among them," *For that reason this his people will return, and full waters will rise up among them;* in the same Psalm: "Behold the men themselves, sinners and flourishing," *They obtained riches in the world;* in the same Psalm: "And I said: Therefore I justified my heart without cause and I washed my hands among the innocent," *But in vain did I consign my heart, and I washed my palms in cleanliness;* in the same Psalm: "If I said, I will report thus, behold, I have condemned the nation of your children," *If I said: I will report, behold, how I condemned the generation of your children;* in the same Psalm: "However, because of their deceptions you subdued them; you cast them down until they could be raised up," *But you will place them on slippery ground; you cast them into afflictions;* in the same Psalm: "suddenly they were overwhelmed; they perished because of their wickedness," *they perished on account of misfortunes,* with no changes earlier; in the same Psalm: "Because my heart was inflamed, and my kidneys were changed," *Because my heart was provoked, and I*

evacuavi; in eodem: 'ut iumentum factus sum apud te, et ego semper tecum,' *at ego pecus sum, et non cognovi. Belua fui apud te;* in eodem: 'Quid enim mihi est in celo? et a te quid volui super terram?' *Quid mihi in celo, et tecum volui in terra?*

18 In LXXIIII: 'posuerunt signa sua signa,' *constituerunt signa sua insignia;* in eodem: 'et non cognoverunt sicut in exitu super summum. Quasi in silva lignorum securibus,' *innotuit ac si afferrentur accessu ad altum in silva lignorum secures;* in eodem: 'exciderunt ianuas eius, in idipsum in securi et ascia deiecerunt eam,' *et nunc sculptilia eius simul in securi et ascia deiecerunt;* in eodem: 'Tu confirmasti in virtute tua mare, contribulasti capita draconum in aquis,' *Tu dirupisti in fortitudine tua mare, contrivisti capita draconum super aquis;* in eodem: 'Tuus est dies et tua est nox, tu fabricatus es auroram et solem,' *Tu fabricatus es lucem et solem,* in reliquis similiter; in eodem: 'Ne tradas bestiis animas confitentium tibi et animas pauperum tuorum ne obliviscaris in finem,' *Ne tradas feris animas turturis tui, vitam pauperum tuorum ne obliviscaris in eternum.*

19 In LXXV: 'Nolite extollere in altum cornu vestrum, nolite loqui adversus Deum iniquitatem,' *Ne elevetis in altum cornu vestrum, ne loquamini in collo robusto;* in eodem: 'et inclinavit ex hoc in hoc; veruntamen fex eius non est exinanita,' *et effusus est ex hoc, tantum feces eius sugent.*

In LXXVI: 'Et factus est in pace locus eius, et habitatio eius in Syon,' *Et erit in Salem tugurium eius et habitatio eius in Syon;* in eodem: 'Illuminans tu mirabiliter a montibus eternis,' *Illustris tu magnifice a montibus rapine;* in eodem: 'Turbati sunt omnes insipientes corde,'

emptied my kidneys; in the same Psalm: "I became like a draft animal before you, and I was always with you," *but I am an animal, and I did not know. I was a wild beast before you;* in the same Psalm: "For what is there for me in heaven? And what do I want from you on earth?" *What is there for me in heaven, and what did I want with you on earth?*

In 74: "they set up their signs as signs," *they established their signs* 18
as ensigns; in the same Psalm: "And they did not know just as on a path at the top. As if in a forest of trees with axes," *it became known as if axes were carried by a path to the top in a forest of trees;* in the same Psalm: "they cut down its doors, they destroyed it at the same time with ax and hatchet," *and now they destroyed his sculptures with both ax and hatchet;* in the same Psalm: "You strengthened the sea with your fortitude, you crushed the heads of dragons in the waters," *You divided the sea with your strength, you pounded the dragons' heads upon on the waters;* in the same Psalm: "Yours is the day and yours the night, you made the dawn and the sun," *You made the light and the sun,* and the same for the rest; in the same Psalm: "Do not hand over the lives of those confessing to you to beasts, and never forget the lives of your poor," *Do not hand over the life of your turtle-dove to the savages, and never forget the life of your poor.*

In 75: "Do not raise your horn up high, do not speak wicked- 19
ness against God," *Do not lift your horn up high, do not speak with a stiff neck;* in the same Psalm: "And he poured it from this to this; nevertheless its dregs are not emptied," *and it was poured from this, but they will drink its dregs.*

In 76: "And his place was made in peace, and his dwelling place in Zion," *And his hut will be in Salem, and his dwelling place in Zion;* in the same Psalm: "You, lighting up wonderfully by the eternal mountains," *You, lit magnificently by the mountains of prey;* in the same Psalm: "All those foolish in their heart were confounded," *Those strong in heart were plundered;* in the same Psalm: "You are frightful,

Spoliati sunt robusti corde; in eodem: 'Tu terribilis es, et quis resistet tibi?' *Tu venerabilis es, et quis stabit coram te?*

20 In LXXVII: 'Memor fui Dei et delectatus sum, et exercitatus sum,' *Recordabor Dei et conturbabor ac loquar;* in eodem: 'Anticipaverunt vigilias oculi mei,' *Assumpsi vigilias oculorum meorum;* in eodem: 'et meditatus sum nocte cum corde meo et exercitabar et scopebam spiritum meum,' *Recordabor psalmodie mee nocte, cum corde meo loquar et inquisivit spiritus meus;* in eodem: 'Nunquid in eternum proiciet Deus? . . . ut complacentior sit adhuc?' *Nunquid in eternum obliviscetur Dominus, et non adiciet ad complacendum amplius?* in eodem: 'Et dixi: Nunc cepi; hec mutatio dextere Excelsi,' *Et dixi: Imbecillitas mea hec est, anni dextere Excelsi;* in eodem: 'multitudo sonitus aquarum; vocem dederunt nubes,' *Excusserunt aquam nubila, vocem dederunt celi;* in eodem: 'vox tonitrui tui in rota; illuxerunt corruscationes tue orbi terre,' *Vox tonitrui in rota; illuminaverunt fulgura orbem.*

21 In LXXVIII: 'Aperiam in parabolis os meum, loquar propositiones ab initio,' *Loquar proverbia antiqua,* in reliquis similiter; in eodem: 'Filii Effrain intendentes et mittentes arcum, conversi sunt in die belli,' *Filii Effrain, armati sagittatores arcus, redierunt in die belli;* in eodem: 'et electos Israel impedivit,' *et electos Israel incurvavit;* in eodem: 'misit in eos cenomiam,' *transmisit in eos feras omnimodas;* in eodem: 'Edificavit sicut unicornis sanctificium suum in terra, quam fundavit in secula,' *Et condidit quasi sanctuarium suum, quasi terram fundavit illud in seculum.*

In LXXVIIII: 'posuerunt Hierusalem in pomorum custodiam,' *posuerunt Hierusalem in acervos;* in eodem: 'quia commederunt Iacob et locum eius desolaverunt,' *quia commederunt Iacob, et habitaculum eius desolaverunt.*

and who will resist you?" *You are venerable, and who will stand before you?*

In 77: "I was mindful of God and I was delighted, and I was 20
worried," *I will remember God and I will be disturbed and I will speak;* in the same Psalm: "My eyes anticipated their watch," *I took the watch of my eyes;* in the same Psalm: "and I thought at night with my heart and I was troubled and I searched my spirit," *I will remember my song at night, I will speak with my heart, and my spirit searched;* in the same Psalm: "Surely God will not abandon forever, will he? . . . so that he may still be favorable?" *Surely God will not be forgetful forever, will he, and will he not add to his kindliness?;* in the same Psalm: "And I said: Now I begin: this is the change of the right hand of the most High," *And I said: this is my weakness, the years of the right hand of the most High;* in the same Psalm: "a multitude of sounds of water; the clouds gave voice," *the dark clouds shook out water, the heavens gave voice;* in the same Psalm: "the sound of your thunder in the heavens; your flashings lit the world," *The sound of thunder in the heavens; lightning illuminated the world.*

In 78: "I will open my mouth in parables, I will speak of themes 21
from long ago," *I will speak ancient proverbs,* with no changes for the rest; in the same Psalm, "The children of Ephraim, aiming and shooting their bow, were turned back on the day of battle," *The children of Ephraim, armed archers of the bow, returned on the day of battle;* in the same Psalm, "and he impeded the chosen men of Israel," *and he bowed down the chosen men of Israel;* in the same Psalm, "he sent a host of flies against them," *he sent every kind of wild animal against them;* in the same Psalm, "Like a unicorn he built his sanctuary on earth, which he established forever," *And he founded it like his own sanctuary, like the earth he established it forever.*

In 79: "They placed Jerusalem as a guard of fruit trees," *They put Jerusalem into heaps;* in the same Psalm, "Because they consumed Jacob and made his place desolate," *because they consumed Jacob and made his dwelling place desolate.*

22 In LXXX: 'Domine Deus virtutum. Quousque irasceris super orationem servi tui?' *Domine Deus exercituum, usque quo fumigasti ad orationem populi tui?* in eodem: 'Vineam de Egypto transtulisti,' *Vitem ex Egypto attulisti;* in eodem: 'Exterminavit eam, aper de silva, et singularis ferus depastus est eam,' *Vastabit eam, aper de silva, et pulchritudo agri depascet eam.*

In LXXXI: 'Testimonium in Ioseph posuit illud, cum exiret de terra Egypti. Linguam quam non noverat audivit,' *Testimonium Joseph posuit eum, cum ipse egrederetur de terra Egypti. Labium quod nescivit, audiam;* in eodem: 'divertit ab oneribus dorsum eius, in cophino servierunt,' *amovi ab onere humerum eius; palme sue ab olla recesserunt;* in eodem: 'Non erit in te Deus recens, neque adorabis deum alienum,' *Non sit in te Deus alienus, et ne adores Deum peregrinum.*

In LXXXII nihil aliene interpretationis est.

In LXXXIII: 'Deus, quis similis erit tibi? Ne taceas neque compescaris, Deus,' *Deus, ne taceas tibi, ne sileas et ne quiescas, Deus.*

23 In LXXXIIII: 'Etenim passer invenit domum, et turtur nidum sibi, ubi reponat pullos suos,' *Insuper avis invenit domum, et hirundo nidum sibi, ubi ponat pullos suos;* in eodem: 'Etenim benedictionem dabit legis lator,' *benedictionibus quoque amicietur doctor;* in eodem: 'Quia misericordiam et veritatem diligit Deus,' *Gratiam et gloriam dabit Dominus.*

In LXXXV: 'et super sanctos suos et in eos qui convertuntur ad cor,' *et ad sanctos suos non revertetur ad stultitiam.*

In LXXXVI nihil alieni in interpretatione reperitur.

In LXXXVII: 'ecce alienigene et Tyrus et populus Ethiopum, ierunt illic,' *Ecce Palestina et Tyrus cum Ethiopia, iste natus est ibi;* in

In 80: "Lord God of strengths, how long will you be angry 22
about the prayer of your servant?" *Lord God of the armies, how long have you burned against the prayer of your people?* in the same Psalm: "You brought over a vineyard from Egypt," *You brought a grapevine from Egypt;* in the same Psalm: "It drove it out, a wild boar from the forest, and each wild animal fed on it," *It will ravage it, the wild boar from the forest, and the beauty of the field will feed on it.*

In 81: "This he placed as a testimony for Joseph, when he came out from the land of Egypt. He heard a language which he did not know," *He placed it as a testimony of Joseph, when he came out from the land of Egypt. I will hear a tongue which he did not know;* in the same Psalm: "he turned his back from the burdens, they served in a basket," *I moved his shoulder from the burden, his palms withdrew from the pot;* in the same Psalm: "There will be no new God in you, nor will you worship a strange god," *May there not be a strange God in you, and may you not worship a foreign God.*

There is no unsuitable translation in 82.

In 83: "O God, who will be like you? Do not be quiet, nor restrain yourself, O God," *O God, do not be quiet, do not be silent and do not be inactive, O God.*

In 84: "For the sparrow has found a home, and the turtledove a 23
nest for itself, a place to put its young," *The bird found a home above, and the swallow a nest for itself, a place to put its young;* in the same Psalm: "For the lawgiver will give a blessing," *the teacher will also be clothed with blessings;* in the same Psalm: "Because God loves mercy and truth," *The Lord will give grace and glory.*

In 85: "and upon his holy ones and toward those who are sincerely changed," *and to his holy ones he will not return to foolishness.*

There is no unsuitable translation in 86.

In 87: "behold, foreigners and Tyre and the people of Ethiopia, they came there," *Behold, Palestine and Tyre with Ethiopia, this man*

eodem: 'Dominus narrabit in scripturis populorum et principum, horum qui fuerunt in ea,' *Dominus numerabit scribens populos, iste natus est ibi semper.*

24 In LXXXVIII: 'Estimatus sum cum descendentibus in lacum, factus sum sicut homo sine adiutorio,' *Deputatus sum cum descendentibus in puteum, factus sum velut vir invalidus;* in eodem: 'Elongasti a me amicum et proximum, et notos meos a miseria,' *Elongasti a me amicum et sodalem, noti mei osculati sunt.*

In LXXXVIIII: 'Tu humiliasti, sicut vulneratum, superbum,' *Tu confregisti, ceu vulneratum Egyptum;* in eodem: 'aquilonem et mare tu creasti,' *Aquilo et meridies, tu creasti ea;* in eodem: 'Quoniam gloria virtutis eorum tu es, et beneplacito tuo ⟨extollitur⟩ cornu nostrum,' *Quia gloria fortitudinis eorum* ⟨tu es⟩, *et in voluntate tua exaltabis cornu nostrum;* in eodem: 'quia Domini est assumptio nostra,' *quia Domini est protectio nostra;* in eodem: 'Semel iuravi in sancto meo, si David mentiar,' *semel iuravi in sancto meo an David mentiar;* in eodem: 'et sicut luna perfecta in eternum,' *quasi luna stabilietur in sempiternum;* in eodem: 'Tu vero reppulisti et despexisti, distulisti Christum tuum,' *Tu autem abscondisti et abominatus es, iratus es cum Christo tuo;* in eodem: 'Quis est homo qui vivet et non videbit mortem? eruet animam suam de manu inferi,' *Quis est vir vivens et non videbit mortem? Eruet animam suam de manu inferni semper;* in eodem: 'Ubi sunt misericordie tue antique, Domine, sicut iurasti David in virtute?' *Ubi sunt misericordie tue prime, Domine? Iurasti David in fide tua.*

25 In LXXXX, qui est primus quarti libri: 'quoniam superveniet mansuetudo, et corripiemur,' *quoniam transivimus cito et advolavimus;* in eodem: 'Quis novit potestatem ire tue, et pre timore tuo iram tuam dinumerare?' *Quis novit fortitudinem furoris tui, et ceu timor tuus*

was born there; in the same Psalm: "The Lord will tell in the writings of peoples and princes, of those who were in it," *The Lord will count, enrolling the peoples, that man was born there, always.*

In 88: "I am reckoned with those going down into the pit, I 24
have become a man without support," *I was reckoned with those going down into the well, I have become like a weak man;* in the same Psalm: "You have removed my friend and neighbor from me and removed my acquaintances from misery," *You have removed my friend and confidant from me, my acquaintances have been kissed.*

In 89: "You humbled the proud man, as if wounded," *You shattered him, like wounded Egypt;* in the same Psalm: "you created the north wind and the sea," *The north wind and midday, you created them;* in the same Psalm: "Since you are the glory of their courage, and our horn is raised at your pleasure," *Because you are the glory of their strength, and at your pleasure you will raise our horn;* in the same Psalm: "because our acceptance is the Lord's," *because our protection is the Lord's;* in the same Psalm: "Once I swore in my sanctuary, if I should lie to David," *Once I swore in my sanctuary if I should lie to David;*[1] in the same Psalm: "and like the moon, perfected for ever," *like the moon it will endure forever;* in the same Psalm: "But you repelled and despised, you put off your anointed one," *You, however, concealed and you detested, you were angry with your anointed one;* in the same Psalm: "Who is the man who is living and will not see death? He will free his soul from the hand of the grave," *Who is the man living and will not see death? He will free his soul from the hand of the grave, forever;* in the same Psalm: "Where are your former mercies, O Lord, as you swore to David in your strength," *Where are your first mercies, O Lord? You swore to David in your faith.*

In 90, which is the first Psalm of the fourth book: "since your 25
gentleness will come, and we will be seized," *since we quickly crossed over and we flew;* in the same Psalm: "Who knows the power of your anger, and to consider your anger in proportion to the fear you inspire?" *Who knows the strength of your rage, and like the fear you*

ira tua? in eodem: 'Dexteram tuam sic notam fac, et eruditos corde in sapientia,' *Ad computationem dierum nostrorum sic doce, et afferemus cor sapientie;* in eodem: 'Convertere, Domine; usque quo? et deprecabilis esto super populos tuos,' *Revertere, Domine, usque quo? et propitiare super servis tuis;* in eodem: 'Repleti sumus mane misericordia tua,' *Satia nos mane misericordia tua;* in eodem: 'Letati sumus pro diebus,' *Letifica nos ceu dies.*

26 In LXXXXI: 'Qui habitat in adiutorio Altissimi, in protectione Dei celi commorabitur,' *Habitans in abscondito excelsi, in umbra omnipotentis commorabitur;* in eodem: 'Dicet Domino: Susceptor meus es tu et refugium meum,' *Dicam Domino: Spes mea, fortitudo mea;* in eodem: 'Quoniam ipse liberabit me de laqueo venantium et a verbo aspero,' *Quia ipse liberabit te de laqueo venantium, de peste confractionum;* in eodem: 'In scapulis suis obumbrabit tibi, et sub pennis eius sperabis,' *In ala sua obumbrabit tibi, et sub alis suis sperabis;* in eodem: 'In manibus portabunt te, ne forte offendas ad lapidem pedem tuum,' *Super palmis portabunt te, ne quando offendat ad lapidem pes tuus.*

27 In LXXXXII: 'Et exaltabitur sicut unicornis cornu nostrum, et senectus mea in misericordia uberi,' *Et exaltabitur ceu unicornis cornu meum, et senectus mea in oleo recenti.*

In LXXXXIII: 'et precinxit se virtute. Etenim firmavit orbem terre, qui non movebitur,' *Accinctus insuper appendet orbem, qui non movebitur.*

In duobus subsequentibus Psalmis nihil aliene interpretationis invenitur.

In LXXXXVI: 'quoniam omnes dii gentium demonia, Dominus autem celos fecit,' *Omnes enim dii populorum sculptilia,* et reliqua eiusmodi.

inspire is your anger? in the same Psalm: "Make your right hand known in this way, and those learned in their heart in wisdom," *Teach us in this way to calculate our days, and let us apply our heart to wisdom;* in the same Psalm: "Turn round, O Lord; how long? and be merciful upon your people," *Return, O Lord, how long? And yield to the prayers of your servants;* in the same Psalm: "We are filled early with your mercy," *Satisfy us early with your mercy;* in the same Psalm: "We are happy according to the days," *Gladden us like the days.*

In 91: "He who lives with the help of the most High, will be 26
remembered with the protection of God of Heaven," *He, living in the secret place of the most High, will dwell in the shadow of the Almighty;* in the same Psalm: "He will say to the Lord: You are my support and my refuge," *I will say to the Lord: My hope, my strength;* in the same Psalm: "Since he will liberate me from the snare of hunters and from a rough word," *Since he will liberate you from the snare of hunters, from the pestilence of ruptures;* in the same Psalm: "He will protect you with his shoulders, and you will trust under his feathers," *He will protect you with his wing, and you will trust under his wings;* in the same Psalm: "They will carry you in their hands lest you strike your foot against a stone," *They will carry you on their palms lest your foot ever strike against a stone.*

In 92: "And our horn will be raised up like a unicorn, and my 27
old age in abundant mercy," *And my horn will be raised up like a unicorn, and my old age in fresh oil.*

In 93: "and he girt himself with courage. For he strengthened the world which will not be moved," *Armed from above he will weigh the world that will not be moved.*

In the following two Psalms no unsuitable translations are found.

In 96: "since all the gods of the nations are demons, whereas the Lord made the heavens," *For all the gods of the peoples are images,* and the same for the rest.

In LXXXXVII: 'adorate eum, omnes angeli eius,' *adorent eum omnes dii;* in eodem: 'quoniam tu, Domine, altissimus super omnem terram,' *Vehementer elatus es super omnes deos.*

In duobus subsequentibus Psalmis nihil aliene interpretationis est.

In C: 'Scitote quoniam Dominus ipse est Deus; ipse fecit nos et non ipsi nos,' *Intelligite quoniam Dominus ipse est Deus, et ipse fecit nos, et nos eius sumus.*

In CI: 'Detrahentem secreto proximo suo, hunc persequebar,' *Detrahentem clanculum proximo suo: hunc necabo.*

28 In CII: 'Quia defecerunt sicut fumus dies mei,' *Quoniam consumpti sunt in fumum dies mei;* in eodem: 'ut audiret gemitum compeditorum, ut solveret filios interemptorum,' *Ut audiret gemitus compeditorum, ut solveret filios mortis.*

In CIII nihil alieni in interpretatione est.

In CIIII: 'Saturabuntur ligna campi, et cedri Libani quas plantavit,' *Saturabuntur ligna Domini,* et reliqua similiter; in eodem: 'Illic passeres nidificabunt; herodii domus dux est eorum,' *Quod illic aves nidificabunt; ciconie abietes domus eius.*

In CV: 'Ut erudiret principes eius sicut semet ipsum,' *Ut vinciret principes suos secundum mentem eius;* in eodem: 'Dixit, et venit cenomia et [s]cyniphes in omnibus finibus eorum,' *Dixit, et venit fera omnimoda, pediculi in omnes terminos eorum.*

29 In CVI: 'et multiplicata est in eis ruina,' *et confregit eos pestis;* in eodem: 'Et stetit Finees et placavit, et cessavit quassatio,' *Stetit autem Finees et diiudicavit, et est retenta pestis.*

In CVII, qui est primus quinti libri: 'Misit verbum suum et sanavit eos, et eripuit eos de interitionibus eorum,' *Et eruit de*

In 97: "worship him, all you his angels," *let all the gods worship him;* in the same Psalm: "since you, O Lord, highest above all the earth," *You were very much raised above all the gods.*

In the following two Psalms there are no unsuitable translations.

In 100: "Know that the Lord himself is God, he made us and not we ourselves," *Understand that the Lord himself is God, and he made us, and we are his.*

In 101: "The one disparaging his neighbor in secret, him I pursued," *The one secretly disparaging his neighbor: him will I destroy.*

In 102: "Because my days have faded like smoke," *Since my days* 28
have disappeared into smoke; in the same Psalm: "so that he could hear the groan of those in shackles, so that he could free the children of the slain," *So that he could hear the groans of those in shackles, so that he could free the children of death.*

There is no unsuitable translation in 103.

In 104: "The trees of the field will be full, and the cedars of Lebanon which he planted," *The timber of the Lord is full,* and the same for the rest; in the same Psalm: "There the sparrows will build their nests; the home of the stork is their leader," *Because there the birds will build their nests; the fir trees of the stork are its home.*

In 105: "So that he could teach his princes just like himself," *So that he could bind his princes according to his purpose;* in the same Psalm: "He spoke, and there came flies and insects in all their borders," *He spoke, and there came every kind of beast, lice into all their borders.*

In 106: "And disaster was increased among them," *And the pesti-* 29
lence crushed them; in the same Psalm: "And Phinehas stood and appeased them, and the shaking ceased," *However Phinehas stood and judged, and the pestilence was restrained.*

In 107, which is the first Psalm of the fifth book: "He sent his word and healed them, and he rescued them from their destructions," *And he rescued them from their grave,* and the same for the

sepulchro ipsorum; in reliquis prioribus similiter; in eodem: 'Et seminaverunt agros et plantaverunt vineas, et fecerunt fructum nativitatis,' *Et fecerunt fructum annone,* in reliquis eodem modo.

In CVIII: 'mihi alienigene amici facti sunt,' *Super Palestinam iubilabo.*

In CVIIII: 'in memoriam redeat iniquitas patrum eius,' *Memoretur iniquitas patrum eius.*

30 In CX: 'Tecum principium in die virtutis tue,' *Populus tuus liberaliter in die exercitus tui;* in eodem: 'in splendoribus sanctorum; ex utero ante luciferum genui te,' *in splendoribus sanctuarii; de vulva orietur tibi ros adolescentie tue;* in eodem: 'Iudicabit in nationibus, implebit ruinas, conquassabit capita in terra multorum,' *Iudicabit in gentibus referctis cadaveribus, percutiet capita in terra multa.*

In tribus subsequentibus Psalmis nihil aliene traductionis est.

In CXIIII: 'facta est Iudea sanctificatio eius, Israel potestas eius,' *Factus est Iudas in sanctificatione eius, Israel potestas eius;* in eodem: 'Montes exultaverunt ut arietes, et colles sicut agni ovium,' *Montes subsilierunt quasi arietes, colles quasi filii ovium;* in eodem: 'Montes, exultastis sicut arietes? et, colles, sicut agni ovium?' *Quid, montes, subsiluistis ceu arietes, colles, quasi filii ovium?*

In CXV: 'Non mortui laudabunt te, Domine, neque omnes qui descendunt in infernum,' *Nec mortui laudabunt Dominum, nec omnes descendentes in taciturnitatem.*

In tribus subsequentibus Psalmis nihil aliene traductionis ostenditur.

31 In CXVIIII: 'Superbi inique agebant usque quaque,' *Superbi deriserunt me usque multum;* in eodem: 'Super inimicos meos prudentem me fecisti,' *Supra inimicos meos instrues me;* in eodem: 'Super omnes docentes me intellexi,' *Supra omnes doctores meos eruditus fui;*

earlier portion; in the same Psalm: "And they sowed the fields and planted vines and they made a new crop," *And they made a crop of grain,* with no change for the earlier portion.

In 108: "Foreigners became my friends," *I will rejoice over Palestine.*

In 109: "May the wickedness of his ancestors return to memory," *May the wickedness of his ancestors be remembered.*

In 110: "The beginning with you on the day of your strength," 30
Your people generously on your army's day; in the same Psalm: "In the
beauties of holy places; from the womb before the morning star I
bore you," *in the beauties of the sanctuary; the dew of your youth will
arise for you from the womb;* in the same Psalm, "He will judge
among the nations, he will accomplish destructions, he will shake
the heads of many in the land," *he will judge among the nations when
the corpses are packed together, he will strike many heads in the land.*

There are no unsuitable translations in the following three Psalms.

In 114: "Judah was made his sanctuary, Israel his strength," *Judah was made in his sanctuary, Israel his strength;* in the same Psalm: "The mountains leaped like rams, the hills like the lambs of sheep," *The mountains leaped up like rams, the hills like the offspring of sheep;* in the same Psalm: "Mountains, did you leap like rams? And hills, like the lambs of sheep? *Why, mountains, did you leap up like rams, hills, like the offspring of sheep?*

In 115: "The dead will not praise you, O Lord, nor all those who descend into hell," *Neither will the dead praise the Lord, nor all those descending into silence.*

No unsuitable translation appears in the following three Psalms.

In 119: "The proud constantly behaved unjustly," *The proud de-* 31
rided me greatly; in the same Psalm: "You made me wise above my
enemies," *You will prepare me above my enemies;* in the same Psalm: "I
have understood beyond everyone teaching me," *I was more learned
than all my teachers;* in the same Psalm: "How sweet are your words

in eodem: 'Quam dulcia faucibus meis eloquia tua! Super mel ori meo,' *Quam dulcia sunt palato meo eloquia tua! Supra mel ori meo;* in eodem: 'Humiliatus sum usque quaque; Domine,' *Afflictus sum usque multum, Domine;* in eodem: 'Iniquos odio habui,' *Curas odivi;* in eodem: 'Adiutor et susceptor meus es tu, et in verbum tuum supersperavi,' *Protectio mea et scutum meum tu es, verbum tuum expectavi;* in eodem: 'Confige timore tuo carnes meas,' *Horripilavit a terrore tuo caro mea;* in eodem: 'Tempus faciendi, Domine; dissipaverunt legem tuam,' *Tempus est faciendi pro Domino; prevaricati sunt legem tuam;* in eodem: 'Ideo dilexi mandata tua super aurum et topatium,' *supra aurum et topatium,* reliqua priora similiter se habent; in eodem: 'Declaratio sermonum tuorum illuminat et intellectum dat parvulis,' *Ostium verborum tuorum dilucidat, et erudit ignavos;* in
32 eodem: 'Os meum aperui et attraxi ⟨spiritum⟩, quia mandata tua desiderabam,' *Os meum aperui et suxi* ⟨auram⟩, *quia mandata tua concupivi;* in eodem: 'Tabescere me fecit zelus meus, quia oblitus sum verba tua,' *Consumpsit me zelus meus, quia obliti sunt verborum tuorum hostes mei;* in eodem: 'Preveni in maturitate et clamavi ⟨quia⟩, in verba tua supersperavi,' *Surrexi in tenebris et clamavi verba tua expectans;* in eodem: 'Erravi sicut ovis que periit,' *Erravi quasi agnus perditus.*

33 In CXX: 'Sagitte potentis acute cum carbonibus desolatoriis,' *Sagitte potentis acute cum carbonibus iuniperorum.*

In CXXI: 'Per diem sol non uret, neque luna per noctem,' *Per diem sol non percutiet te, neque luna per noctem.*

In CXXII: 'Hierusalem, que edificatur ut civitas, cuius participatio eius in id ipsum,' *Hierusalem edificata ut civitas, que colligata est sibi simul;* in eodem: 'Rogate que ad pacem sunt Hierusalem et abundantia diligentibus te,' *Petite pacem Hierusalem, pacificentur*

to my throat! Beyond honey to my mouth," *How sweet are your words to my taste! Beyond honey to my mouth;* in the same Psalm: "I am constantly brought low, O Lord," *I am afflicted greatly, O Lord;* in the same Psalm: "I have hated the wicked," *I hated anxieties;* in the same Psalm: "You are my helper and my support, and I have trusted in your word," *You are my protection and my shield, I have waited for your word;* in the same Psalm: "Transfix my flesh with fear of you," *My skin bristles for fear of you;* in the same Psalm: "It is time for action, O Lord; they have destroyed your law," *It is the time for acting on behalf of the Lord; they have compromised your law;* in the same Psalm: "Therefore I loved your commandments above gold and topaz," *beyond gold and topaz,* with no changes for the earlier portion; in the same Psalm: "The pronouncement of your words gives light and gives understanding to the young," *The utterance of*
your words gives light and teaches the ignorant; in the same Psalm: "I 32
opened my mouth and drew my breath, because I desired your commandments," *I opened my mouth and sucked in the air, because I longed for your commandments;* in the same Psalm: "My zeal has made me weak, because I forgot your words," *My zeal has consumed me, because my enemies have forgotten your words;* in the same Psalm: "I arrived early and I cried out because I trusted in your words," *I arose in darkness and cried out while waiting for your words;* in the same Psalm: "I wandered like a sheep which is lost," *I wandered like a lost lamb.*

In 120: "Sharp arrows of the Almighty with abandoned coal," 33
Sharp arrows of the Almighty with the coal of junipers;

In 121: "The sun will not burn by day, nor the moon by night," *The sun will not strike you by day, nor the moon by night.*

In 122: "Jerusalem, which is built as a city, the sharing of which is for it itself," *Jerusalem built as a city which has been gathered together to itself;* in the same Psalm: "Ask for things which are for the peace of Jerusalem and abundance for those loving you," *Entreat for the peace of Jerusalem, may those who love you be appeased;* in the same

dilectores tui; in eodem: 'Fiat pax in virtute tua et abundantia in turribus tuis,' *Sit pax in muris tuis, pax in palatiis tuis.*

34 In CXXIII: 'quia multum repleta est anima nostra, obprobrium abundantibus et despectio superbis,' *Multum satiata est sibi anima nostra obprobrio requiescentium, despectione superborum.*

In CXXIIII: 'forsitan pertransisset anima nostra aquam intollerabilem,' *tunc transissent super animam nostram aque superbe.*

In CXXV nihil aliene interpretationis est.

In CXXVI: 'In convertendo Dominus captivitatem Syon, facti sumus sicut consolati,' *Cum converterit Dominus captivitatem Syon, facti sumus ceu somniantes;* in eodem: 'Converte, Domine, captivitatem nostram sicut torrens in austro,' *Converte, Domine, captivitatem nostram ceu rivos in austrum.*

In duobus subsequentibus Psalmis nihil aliene traductionis est.

35 In CXXVIIII: 'Supra dorsum meum fabricaverunt fabricatores, prolongaverunt iniquitatem suam,' *Super dorsum meum araverunt aratores, prolongaverunt sulcum suum.*

In CXXX: 'Quia apud te propitiatio est, et propter legem tuam sustinui te, Domine,' *Quoniam tecum est propitiatio, unde venerandus es;* in eodem: 'anima mea in Domino. A custodia matutina usque ad noctem,' *anima mea ad Dominum supra custodes ad dilucula, custodes ad dilucula.*

In CXXXI: 'neque ambulavi in magnis neque in mirabilibus super me,' *et non ambulavi in magnis et in mirabilibus supra me;* in eodem: 'Si non humiliter sentiebam, sed exaltavi animam meam,' *Si non proposui et silere feci animam meam;* in eodem: 'sicut ablactatus super matrem suam, ita retributio in anima,' *Quasi ablactatus super matrem suam. Quasi ablactatus super me anima mea.*

Psalm: "May there be peace in your courage and abundance in your towers," *May there be peace in your walls, peace in your palace.*

In 123: "Because our soul is very full, reproach for those who are 34
rich, contempt for the proud," *Our soul is very full with reproach for those resting and with contempt for the proud.*

In 124: "perhaps our soul would have passed over the unendurable water," *then proud waters would have crossed over our soul.*

There is no unsuitable translation in 125.

In 126: "The Lord in turning back the servitude of Zion, we became like people comforted," *When the Lord turned back the servitude of Zion, we became like people sleeping;* in the same Psalm: "Turn back, O Lord, our servitude like a torrent in the south," *Turn back, O Lord, our servitude like streams to the south.*

There are no unsuitable translations in the following two Psalms.

In 129: "Builders have built upon my back, they have extended 35
their injustice," *Plowmen have plowed on my back, they have lengthened their furrow.*

In 130: "Because forgiveness is with you, and on account of your law I upheld you, O Lord," *Since forgiveness is with you, whence you are venerable;* in the same Psalm: "my soul in the Lord. From the morning watch all the way until night," *my soul to the Lord more than guards to the dawn, guards to the dawn.*

In 131: "I have neither walked among great nor marvelous things that are above me," *and I have not walked among great and marvelous things that are above me;* in the same Psalm: "If I was not feeling humble, but I raised my soul," *If I did not resolve and make my soul silent;* in the same Psalm: "as if weaned upon his mother, thus repayment in his soul," *As if weaned upon his mother. As if weaned upon me in my soul.*

36 In CXXXII: 'Memento, Domine, David et omnis mansuetudinis eius,' *Memento, Domine, David et omnis afflictionis sue;* in eodem: 'Iuravit Dominus David veritatem et non frustrabitur eam,' *Iuravit Dominus David veritatem, non recedet ab ea;* in eodem: 'Viduam eius benedicens benedicam, pauperes eius saturabo panibus,' *Commeatus eius benedicens benedicam,* et in aliis similiter; in eodem: 'Illuc perducam cornu David,' *Ibi florere faciam cornu David;* in eodem: 'inimicos induam confusione; super ipsum autem efflorebit sanctificatio mea,' *Inimicos eius induam pudore, et super ipsum florebit corona eius.*

In duobus subsequentibus Psalmis nihil alienum reperitur.

37 In CXXXV: 'quoniam Iacob elegit sibi Dominus, Israel in possessione sibi,' *Quia Iacob elegit sibi Dominus, Israel in peculium suum;* in eodem: 'qui producit ventos de thesauris suis,' *extrahens ventum de muniminibus.*

In CXXXVI: 'Qui firmavit terram super aquas,' *Qui extendit terras super aquas;* in eodem: 'et solem in potestate diei,' *Et solem ut presit diei;* in eodem: 'et excussit Pharaonem in mari Rubro,' *Et convolvit Pharaonem et exercitum ipsius in mari Rubro.*

In CXXXVII: 'si non proposuero Hierusalem in principio letitie mee,' *Si non extulero Hierusalem super caput letitie mee.*

In CXXXVIII nihil alieni est.

38 In CXXXVIIII: 'novissima et antiqua tu formasti,' *retrorsum et ante formasti me;* in eodem: 'Mirabilis facta est scientia tua ex me; confortata est, et non potero ad eam,' *Abscondita est scientia a me, excelsa est: non potero ad eam;* in eodem: 'Confitebor tibi, quia terribiliter magnificatus es; mirabilia opera tua,' *Confitebor tibi, quoniam ob venerabilia admiratus fui de admirabilibus operibus tuis;* in eodem: 'Imperfectum meum viderunt oculi tui,' *Informem me viderunt oculi*

In 132: "Remember, O Lord, David and all his mercy," *Remember, O Lord, David and all his affliction;* in the same Psalm: "The Lord has sworn by the truth to David and he will not make it vain," *The Lord has sworn by the truth to David, and he will not retreat from it;* in the same Psalm: "Blessing his widow I will bless him, and I will fill his poor with bread," *Blessing his provisions I will bless him,* with no changes for the rest; in the same Psalm: "I will lead the horn of David there," *There I will make the horn of David flower;* in the same Psalm: "I will dress my enemies in confusion; however, my sanctuary will flourish over him," *I will dress his enemies in shame, and his crown will flourish upon him.* 36

In the following two Psalms no unsuitable translations are found.

In 135: "Since the Lord chose Jacob for himself, Israel for his possession," *Because the Lord chose Jacob for himself, Israel for his property;* in the same Psalm: "who brings forth winds from his storehouses," *drawing forth wind from his defenses.* 37

In 136: "Who strengthened the earth upon the waters," *Who stretches out the lands upon the waters;* in the same Psalm: "And the sun in the power of the day," *And the sun that it rule over the day;* in the same Psalm: "and he shook Pharaoh in the Red Sea," *And he rolled Pharaoh and his army in the Red Sea.*

In 137: "if I will not place Jerusalem at the forefront of my joy," *If I will not elevate Jerusalem above the height of my joy.*

There is no unsuitable translation in 138.

In 139: "you shaped the newest and the ancient," *behind and before you formed me;* in the same Psalm: "Your knowledge has become wonderful beyond me; it is strong; I will not be able to reach it," *Knowledge is hidden from me, it is high; I will not be able to reach it;* in the same Psalm: "I will confess to you, because you are terribly grand; your works are wonderful," *I will confess to you, since on account of venerable qualities I am astonished at your wonderful works;* in the same Psalm: "Your eyes have seen my imperfection," *Your eyes* 38

tui; in eodem: 'Mihi autem nimis honorificati sunt amici tui, Deus,' *Mihi autem quam pretiose facte sunt cogitationes tue, Deus;* in eodem: 'nimis confortatus est principatus eorum,' *quam adauctus est numerus eorum;* in eodem: 'quia dicitis in cogitatione: accipient in vanitate civitates suas,' *qui exaltant te cum impudentia, extulerunt falso adversarii tui;* in eodem: 'Perfecto odio oderam illos,' *Supremo odio oderam eos;* in eodem: 'Proba me, Deus, et scito cor meum; interroga me et cognosce semitas meas,' *Scrutare me, Deus, et cognosce cor meum. Discerne me, et scito cogitationes meas.*

39 In CXXXX: 'Vir linguosus non dirigetur in terra,' *Vir linguosus non confirmabitur in terra;* in eodem: 'virum iniustum mala capient in interitu,' *virum iniquum, malum illaqueabit eum ad impulsiones;* in eodem: 'Cognovi quia faciet Dominus iudicium inopis et vindictam pauperum,' *Novi quod faciet Dominus causam inopis, iudicia pauperum.*

In CXLI: 'Ne declines cor meum in verba malitie, ad excusandas excusationes in peccato,' *Ne declines cor meum in verbum malum, ad causandum causas in impietate;* in eodem: 'cum hominibus operantibus iniquitatem, et non communicabo cum electis eorum,' *cum hominibus operantibus iniquitatem non epulabor in delitiis eorum;* in eodem: 'oleum autem peccatoris non impinguet caput meum,' *oleum capitis non infringat caput meum;* in eodem: 'audient verba mea, quoniam poterunt,' *audiant verba mea, quoniam dulcescentia fuere;* in eodem: 'Sicut crassitudo terre erupta est super terram,' *Ceu incisor et divisor in terra;* in eodem: 'dissipata sunt ossa nostra secus infernum,' *dissipata sunt ossa nostra in ore inferni;* in eodem: 'Cadent in retiaculo eius peccatores: singulariter sum ego donec transeam,' *Incident in rete eius impii simul, ego semper transibo.*

have seen me ugly; in the same Psalm: "However, your friends are too respected by me, O God," *However, how valuable have your thoughts become to me, O God;* in the same Psalm: "Their supremacy is too strong," *how increased is their number;* in the same Psalm: "because you speak in thought: they will receive their cities in vain," *who exalt you with impudence, your adversaries have elevated you falsely;* in the same Psalm: "I hated them with a perfect hatred," *I hated them with an extreme hatred;* in the same Psalm: "Test me, O God, and know my heart; ask me and know my paths," *Examine me, O God, and know my heart. Set me apart and know my thoughts.*

In 140: "A man with an idle tongue will not be guided on the 39
earth," *A man with an idle tongue will not be established on the earth;* in the same Psalm: "Evils will seize the unjust man with destruction," *the unjust man, evil will ensnare him in impulses;* in the same Psalm: "I know that the Lord will support the justice of the weak and the defense of the poor," *I know that the Lord will support the cause of the weak, the justice of the poor.*

In 141: "May you not turn my heart to words of malice, to making excuses in sin," *May you not turn my heart to an evil word, to pleading causes in impiety;* in the same Psalm: "with men doing wickedness, and I will not partake in their choices," *with men doing wickedness I will not feast on their favorites;* in the same Psalm: "however, the oil of a sinner will not fatten my head," *may the oil of his head not bruise my head;* in the same Psalm: "they will hear my words, since they were able," *let them hear my words, since they were sweet;* in the same Psalm: "Just as the thickness of the earth broke out over the earth," *Like a cutter and cleaver on the earth;* in the same Psalm: "Our bones have been scattered beside the grave," *our bones have been scattered at the mouth of the grave;* in the same Psalm: "Sinners will fall in his net: I am separate until I cross over," *The impious will fall into his net at once, I will always cross over.*

40 In CXXXXII: 'In deficiendo ex me spiritum meum, et cognovisti semitas meas,' *Cum anxius in me fuerit spiritus meus, tu nosti callem meum;* in eodem: 'Considerabam ad dexteram et videbam, et non erat qui cognosceret me,' *Respice ad dexteram et vide, quia non est, qui cognoscat me;* in eodem: 'Libera me a persequentibus me, quia confortati sunt super me,' *Libera me a persecutoribus meis, quia corroborati sunt supra me;* in eodem: 'me expectant iusti donec retribuas mihi,' *Me coronabunt iusti, tu retribueris mihi.*

In CXLIII: 'et in misericordia tua disperdes inimicos meos, et perdes omnes qui tribulant animam meam,' *Et in misericordia tua dissipabis inimicos meos, et perdes omnes opprimentes animam meam.*

41 In CXLIV: 'filie eorum composite sunt, circunornate sicut similitudo templi,' *Filie nostre quasi anguli ornati ad similitudinem templi;* in eodem: 'promptuaria eorum plena, eructantia ex hoc in illud,' *Anguli pleni egrediuntur ex angulo in angulum;* in eodem: 'oves eorum fetose, abundantes in gressibus suis,' *Oves nostre, in milibus et decem milia in areis nostris.*

In CXLV: 'ut notam faciant filiis hominum potentiam tuam,' *Ut notificent filiis hominum potentias suas;* in eodem: 'et gloriam magnificentie regni tui,' *et gloriam decoris regni sui;* in eodem: 'aperis tu manum tuam, et imples omne animal benedictione,' *Aperias tu manus tuas et satures omne animal complacentia.*

In CXLVI nihil aliene interpretationis est.

In CXLVII: 'Non fecit taliter omni nationi et iudicia sua non manifestavit eis,' *Non fecit sic omni genti, et iudicia sua non cognoscent.*

In tribus reliquis nihil aliene traductionis reperitur.

In 142: "In causing my spirit you fail me, you also knew my 40
paths," *When my spirit was anxious in me, you knew my footpath;* in the same Psalm: "I looked to the right and I saw, and there was no one who knew me," *Look to the right and see, because there is no one who knows me;* in the same Psalm: "Deliver me from those pursuing me, because they have grown in strength above me," *Deliver me from my persecutors, because they have grown strong beyond me;* in the same Psalm: "The just are waiting for me, until you repay me," *The just will surround me, you will repay me.*

In 143: "In your compassion you will ruin my enemies, and you will destroy all those who trouble my soul," *And in your compassion you will scatter my enemies, and you will destroy all those oppressing my soul.*

In 144: "their daughters have been brought together, decorated 41
like a temple," *Our daughters like cornerstones decorated in the likeness of a temple;* in the same Psalm: "their storerooms full, spilling out from here to there," *the corners are full, spreading out from corner to corner;* in the same Psalm: "their sheep prolific, overflowing on their paths," *our sheep, in the thousands and tens of thousands in our fields.*

In 145: "so that they may make your power known to the children of men," *So that they may make their powers known to the children of men;* in the same Psalm: "and the glory of the magnificence of your kingdom," *and the glory of the splendor of his kingdom;* in the same Psalm: "You open your hand, and you fill every animal with your blessing," *May you open your hands, and glut every animal with gratification.*

There is no unsuitable translation in 146.

In 147: "He did not do this for every nation and he did not reveal his judgments to them," *He did not act in this way for every nation, and they will not learn their judgments.*

In the remaining three Psalms no unsuitable translation is found.

⟨*II. De diversis Psalmorum titulis*⟩

42 Cum igitur de alienis interpretationibus in hoc quarto libro superius ad sufficientiam dixisse videamur, reliquum est ut secundum propositum ordinem de diversis cunctorum Psalmorum titulis in calce eius parumper prosequamur.

Primus itaque Psalmus cum loco prefationis totius voluminis habeatur, non iniuria omni titulo caruisse traditur.

Secundus pro titulo habet 'Psalmus David,' qui apud Hebreos non reperitur.

In III nulla inter titulos differentia est.

In IIII: 'In finem, in carminibus. Psalmus David,' *Victori. In organis. Psalmus David.*

In V: 'In finem, pro ea que consequitur hereditate,' *Victori. In sonitibus. Neailoth. Psalmus David.*

In VI: 'In finem, Psalmus David, pro octava,' *Victori. In organis, super instrumentum octave. Psalmus David.*

43 In VII: 'In finem. Psalmus David, quem cantavit pro verbis Chusi filii gemini,' *Sonitus Scigaion David, quem cantavit Domino ob causas Chusi Beniamin.*

In VIII: 'In finem. Psalmus David, pro torcularibus,' *Victori. Super sonitum Aghithit. Psalmus David.*

In VIIII: 'In finem, pro occultis filii. Psalmus David,' *Victori, super mortem Laben. Psalmus David.*

In X licet apud Septuaginta non sit Psalmus separatus, est tamen apud Hebreos seorsum distinctus, et titulo caret.

In XI: 'In finem. Psalmus David,' *Victori. David.*

44 In XII: 'In finem. Psalmus David. Pro octava,' *Victori, super instrumentum octave. Psalmus David.*

In XIII: 'In finem. Psalmus David,' *Victori. Psalmus David.*

In XIIII: 'In finem. Psalmus David,' *Victori. David.*

II. About variant titles of the Psalms

Although we appear to have said enough above about unsuitable translations in this fourth book, according to our proposed plan, it remains at the tail end for us briefly to describe the different titles of all the psalms.[2] 42

Although the first Psalm assumes the position of preface for the whole volume, it is traditionally said that it properly lacked any title.

The second has for its title "Psalm of David" which is not found in the Hebrew.

In the third Psalm there is no difference between the titles.

In 4: "To the end, in songs. A Psalm of David," *For the victor. On instruments. A Psalm of David.*

In 5: "To the end, for that inheritance which follows," *For the victor. With sounds. Neailoth. A Psalm of David.*

In 6: "To the end, a Psalm of David, for the eighth," *For the victor. On instruments, upon the instrument of the eighth. A Psalm of David.*

In 7: "To the end. A Psalm of David, which he sang on behalf 43
of the words of Cush, the twin son," *The sound of the Shiggaion of David, which he sang to the Lord by reason of Cush, the Benjamite.*

In 8: "To the end. A Psalm of David, for the winepress," *For the victor. On the sound of the Gittith. A Psalm of David.*

In 9: "To the end, for the secrets of the son. A Psalm of David," *For the victor, on the death of Laben. A Psalm of David.*

Although in 10 the Psalm is not separated in the Septuagint, nevertheless it is divided in two in the Hebrew and lacks a title.

In 11: "To the end. A Psalm of David," *For the victor. Of David.*

In 12: "To the end. A Psalm of David. On the eighth," *For the* 44
Victor, on the instrument of the eighth. A Psalm of David.

In 13: "To the end. A Psalm of David," *For the victor. A Psalm of David.*

In 14: "To the end. A Psalm of David," *For the victor. Of David.*

In XV nulla est differentia, cum utrobique inscribatur 'Psalmus David.'

In XVI: 'Tituli inscriptio ipsi David,' *Sonitus. Mictam. David.*

In XVII nullam in titulis differentiam continet, cum utrinque 'Oratio David' habeatur.

45 In XVIII: 'In finem. Puero Domini David, qui locutus est Domino verba cantici, in die qua eripuit eum Dominus de manu inimicorum eius et de manu Saul, et dixit,' *Victori, servo Domini, David, quando locutus est Domino verba cantici huius, in die qua liberavit eum Dominus ab omnibus inimicis eius et de manibus Saul.*

In XVIIII: 'In finem. Psalmus David,' *Victori. Psalmus David.*

In XX: 'In finem. Psalmus David,' *Victori. Psalmus David.*

In XXI: 'In finem. Psalmus David,' *Victori. Psalmus David.*

In XXII: 'In finem. Psalmus David. Pro assumptione vel susceptione vel pro cerva matutina,' *Victori, super potentiam matutinam. Psalmus David.*

In XXIII nequaquam in titulo differt, cum utrobique scriptum sit 'Psalmus David.'

46 In XXIV: 'Psalmus David, in prima Sabati,' *David. Psalmus.*

In XXV: 'In finem. Psalmus David,' *David.*

In XXVI: 'Psalmus David,' *David.*

In XXVII: 'In finem. Psalmus David, priusquam liniretur,' *David.*

In XXVIII: 'Psalmus David,' *David.*

In XXVIIII: 'Psalmus David in consecratione tabernaculi,' *Psalmus. David.*

In 15 there is no difference, since they are both entitled "A Psalm of David."

In 16: "An inscription of the title for David himself," *Sound. A mictam. Of David.*

In 17 there is no difference between the titles, since both have "A prayer of David."

In 18: "To the end. For the son of the Lord, David, who spoke 45
the words of the song to the Lord, on the day on which the Lord seized him from the hand of his enemies and from the hand of Saul, and he said," *For the Victor, the servant of the Lord, David, when he spoke the words of this song to the Lord, on the day on which the Lord delivered him from all his enemies and from the hands of Saul.*

In 19: "To the end. A Psalm of David," *For the victor. A Psalm of David.*

In 20: "To the end. A Psalm of David," *For the victor. A Psalm of David.*

In 21: "To the end. A Psalm of David," *For the victor. A Psalm of David.*

In 22: "To the end. A Psalm of David. For the acceptance or undertaking or for the morning deer," *For the Victor, on the morning power. A Psalm of David.*

In 23 there is absolutely no difference in the title, since both have the title "A Psalm of David."

In 24: "A Psalm of David, in the first hour of the Sabbath," *Of* 46
David. A Psalm.

In 25: "To the end. A Psalm of David," *Of David.*

In 26: "A Psalm of David," *Of David.*

In 27: "To the end. A Psalm of David, before he was anointed," *Of David.*

In 28: "A Psalm of David," *Of David.*

In 29: "A Psalm of David in the consecration of the tabernacle," *A Psalm. Of David.*

In XXX: 'Psalmus David in dedicatione domus David,' *Psalmus cantici in dedicatione domus. David.*

47 In XXXI: 'In finem. Psalmus David, pro exstasi,' *Victori. Psalmus. David.*

In XXXII: 'Intellectus David,' *David. Sonitus. Maschil.*

In XXXIII: 'In finem. Psalmus David.' Verum apud Hebreos titulo caret.

In XXXIIII: 'Psalmus David, cum mutaret vultum suum coram Abimelech,' *David, dum mutaret sensum suum coram Abimelech, et expulit eum, et abiit.*

In XXXV: 'In finem. Psalmus ipsi David,' *David.*

In XXXVI: 'In finem. Servo Domini Psalmus David,' *Victori. Ad servum Domini David.*

In XXXVII: 'Psalmus,' *David.*

48 In XXXVIII: 'Psalmus David, in rememoratione Sabati,' Psalmus *David. Ad commemorandum.*

In XXXVIIII: 'In finem, cantici David pro Idudum,' *Victori. Iedudum. Psalmus. David.*

In XL: 'In finem. Psalmus David,' *Victori. David. Psalmus.*

In XLI: 'In finem. Psalmus David,' *Victori. Psalmus. David.*

In XLII, qui est primus secundi libri, sic inscribitur: 'In finem. Intellectus filiis Chore,' *Victori. Sonitus. Maschil. Filiorum Chore.*

In XLIII: 'In finem. Psalmus David,' sed hebraice titulo caret.

In XLIIII: 'In finem. Filiis Chore ad intellectum,' *Victori. Filiorum Chore. Sonitus. Maschil.*

In 30: "A Psalm of David in the dedication of the house of David," *A Psalm of the song in the dedication of the house. Of David.*

In 31: "To the end. A Psalm of David, for religious frenzy," *For* 47
the victor. A Psalm. Of David.

In 32: "The understanding of David," *Of David. A sound. A maskil.*

In 33: "To the end. A Psalm of David." But a title is absent in the Hebrew.

In 34: "A Psalm of David, when he changed his expression before Abimelech," *Of David, when he changed his opinion before Abimelech, and drove him away, and he departed.*

In 35: "To the end. A Psalm for David himself," *Of David.*

In 36: "To the end. A Psalm for the servant of the Lord, David," *For the victor. To the servant of the Lord, David.*

In 37: "A Psalm," *Of David.*

In 38: "A Psalm of David, in remembrance of the Sabbath," *A* 48
Psalm. Of David. For remembering.

In 39: "To the end, of a song of David for Jeduthun," *For the victor. For Jeduthun. A Psalm. Of David.*

In 40: "To the end. A Psalm of David," *For the victor. Of David. A Psalm.*

In 41: "To the end. A Psalm of David," *For the victor. A Psalm. Of David.*

In 42, which is the first Psalm of the second book, it is entitled thus: "To the end. Understanding for the children of Korah," *For the victor. Sound. A maskil. Of the children of Korah.*

In 43: "To the end. A Psalm of David," but a title is absent in the Hebrew.

In 44: "To the end. For the children of Korah for understanding," *For the victor. Of the children of Korah. Sound. A maskil.*

49 In XLV: 'In finem, pro iis qui commutabuntur. Filiis Chore ad intellectum. Canticum pro dilecto,' *Victori 'Super Rosis' Filiorum Chore. Sonitus. Maschil. Cantici amorum.*

In XLVI: 'In finem. Psalmus David. Pro arcanis,' *Victori. Filiorum Chore. 'Super Sonitum' Alamoth. Cantici.*

In XLVII: 'In finem. Psalmus David. Filiis Chore,' *Victori. Filiorum Chore. Psalmus.*

In XLVIII: 'Psalmus David vel laus cantici filiorum Chore, secunda sabati,' *Canticum. Psalmi. Filiorum Chore.*

In XLVIIII: 'In finem, filiis Chore. Psalmus David,' *Victori. Filiorum Chore. Psalmus.*

In L nullam in titulis differentiam continet, cum utrinque 'Psalmus Asaph' reperiatur.

50 In LI: 'Cum venit ad eum Nathan propheta, quando intravit ad Bersabe,' *Victori. Psalmus. David, dum accessit ad eum Nathan propheta, quando venit ad Bersabe.*

In LII: 'In finem. Intellectus David, cum venit Doech idumeus et nuntiasset Saul: Venit David in domum Abimelech,' *Victori. Sonitus. Maschil, dum veniret Doeg idumeus ac nuntiaret Saul et diceret ei: Accessit David ad domum Abimelech.*

In LIII: 'In finem. Intellectus David. Pro Amalech,' *Victori. 'Super Instrumentum' Malath. Sonitus. Maschil. David.*

51 In LIIII: 'In finem, in carminibus. In titulis David, cum venissent Ziphei ad Saul et nuntiassent Saul: Nonne David absconditus est apud nos?' *Victori, in organis. Sonitus. Maschil, dum venirent Aziphei et dicerent Sauli: Iam David absconditur inter nos.*

In LV: 'In finem, in carminibus. Intellectus David,' *Victori, in organis. Sonitus. Maschil. David.*

In 45: "To the end. For those who will be changed. For the 49
children of Korah for understanding. A song for the beloved," *For
the victor "On Roses" of the children of Korah. Sound. A maskil. Of the
song of loves.*

In 46: "To the end. A Psalm of David. For the secrets," *For the victor. Of the children of Korah. "On sound" of Alamoth. Of the song.*

In 47: "To the end. A Psalm of David. For the children of Korah," *For the victor. Of the children of Korah. A Psalm.*

In 48: "A Psalm of David or praise of the song of the children of Korah, at the second hour of the Sabbath," *A song. Of the Psalm. Of the children of Korah.*

In 49: "To the end, for the children of Korah. A Psalm of David," *For the victor. Of the children of Korah. A Psalm.*

In 50 there is no difference between the titles, since the title "Psalm of Asaph" is found in both.

In 51: "When Nathan the prophet came to him, when he en- 50
tered in to Bathsheba," *For the victor. A Psalm. Of David, when the
prophet Nathan approached him, when he went to Bathsheba.*

In 52: "To the end. An understanding of David, when Doeg the Edomite came and announced to Saul: David has come into the house of Ahimelech," *For the victor. A Sound. A maskil, when Doeg the Edomite came and announced to Saul and said to him: David has approached the house of Ahimelech.*

In 53: "To the end. An understanding of David. For Amalech," *For the victor. "On the instrument" Malath. Sound. A maskil. Of David.*

In 54: "To the end, with poems. Among the titles of David, 51
when the Ziphites came to Saul and announced to Saul: "Has
David not hidden himself with us?" *For the victor, with instruments.
Sound. A maskil, when the Aziphites came and said to Saul: Now David
is hiding among us.*

In 55: "To the end, with poems. An understanding of David," *For the victor, with instruments. Sound. A maskil. Of David.*

In LVI: 'In finem, pro populo qui a sanctis longe factus est. In tituli inscriptione ipsi David, cum tenerent eum allophili in Geth,' *Victori. Super 'Columbam Mutam' procul a David. Sonitus. Micthan, dum caperent eum Philistei in Gath.*

52 In LVII: 'In finem, ne disperdas. David in tituli inscriptione cum fugeret a facie Saul in spelunca,' *Victori. 'Ne disperdas.' David. Sonitus. Michtam, dum ipse fugeret a facie Saul in speluncam.*

In LVIII: 'In finem, ne disperdas. David in tituli inscriptione,' *Victori. 'Ne disperdas.' David. Sonitus. Micthan.*

In LVIIII: 'In finem, ne disperdas. David in tituli inscriptione quando misit Saul, ut custodirent domum eius, ut interficerent eum,' *Victori. 'Ne disperdat.' David. Sonitus. Micthan, dum mitteret Saul ad observandum eum, ut occiderent eum.*

53 In LX: 'In finem. Pro iis qui commutabuntur, in tituli inscriptione ipsi David, in doctrinam, cum succendit Mesopotamiam Syrie Sobath, et convenit Ioab et percussit Edon in valle salinarum duodecim milia,' *Victori. Super 'Rosam testificationis.' Sonitus. Micthan. David. Ad docendum, dum demoliretur Aram Narain. Et Aram Zeva, et redivit Ioab et percussit Edon in valle salis duodecim milia.*

In LXI: 'In finem, in hynnis. Psalmus David,' *Victori. Super 'Organis.' David.*

In LXII: 'In finem, pro Iditum. Psalmus David,' *Victori. Super Iedudum. Psalmus. David.*

54 In LXIII: 'Psalmus David, cum esset in deserto Idumee,' *Psalmus. David, cum esset in deserto Iuda.*

In LXIIII: 'In finem. Psalmus David,' *Victori. Psalmus. David.*

In LXV: 'In finem. Psalmus David, canticum Aggei, Hieremie vel Ezechielis de verbo peregrinationis, ut inciperent proficisci,' *Victori. Psalmus. David. Cantici.*

In 56: "To the end, for the people who became far from sanctuary. On the inscription of the title for David himself, when the Allophils held him in Geth," *For the victor, upon "The Silent Dove" far from David. Sound. A mictham, while the Philistines held him in Gath.*

In 57: "To the end, do not destroy. Of David in the inscription 52
of the title when he fled from the face of Saul in a cave," *For the victor. "Do not destroy." Of David. Sound. A michtham, when he fled from the face of Saul into a cave.*

In 58: "To the end, do not destroy. Of David in the inscription of the title," *For the victor. "Do not destroy." Of David. Sound. A mictham.*

In 59: "To the end, do not destroy. Of David in the inscription of the title when Saul sent so that they could watch his house to kill him," *For the victor. "Do not destroy." Of David. Sound. A mictham, when Saul sent to watch him so that they might kill him.*

In 60: "To the end. For those who will be changed, in the in- 53
scription of the title for David himself, for instruction, when Sobath of Syria set fire to Mesopotamia, and Joab came and struck Edom, twelve thousand strong, in the Valley Of Salt," *For the victor, On "The Rose of testimony." Sound. A mictham. Of David. For teaching, when he demolished Aram Narain. And Aram Zeva, and Joab returned and struck Edom, twelve thousand strong, in the Valley of Salt.*

In 61: "To the end, with hymns. A Psalm of David," *For the victor. On "instruments." Of David.*

In 62: "To the end, for Jeduthun. A Psalm of David," *For the victor. Upon Jeduthun. A Psalm. Of David.*

In 63: "A Psalm of David, when he was in the wilderness of 54
Idumea," *A Psalm. Of David, when he was in the wilderness of Judah.*

In 64: "To the end. A Psalm of David," *For the victor. A Psalm. Of David.*

In 65: "To the end. A Psalm of David, a song of Haggai, Jeremiah or Ezekiel about the word of traveling, so that they could begin to set out," *For the victor. A Psalm. Of David. Of a song.*

In LXVI: 'In finem. Canticum Psalmi resurrectionis,' *Victori. Canticum Psalmi.*

In LXVII: 'In finem, in hymnis. Psalmus cantici David,' *Victori. Pro organis. Psalmus. Cantici.*

In LXVIII: 'In finem. Psalmus cantici. David,' *Victori. David. Psalmus. Cantici.*

55 In LXVIIII: 'In finem, pro iis qui commutabuntur. Ipsi David,' *Victori. Super 'Rosis.' David.*

In LXX: 'In finem. Psalmus David in rememoratione quod salvum fecit eum Dominus,' *Victori. David ad commemorandum.*

In LXXI 'Psalmus David, filiorum Ionadab et priorum captivorum,' apud Hebreos titulo caret.

In LXXII: 'In Salomonem,' *Salomonis.*

In LXXIII, qui est principium tertii libri, sic pro titulo habet: 'Defecerunt laudes vel hynni David, filii Iesse,' *Explicunt orationes David, filii Iesse. Psalmus. Asaph.*

In LXXIIII: 'Intellectus Asaph,' *Sonitus. Maschil. Asaph.*

56 In LXXV: 'In finem, ne disperdas. Psalmus cantici Asaph,' *Victori. 'Ne disperdas.' Psalmus. Asaph. Cantici.*

In LXXVI: 'In finem, in carminibus. Canticum Assyriorum. Psalmus David,' *Victori. In organis. Psalmus. Asaph. Cantici.*

In LXXVII: 'In finem, pro Idudum. Psalmus David,' *Victori. Super Iedudum. Asaph. Psalmus.*

In LXXVIII: 'Intellectus Asaph,' *Sonitus. Maschil. Asaph.*

In LXXVIIII nullam in titulis differentiam habet, cum utrobique 'Psalmus Asaph' inveniatur.

In LXXX: 'In finem, pro iis qui commutabuntur. Psalmus. Pro Assyriis testimonium Asaph,' *Victori. Pro 'Rosis testificationis.' Asaph. Psalmus.*

In 66: "To the end. A Song of the Psalm of resurrection," *For the victor. A song of the Psalm.*

In 67: "To the end, with hymns. A Psalm of the song of David," *For the victor. On instruments. A Psalm. Of the song.*

In 68: "To the end. A Psalm of the song. Of David," *For the victor. Of David. A Psalm. Of the song.*

In 69: "To the end, for those who will be changed. For David 55
himself," *For the victor. On "Roses." Of David.*

In 70: "To the end. A Psalm of David in remembrance that the Lord made him safe," *For the victor. Of David for remembrance.*

In 71: "A Psalm of David, of the sons of Jonadab and the first captives," there is no title in the Hebrew.

In 72: "To Solomon," *Of Solomon.*

In 73, which is the first Psalm of the third book, the title is this: "Praises or the hymns of David, son of Jesse, have ceased," *The prayers of David, the son of Jesse, are completed. A Psalm. Of Asaph.*

In 74: "The understanding of Asaph," *Sound. A maskil. Of Asaph.*

In 75: "To the end. Do not destroy. A Psalm of the song of 56
Asaph," *For the victor, "Do not destroy." A Psalm. Of Asaph. Of a song.*

In 76: "To the end, with poems. A Song of the Assyrians. A Psalm of David," *For the victor. On instruments. A Psalm. Of Asaph. Of a song.*

In 77: "To the end, for Jeduthun. A Psalm of David," *For the victor. On Jeduthun. Of Asaph. A Psalm.*

In 78: "The understanding of Asaph," *Sound. A maskil. Of Asaph.*

In 79 there is no difference between the titles, since in both "A Psalm of Asaph" is found.

In 80: "To the end, for those who will be changed. A Psalm. For the Assyrians the testimony of Asaph," *For the victor. For "the roses of testimony." Of Asaph. A Psalm.*

57 In LXXXI: 'In finem. Pro torcularibus. Psalmus ipsi Asaph. Quinta sabati,' *Victori. Sonitus Agithith. Asaph.*

In LXXXII nullam titulorum discrepantiam amplectitur, cum utrobique 'Psalmus Asaph' reperiatur.

In LXXXIII: eodem modo se habet, cum utrobique 'Canticum Psalmi Asaph' inscribatur.

In LXXXIIII: 'In finem. Pro torcularibus filiis Chore. Psalmus,' *Victori. Super 'Sonitum Agithith.' Filiorum Chore. Psalmus.*

58 In LXXXV: 'In finem, filiis Chore,' *Victori. Filiorum Chore. Psalmus.*

In LXXXVI nullam in titulis differentiam habet, cum utrobique 'Oratio David' scriptum ostendatur.

In LXXXVII: 'Filiis Chore. Psalmus cantici,' idem hebraice legitur.

In LXXXVIII: 'Canticum Psalmi, filiis Chore, in finem, pro Melech, ad respondendum intellectus Eman Esraelite,' *Canticum Psalmi Victori. Filiorum Chore. Victori. Super 'Instrumentum Malaath,' ad affligendum. Sonitus. Maschil. Eman Aesrai.*

In LXXXIX: 'Intellectus Ethan esraelite,' *Sonitus. Maschil. Eedan Aesrai.*

59 In LXXXX, qui est primus quarti libri: 'Oratio Moysi, hominis Dei,' *Oratio Moysi, viri Dei.*

In LXXXXI: 'Laus cantici ipsi David,' hebraice titulo caret.

In XCII nullam in titulis differentiam habet, cum utrobique 'Psalmus cantici, in die sabati' scriptum reperiatur.

In XCIII: 'Laus cantici David, in die ante sabatum, quando fundata est terra,' apud Hebreos autem titulo caret.

In 81: "To the end. For winepresses. A Psalm for Asaph himself. At the fifth hour of the Sabbath," *For the victor. Sound of Gittith. Of Asaph.* 57

In 82 there is no difference between the titles, since in both "A Psalm of Asaph" is found.

In 83 the same holds true, since in both "A song of the Psalm of Asaph" is written.

In 84: "To the end. For winepresses for the children of Korah. A Psalm," *For the victor. On the "Sound of Gittith." Of the children of Korah. A Psalm.*

In 85: "To the end, for the children of Korah," *For the victor. Of the children of Korah. A Psalm.* 58

In 86 there is no difference between the titles, since in both "The prayer of David" appears written.

In 87: "For the children of Korah. A Psalm of the song," the same is read in Hebrew.

In 88: "A song of the Psalm, for the children of Korah, to the end, for Melech, an understanding of Heman the Israelite for responding," *A song of the Psalm for the victor. Of the children of Korah. For the victor. On "The instrument of Mahalath," for overthrowing. Sound. A maskil. Of Heman the Ezrahite.*

In 89: "An understanding of Ethan the Israelite," *Sound. A maskil. Of Ethan the Ezrahite.*

In 90, which is the first Psalm of the fourth book: "A prayer of Moses, a person of God," *A prayer of Moses, a man of God.* 59

In 91: "Praise of the song for David himself," it lacks a title in the Hebrew.

In 92 there is no difference between the titles, since "A Psalm of the song on the day of the Sabbath" is found written in both.

In 93: "Praise of the song of David, on the day before the Sabbath, when the earth was created," but it lacks a title in the Hebrew.

In XCIIII: 'Psalmus David, quarta sabati,' attamen hebraice nullum titulum habet.

In XCV: 'Laus cantici ipsi David,' apud Hebreos vacat titulus.

In XCVI: 'Psalmus David, quando domus edificabatur post captivitatem,' apud Hebreos titulo caret.

60 In XCVII: 'Psalmus David, quando terra restituta est ei,' hebraice vacat titulus.

In XCVIII: 'Psalmus David,' *Psalmus.*

In XCIX: 'Psalmus David,' apud Hebreos deficit titulus.

In C nullam in titulis differentiam habet, cum utrobique 'Psalmus in confessione' pro titulo reperiatur.

In CI: 'Psalmus ipsi David,' *David. Psalmus.*

In CII: 'Oratio pauperis, cum anxiaretur et coram Domino fudit precem suam,' *Oratio pauperis, quando afflictus fuerit, et coram Domino effuderit eloquium suum.*

In CIII: 'Psalmus ipsi David,' *David.*

In CIIII: 'Psalmus David,' apud Hebreos autem titulo caret.

61 In CV: 'Alleluia. Alleluia,' apud Hebreos deficit titulus, cum in fine precedentis Psalmi scriptum reperiatur.

In CVI nullam in titulis differentiam habet, cum utrobique 'Alleluia. Alleluia' pro titulo habeatur.

In CVII, et est primus quinti libri, pro titulo habet: 'Alleluia. Alleluia,' quo Hebrei carere reperiuntur, sed in fine precedentis Psalmi semel 'Alleluia' reperitur.

In CVIII: 'Canticum Psalmi ipsi David,' *Canticum Psalmi. David.*

In CVIIII: 'In finem. Psalmus David,' *Victori. David. Psalmus.*

In CX: 'Psalmus David,' *David. Psalmus.*

In CXI: 'Alleluia,' *Laudate Dominum.*

In 94: "A Psalm of David, at the fourth hour of the Sabbath," but nevertheless it has no title in the Hebrew.

In 95: "Praise of the song for David himself," there is no title in the Hebrew.

In 96: "A Psalm of David, when his home was built after the captivity," a title is lacking in the Hebrew.

In 97: "A Psalm of David, when the land was given back to 60
him," a title is lacking in the Hebrew.

In 98: "A Psalm of David," *Psalm.*

In 99: "A Psalm of David," a title is lacking in the Hebrew.

In 100 there is no difference between the titles, since "A Psalm in confession" is found in both as the title.

In 101: "A Psalm for David himself," *Of David. A Psalm.*

In 102: "The prayer of a poor man, when he was nervous and poured out his prayer before the Lord," *The prayer of a poor man, when he was afflicted and poured out his utterance before the Lord.*

In 103: "A Psalm for David himself," *Of David.*

In 104: "A Psalm of David," however a title is lacking in the Hebrew.

In 105: "Halleluiah. Halleluiah," a title is lacking in the Hebrew, 61
since it is included at the end of the preceding Psalm.

In 106 there is no difference between the titles, since "Halleluiah. Halleluiah" is the title for both.

In 107, which is the first Psalm of the fifth book, the title is "Halleluiah. Halleluiah," which is found to be lacking in the Hebrew, but one "Halleluiah" is found at the end of the preceding Psalm.

In 108: "A song of the Psalm for David himself," *A song of the Psalm. Of David.*

In 109: "To the end. A Psalm of David," *For the victor. Of David. A Psalm.*

In 110: "A Psalm of David," *Of David. A Psalm.*

In 111: "Halleluiah," *Praise the Lord.*

62 In CXII: 'Alleluia. Reversionis Aggei et Zacharie,' *Laudate Dominum.*

In CXIII: 'Alleluia,' *Laudate Dominum.*

In CXIIII: 'Alleluia,' in hebreo deficit titulus, qui est in fine precedentis Psalmi.

In CXV cum apud Septuaginta non sit Psalmus a proximo separatus, sed cum eo coniunctus, titulum habere non potest. Quo etiam apud Hebreos caret.

In CXVI: 'Alleluia,' hebraice vero titulo caret, et continuus est usque ad alium qui incipit 'Laudate Dominum' licet apud Grecos et Latinos in hoc verbo, credidi, ab invicem separetur.

63 Duo alii subsequentes 'Alleluia' pro titulis habent, qui apud Hebreos deficiunt, et in fine precedentium Psalmorum reperiuntur.

In CXIX habet pro titulo apud Septuaginta 'Alleluia.' Quo Hebrei carent: apud eos enim est unus atque continuus usque ad alium Psalmum, qui incipit 'Ad Dominum, in tribulatione mea, invocavi.' Si vero apud Grecos vel Latinos per XXII Psalmos, secundum hebreos caracteres (hoc enim ordine apud eos scribitur), in quibusdam mendosis codicibus variis titulis forte distinctus inveniretur, menda esset.

Duo subsequentes Psalmi nullam in titulis differentiam habent, cum utrobique 'Canticum graduum' scriptum reperiatur.

64 In CXXII: 'Canticum graduum,' *Canticum graduum. David.*

In CXXIII nulla in titulis differentia est, cum utrobique 'Canticum graduum' legatur.

In CXXIIII: 'Canticum graduum,' *Canticum graduum. David.*

In duobus subsequentibus nulla in titulis differentia invenitur.

In CXXVII nullam in titulis discrepantiam continet. Utrobique enim 'Canticum graduum Salomonis' pro titulo habetur.

In 112: "Halleluiah. Of the return of Haggai and Zechariah," *Praise the Lord.* 62

In 113: "Halleluiah," *Praise the Lord.*

In 114: "Halleluiah," a title is lacking in the Hebrew and is found at the end of the preceding Psalm.

In 115, since in the Septuagint the Psalm is not divided from the previous Psalm but is joined with it, it cannot have a title. The title is also lacking in the Hebrew.

In 116: "Halleluiah," but the title is lacking in the Hebrew and continues to the next which begins "Praise the Lord," although in the Greek and Latin it is separated from the next by these words, "I believed."

The two other following Psalms have "Halleluiah" as a title, 63
which is absent in the Hebrew, and is found at the end of the preceding Psalms.

In 119 the Septuagint has as a title "Halleluiah." This is missing in the Hebrew; for in the Hebrew it is one and continuous Psalm all the way to the other Psalm which begins "I called upon the Lord in my tribulation." But if through the twenty-two Psalms according to the Hebrew letters (for they are written in this order in the Greek and Latin) this Psalm were found separated in some defective manuscripts with different titles, it would be a mistake.

The following two Psalms have no difference in title, since in both "Song of steps" is found written.

In 122: "Song of the steps," *Song of steps. Of David.* 64

In 123 there is no difference between the titles, since in both "Song of steps" is read.

In 124: "Song of steps," *Song of steps. Of David.*

In the following two Psalms no difference between the titles is found.

In 127 there is no discrepancy between the titles. For in both "Song of the steps of Solomon" is the title.

Tres subsequentes eos retinent titulos, cum penes unumquemque 'Canticum graduum' conscribatur.

In CXXXI: 'Canticum graduum,' *Canticum graduum. David.*

65 In CXXXII nullam in titulis differentiam habet, cum utrobique 'Canticum graduum' legamus.

In CXXXIII: 'Canticum graduum,' *Canticum graduum. David.*

In subsequenti Psalmo nulla in titulis diversitas extat, cum utrobique 'Canticum graduum' scriptum videamus.

In CXXXV: 'Alleluia,' *Laudate Dominum.*

In CXXXVI: 'Alleluia,' quod in fine precedentis Psalmi apud Hebreos duntaxat reperitur, et alio titulo caret.

66 In CXXXVII: 'Psalmus David, propter Hieremiam,' hebraice vero titulo caret.

In CXXXVIII: 'Psalmus ipsi David,' *David.*

In CXXXIX: 'Psalmus David,' *Victori. David. Psalmus.*

In CXXXX: 'Psalmus David,' *Victori. Psalmus. David.*

In CXXXXI nulla in titulis differentia apparet, cum utrobique 'Psalmus David' reperiatur.

67 In CXLII: 'Intellectus David, cum esset in spelunca, oratio,' *Sonitus. Maschil. David, cum esset in spelunca. Oratio.*

In CXLIII: 'Psalmus David, quando persequebatur eum filius suus Absalon,' *Psalmus. David.*

In CXLIIII: 'Psalmus David adversus Goliam,' *David.*

In CXLV: 'Laudatio ipsi David,' *Laudatio. David.*

In CXLVI: 'Alleluia,' *Laudate Dominum,* licet ambigatur utrum apud Hebreos sit titulus, cum principium Psalmi esse videatur.

68 In CXLVII: 'Alleluia,' *Laudate Dominum,* sicut paulo superius dicebatur. In hoc Psalmo apud Hebreos est continuatio usque ad alterum subsequentem qui incipit 'Laudate Dominum,' licet apud Septuaginta per innovationem alterius Psalmi hoc titulo prenotati: 'Alleluia, Aggei et Zacharie,' cuius principium est 'Lauda, Hierusalem, Dominum.'

The following three Psalms have these titles, since for each "Song of the steps" is written.

In 131: "Song of the steps," *Song of the steps. Of David.*

In 132 there is no difference between the titles, since we read 65
"Song of the steps" for both.

In 133: "Song of the steps," *Song of the steps. Of David.*

In the following Psalm there is no difference between the titles, since for both we read "Song of the steps."

In 135: "Halleluiah," *Praise the Lord.*

In 136: "Halleluiah," which in the Hebrew is found only at the end of the preceding Psalm, and it lacks another title.

In 137: "Psalm of David, according to Jeremiah," but a title is 66
lacking in the Hebrew.

In 138: "A Psalm for David himself," *Of David.*

In 139: "Psalm of David," *For the victor. Of David. A Psalm.*

In 140: "A Psalm of David," *For the victor. A Psalm. Of David.*

In 141 no difference between the titles appears, since in both "A Psalm of David" is found.

In 142: "The understanding of David, sine he was in the cave, a 67
prayer," *Sound. A maskil. Of David, when he was in the cave. A prayer.*

In 143: "A Psalm of David, when his son Absalom was pursuing him," *A Psalm. Of David.*

In 144: "A Psalm of David against Goliath," *Of David.*

In 145: "Praise for David himself," *Praise. Of David.*

In 146: "Halleluiah," *Praise the Lord,* although it is unclear whether this is the title in the Hebrew, since it seems to be the beginning of the Psalm.

In 147: "Halleluiah," *Praise the Lord,* as was said just above. In 68
the Hebrew this Psalm continues to the following one which begins "Praise the Lord," although in the Septuagint it marks the beginning of another Psalm with this title: "Halleluiah, of Haggai and Zechariah," the beginning of which is "Praise the Lord, Jerusalem."

In tribus reliquis et ultimis 'Alleluia' pro titulis habentur, et apud Hebreos in omnibus 'Laudate Dominum' reperitur. De quo dubitatio est utrum sint tituli vel principia Psalmorum, quemadmodum supra dicebatur.

⟨EXPLICIT LIBER QVARTVS⟩

The three remaining Psalms and the final one have "Halleluiah" for a title, and in Hebrew for all of them is found "Praise the Lord." But there is doubt whether these are the titles or the beginnings of the Psalms, as was said above.

END OF BOOK FOUR

LIBER QVINTVS

1 Instituentibus nobis, gloriosissime princeps, inceptam ac iam propemodum absolutam huius nostri operis materiam prosequi et mandare huic quinto, quemadmodum institueramus, libro, nuntiatum est maiestatem tuam mala valitudine ea scilicet tempestate detineri, qua Beneventi venationis gratia commorabaris. Quo quidem adverso et permolesto nuntio usque adeo per aliquot dies turbati et consternati sumus, ut nihil omnino scribere valeremus.
2 Cuius quidem tante turbationis nostre causas cum inter nos sepenumero consideraremus, duas vel maxime fuisse inveniebamus. Una erat generalis quedam, cunctorum populorum, qui sub tuo imperio degebant, consternatio atque extrema omnium statuum suorum eversio, quam quidem mox futuram ac e vestigio subsecuturam non iniuria putabamus ac coniectura augurabamur, si ea valitudo, ut ab origine inceperat, paulo diutius commorata inva-
3 luisset. Quorum quidem acerbissimorum tot tantorumque subditorum tuorum casu⟨u⟩m apprime miserati, mente non mediocriter, sed multum admodum angebamur. Homines enim sumus, nec quicquam humani a nobis alienum existimamus. Altera accedebat privata persone statusque mei periclitatio, quam equidem tandem aliquando fore intelligebam, si mors (Deus avertat!) te a tergo ino-
4 pinata invasisset. Sed cum infinita omnipotentis Dei gratia atque affectatis plurimorum populorum precibus assiduisque orationibus, te paucis post diebus ex gravi quo carpebaris morbo, ita convaluisse cognovi, ut pristinam corporis tui sani ac robusti incolumitatem atque salutem penitus omninoque recuperaveris; Domino Deo nostro, cuius favoribus adiutus, repente convalueras, in primis magnas et ingentes gratias egi, quoniam non solum vehemens illa et acerba turbatio, que mentem meam ita consternaverat,

BOOK FIVE

Most illustrious prince, when I was putting in order the material 1
for this work of mine which I had begun and almost finished, and
I was continuing to set it down in this fifth book, according to
plan, word was brought to me that Your Majesty had taken ill during your hunting expedition at Benevento. For several days I was
so agitated and alarmed by this distressing news that I was unable
to write anything at all. I repeatedly examined the reasons for my 2
profound distress, and I discovered two reasons in particular. One
was the universal alarm experienced by all your subjects and the
complete upheaval of public order which we reasonably thought
and prophesied would soon occur and immediately follow if your
affliction lingered on as it had begun and gained strength. I felt 3
great compassion for your subjects' great, numerous and exceedingly bitter misfortunes, but I experienced a great deal of anxiety.
For I am a man and I do not consider any thing that happens to
mankind foreign to me.[1] A second and private trial involving my
own person and status also loomed, a trial I realized would occur
at some point if death (may God prevent it!) assailed you unex-
pectedly. But by the infinite grace of all-powerful God and the 4
ceaseless, heartfelt prayers of many of your peoples, I learned that
within a few days you had been so fully restored from the serious
malady that assailed you, that you completely recovered your former health and physical vigor. I most fervently thanked, above all,
our Lord God, aided by whose favor you suddenly recovered, since
not only did the powerful and bitter anxiety that had plagued my
mind completely disappear, but I was also filled with the greatest

prorsus evanuit, sed maximo quoque gaudio et incredibili letitia
5 perfusus sum. Cum vero paulo post recuperatam pristinam valitudinem, non sine infinito totius populi applausu atque admirabili festivitate, Neapolim ad nos redires, me continere non potui, quin medicos tuos de causis illius detestande egritudinis diligenter et accurate percontarer.

6 Ceterum cum unam et solam predicte egrotationis causam, nimios scilicet quosdam atque importunos inter venandum labores fuisse accepissem, non ab re fore arbitratus sum si, ut hoc loco ob singularem quandam ac precipuam meam in te caritatem, observantiam ac venerationem te rogare, te exhortari, te denique exorare cogor, ita tibi suppliciter obsecravero, ut his saltem nimiis, ubi ab omnibus pre eximia animi tui voluptate mentisque tranquillitate
7 non potes, venandi laboribus mitius ac parcius indulgeas. Si enim omnes homines communi nature lege non sibi solis, sed patrie, sed amicis, sed propinquis et affinibus et cunctis denique vulgo hominibus ⟨nati sunt⟩, ut preclare scriptum est a Platone et in optimis etiam (quod multo maius ac prestantius est) christiane religionis institutis plane et aperte continetur divinitusque explicatur; quanto magis reges, qui non pervulgata et communi aliorum mortalium lege, sed precipuo ac divino nature privilegio et procreati et orti sunt, in quorum quidem salute una cunctorum subditorum populorum status vel maxime conservatur?

8 At vero si forte eam celebratam Gaii Cesaris sententiam, quam crebro dictis suis usurpabat, tua responsione assummeres diceresque instar illius: 'Satis diu vixi vel nature vel glorie,' tibi forte ita dicenti id ipsum respondere non extimescerem quod Ciceronem, prestantissimum oratorem egregiumque philosophum, predicto Cesari respondisse constat. In ea enim celeberrima oratione, que *Pro M. Marcello* inscribitur et coram eo habita est, verba hec posuit:

joy and extraordinary happiness. When, shortly after the recovery 5
of your former health, you returned to us at Naples to the limit-
less cheers and celebration of the whole populace, I was unable to
refrain from persistently inquiring from your doctors the specific
causes of that deplorable affliction.

When I had discovered that there was a single reason for the 6
aforementioned sickness and that it was due to the excessively
harsh exertions of hunting, I did not think it inappropriate, in this
place, compelled as I am by my especially deep love for you, to
beg, exhort, and entreat you, so I humbly implore you at least to
moderate and reduce your excessively strenuous expeditions, since,
due to the pleasure and peace of mind you derive from it, you cannot give up hunting altogether. For if by the universal law of na- 7
ture all men have been born not for themselves alone, but for their
country, friends, kinsmen, and finally for all men in general, as
Plato famously wrote[2] and as it is also clearly expressed in the best
doctrines of the Christian religion (which is a so much greater and
more excellent authority) and is divinely revealed, how much more
[obligated to others] are kings, who are neither procreated nor
born according to the universal law of other mortals, but by a
special divine privilege of nature, since the well-being of all their
subjects is preserved by the good health of their kings alone?

But if by chance you were in reply to invoke that famous saying 8
Gaius Caesar often used—"I have lived long enough for nature or
for glory"—I would not hesitate when you did so to respond as
we know Cicero, that most extraordinary orator and sage philosopher, responded to Caesar. In his famous speech *For Marcus Marcellus*, delivered in Caesar's presence, he said the following:

9 Itaque illam tuam preclarissimam et sapientissimam vocem invitus audivi: 'Satis diu vel nature vixi vel glorie.' At, quod maximum est, certe patrie parum. Quare omitte, queso, istam doctorum hominum in contemnenda morte prudentiam: noli nostro periculo esse sapiens. Sepe enim venit ad aures meas te idem istud nimis dicere crebro tibi satis te vixisse. Credo, sed tum id audirem, si tibi soli viveres aut si tibi soli natus esses.

10 Quod si Cicero Cesari, dum apud eum oraret, se ita respondisse testatur, cur ego extimescere aut subvereri debeo, ne id ipsum
Maiestati tue, si forte commemoratam Cesaris sententiam usur-
pares, plane aperteque respondeam, quin immo tantum abest ut
huiusmodi responsionem extimescam, quod prompte et aperta, ut
11 dicitur, fronte in hunc modum respondere non dubitarem? Noli,
fortunatissime Alfonse, noli, queso, tot tantorumque subditorum
periculo in contemnenda morte et in negligenda incolumitate esse
sapiens; sed ita vive, ita tibi indulge, ita denique valitudinem tuam
cura, ut cum singulari quadam et precipua tantarum gentium uti-
litate simul ac maxima et pene infinita nominis tui gloria diutius
12 vivere possis et valeas. Quod uno solo cunctorum medicorum
consensu nimirum assequeris, si nimiis ac profecto (pace tua dicam) interdum importunis quotidianarum ac continuarum vena-
tionum laboribus parumper modiceque peperceris. Id ut non solum pro salute tua, sed etiam pro certa et expressa tot tantorumque
subditorum tuorum conservatione accurate efficere ac diligenter
prestare digneris, ego ascriptitius ac dedititius Maiestatis tue servus, te in maiorem modum exhortor ac suppliciter rogo et obsecro.
13 Nec enim absurdum est ut tu, qui magne orbis parti imperare le-
gesque imponere videris, pro salute tua imperatique, ut dixerim,

> Unwillingly have I heard your extraordinarily distinguished 9
> and sagacious voice proclaim: "I have lived long enough for nature or for glory." But what is most important, certainly not long enough for your country. And so I ask you to forego that wisdom of learned men who have contempt for death. Do not be wise at our expense. For often has it been reported to me that you frequently say that you have lived long enough. I believe that, but I would take it seriously only if you were living for yourself alone, or if you had been created for yourself alone.[3]

If Cicero attests that he made this response to Caesar when he 10
was speaking in his presence, why should I feel apprehensive about making the same response clearly and explicitly to Your Majesty, if you were to employ the aforementioned saying of Caesar? On the contrary: so little do I fear a response of this kind that I would not hesitate to respond readily, and, as they say, with head held high.
Most blessed Alfonso, please do not, I beg you, be wise at the ex- 11
pense of your many important subjects by despising death and neglecting your safety. But live, have regard for yourself, and take care of your health in such a way that you can live and flourish longer as an exceptional benefit for your many great peoples, acquiring at the same time the greatest and virtually infinite glory for
your name. By the universal agreement of all your doctors, you 12
will clearly achieve this goal if for a little while you moderate your excessive and sometimes, may I say, misguided efforts to hunt on a daily and uninterrupted basis. I, as an enrolled and dedicated servant of Your Majesty, exhort you on bended knee and humbly ask and beseech you that you deign to do this not only for your safety, but also for the certain and manifest preservation of all your many
subjects. Nor is it inappropriate that you, who are seen to com- 13
mand a great part of the world and to mandate laws, be willing to

orbis conservatione medicorum duntaxat preceptis institutisque parere et obtemperare velis. Nunc ad propositum incepti et pene absoluti operis redeamus, si prius quid paulo post commemoratam convalescentiam tuam circa usitatam provisionis mee solutionem acciderit, breviter enarravero.

14 Unde quantum ego ex predicta egrotatione iure cruciari, et
versa vice quantum ex recuperata salute letari debuerim, manifestissime declarabitur. Nam cum oportunum ordinarie solutionis
tempus iam preteriisset atque idcirco ut mihi convenienter solveretur, a novo quodam thesaurario, ad quem solvendi gratia nuper
remissus eram et quem honoris causa nominare nolui, quoad pote-
ram, paulo diligentius crebriusque curarem, nihil aliud nisi bona
15 certaque eiusdem solutionis mee verba reportabam. Sed cum id
ipsum aliquandiu postulans atque efflagitans, sepius frustra tentas-
sem, tandem aliquando factum est ut mihi eum gravioribus verbis
semel urgenti, in hunc modum particularius atque exactius se inter
legendum privilegia mea propterea solvere non posse responderet,
quoniam duobus illis magnis ac dignis et sacri regii consilii et pu-
blici, ut ita dixerim, erarii tui magistratibus, quibus me ornare
atque illustrare volueras, quotidianis persone mee officiis haudqua-
16 quam subministraveram. Cui quidem sic obicienti me ad illa officia
quotidiana quadam persone mee assistentia ex ipsa privilegiorum
solemnitate minime obnoxium esse foreque aperta fronte respon-
dissem atque ille in sententia sua pertinacius obduraret, demum
ad Maiestatem tuam, certum quendam cunctarum turbationum
17 mearum portum, magna iactatus tempestate confugi. Atque re
ipsa paucis, ut scis, verbis diligenter enarrata, ita grate, ita liberaliter, ita denique magnifice respondisti, ut coram multis illustribus

obey and submit at least to the rules and prescriptions of your doctors for your health and for the preservation of the territory you rule. Now let us return to the theme of my work, which has been begun and nearly completed, but only after briefly relating what happened a little after your convalescence with regard to the regular payment of my stipend.

It will become entirely clear from this how much I ought with 14
cause to have been tormented by your illness, and vice versa how much I ought to have rejoiced when you became well again. For when the normal time for my regular payment had already passed and on that account I was endeavoring, as far as possible, a little more diligently and frequently to be appropriately remitted by a new treasury official, to whom I had been sent for payment and whom, for honor's sake, I have refused to name, all I came away with was nothing other than fair words and promises about this
very payment. When my repeatedly asking for payment and in- 15
deed demanding it had proven ineffective, it finally happened that he responded to an even more aggressive tack from me with the following: that after reading the specifics of the privilege detailing the circumstances of my stipend, he determined that he could not pay me because in my two distinguished appointments, to the sacred royal council and the public treasury, by which you had wished to grace and honor me, I had not at all tended to my official duties on a daily basis. When I had responded to his objec- 16
tions with head held high that I was not, nor would be, at all responsible for engaging in those duties in person on a daily basis according to the terms of the privilege and he was stubbornly sticking to his position, I finally took refuge in your majesty, a safe haven from all my troubles, as though I had been tossed by a great
storm. When the situation was briefly explained to you, as you 17
know, you responded so generously and graciously that in the presence of your many grand princes and aristocrats who happened to

principibus proceribusque tuis, quibus forte eo allocutionis mee tempore circundatus eras, cum maximis laudibus meis te non solum me exhibite provisionis muneribus ac emolumentis, sed duabus quoque predictorum magistratuum dignitatibus prosequi et honorare voluisse apertissime atque dignissime declarares; ac propterea ut mihi actutum solveretur, te paulo post curaturum largissime pollicitus fuisti atque dignissime ac regaliter obtulisti, et id
18 ipsum iuxta pollicitationes oblationesque tuas illico effecisti. Nam confestim vive vocis oraculo illi ipsi edixisti ut, quemadmodum in privilegio plane et aperte expresseras, mihi celeriter simul ac sine strepitu et figura, ut dicitur, iudicii liberaliter solveret. Quod ubi ipse audivit, non ulterius cunctandum aut refragandum ratus, mihi celerrime ac largissime solvere non detrectavit. Sed quorsum hec, hoc presertim loco, forte dicet quispiam? Ut scilicet me ex mala valitudine tua non immerito apprime cruciari, et versa vice ex recuperata salute multum admodum letari debuisse, quemadmodum supra dixi, plane et aperte intelligatur. Verum ad institutum nostrum, unde paulo longius digressi sumus, bonis ominibus revertamur.

19 Cum igitur in primo huius nostri *Apologetici* libro de diversis cunctorum auctorum obtrectatoribus omniumque sanctorum scriptorum veterum vita et moribus breviter tractaverimus, ac secundo de variis sacrarum Scripturarum interpretibus, et tertio et quarto de singulis quibusque Psalterii inter celebratam Septuaginta seniorum traductionem et Hebraicam veritatem differentiis ac diversitatibus abunde affatimque disseruerimus, reliquum est ut hoc quinto et ultimo de interpretatione recta non nulla memoratu
20 digna in medium afferamus. De hac igitur interpretatione recta deinceps tractaturi, ab eius diffinitione non iniuria ordiemur. Omnis enim que a ratione de aliqua re suscipitur institutio, secundum celebratam illam Ciceronis nostri sententiam, debet a diffinitione proficisci, ut intelligatur quid sit illud de quo disputetur.

surround you when I made my plea, you openly and worthily declared not only that you had wished to honor me with the favor and benefit of the tendered stipend but also with the prestige of the aforementioned appointments. Therefore you most handsomely, worthily, and royally promised and offered that you would soon take measures that payment be made to me immediately. This you brought about at once in accordance with your promises
and offers. For you immediately proclaimed to that person by the 18
oracle of your living voice that, just as you had clearly and openly expressed in the privilege, a generous payment should be paid to me forthwith and without further ado. When that person heard this, thinking he ought not to delay or postpone further, he agreed to pay me quickly and generously. But someone perhaps might ask what is the point of this, especially in this place? So that it can plainly and clearly be understood that I ought to have been tormented to the highest degree by your illness, and *vice versa*, that I ought to have rejoiced wholeheartedly when you recovered, as I mentioned above. But now let me return under good omens to my subject after this rather long digression.

In the first book of this my *Apologeticus* I briefly discussed the 19
different detractors of all authors and about the life and character of all the old sacred writers; in the second book I discussed the different translators of the sacred Scriptures; in the third and the fourth I fully examined the differences and divergences between the well-known rendering of the Psalter by the Seventy Elders and the true, original text in Hebrew; it remains in this fifth and final book to offer some comments about correct translation that are
worth saying. Because I am going to discuss what constitutes cor- 20
rect translation, it makes sense for me to begin with its definition. For any teaching that is methodically undertaken about any subject should, according to that famous precept set down by Cicero, start with a definition so that the subject is clearly understood.[4]

21 Est ergo interpretatio recta idonea quedam et commoda de quacunque celebrata ac preceptis et regulis instituta lingua in aliam pariter vel pene similem, iuxta subiectam de qua tractatur materiam, conversio. Nam si ex quatuor celeberrimis idiomatibus (Hebreo, Caldeo, Greco ac Latino), reliquis omnibus pretermissis, de uno aliquo in aliud secundum diversitatem materie recte con-
22 verteretur, profecto recta illa interpretatio nuncuparetur. At vero si de aliquo predictorum in maternum sermonem forte transferretur, quanquam cuncta alia convenirent que ad rectam interpretationem requiruntur, non tamen proprie recta interpretatio diceretur; recta quippe conversio certam quandam eloquii illius lingue, in quam traducitur, dignitatem exigere et postulare videtur. Multa quoque alia ad hanc, de qua loquimur, necessario concurrant oportet.

23 Primo, etenim habenda est illius lingue, de qua transfertur, cognitio, neque ea parva ac vulgaris, sed minuta et trita et accurata et multa ac diuturna poetarum, oratorum, historicorum, philosophorum, et, si e sacris Scripturis traducendum foret, celebratorum doctorum lectione quesita; siquidem qui hos omnes non legerit, evolverit ac diligenter accurateque versarit, is proprietatem signi-
24 ficataque verborum probe tenere intelligereque non poterit. Sine quorum omnium certa et exacta intelligentia nullus bene interpretari ex eo valet, quia omnes presertim elegantes scriptores tropis figurisque dicendi frequenter utuntur. Que si ut sonant verba, ita interpretarentur, non modo ridicula et stulta, sed quandoque falsa redderetur conversio. Qualia sunt apud nos: 'Gero tibi morem' et 'desiderati milites' et 'boni consulas' et 'opere pretium fuerit' et

And so correct translation is a suitable and appropriate conversion from one distinguished language with established rules and precepts into another language equally established and more or less similar, in accordance with the subject matter being treated. For if from the four most distinguished languages — Hebrew, Aramaic,[5] Greek, and Latin — (leaving all the remaining ones aside) one were rightly changed into another in accordance with the variety of subject matter, that would certainly be called a correct trans- 21
lation. But if there were a translation from one of the languages 22
mentioned above into a vernacular language, even if all other points were fitting which are required for a correct translation, this would nonetheless not properly be called a correct translation. For a correct conversion seems to require and demand a certain elevation of the diction of that language into which it is done. Many other considerations inevitably converge on the topic we are discussing.

First of all,[6] a knowledge of the language from which the trans- 23
lation is being made is absolutely necessary, and not a modest or common knowledge, but intimate and expert and acquired through a careful, comprehensive, and daily practice of reading the poets, orators, historians, philosophers, and, if a translation is to be made from the sacred Scriptures, through reading the illustrious Doctors of the Church. He who does not read all of these and diligently and precisely engage with them, will not be able to rightly grasp and understand the proper meaning of the words.[7]
Without a certain and precise understanding of all these writers 24
no one is able to translate well, because in particular all accomplished writers often use tropes and figures of speech. If words should be translated based on their literal meaning, not only would the translation be laughable and foolish but sometimes wrong. For instance, we employ the following expressions: "I humor you," "soldiers lost in battle," "may you regard favorably," "it

'negotium facesso' et 'dabis improbe penas', et plura alia huiusmodi, quibus idoneorum auctorum libri referti comperiun-
25 tur. Hec profecto omnia longe aliud ex consuetudine figurisque
loquendi significant quam propria ipsius locutionis verba significare videantur, ut est. Duobus enim et quidem celebratis duntaxat
exemplis contenti erimus: 'Desiderati milites centum' et 'armata
iuventus.' 'Desiderati' namque 'milites', si verba tantummodo at-
tendas, aliud important si tritam vero loquendi consuetudinem,
26 'perierunt.' 'Iuventus' quoque et 'iuventa' duo diversa sunt, quorum alterum 'multitudinem,' alterum 'etatem' significat, ceu idoneis
Virgilii Liviique auctoritatibus plane et aperte confirmatur. Maro
enim *Eneidos* quinto ita canit:

> si nunc foret illa iuventa

et alibi:

> primevo flore iuventus
> exercebat equos.

Livius etiam quodam loco *Ab urbe condita,* sic scribit: 'Armata iuventus excursionem in agrum romanum fecit.'

27 Si ergo ad rectam interpretationem notitia illius lingue, e qua transfertur, ut diximus, necessaria est, profecto multo magis necessaria videbitur et illius cognitio in quam transferetur. Nam quicunque recte interpretari voluerit, propositum suum nequaquam assequi poterit nisi linguam eam, in quam traducere proposuerit, sic tenuerit, ut in ipsa quodammodo dominetur et totam, ut ita dixerim, ita in potestate habeat, ut cum par verbum verbo reddendum fuerit, quod plerunque accidit, vel id nullatenus mendicare

will be worth the effort," "I am bringing a case against," and "you
will suffer immensely," and there are many other expressions of
this kind.[8] The books of good authors are filled with them. All of 25
these examples, through idioms and figures of speech, mean something far different from what the proper words of the locution itself seem to indicate. Two well known expressions will do to make
the point: "a hundred soldiers longed for," and "armed youth."
"Longed-for soldiers," if you focus on the words only, indicates one
thing, but if you pay attention to the customary usage, it means
"the soldiers perished." Likewise "youths" and "youth" are two dif- 26
ferent things, the latter indicating an age group and the former
indicating a group of young men. This is clearly illustrated by the
good authors Vergil and Livy. Vergil writes the following in the
fifth book of *The Aeneid:*

> If now I had that youth,

and elsewhere,

> The youths in their first prime
> were exercising their horses.[9]

Livy says somewhere in his [*History of Rome*] *from the Founding of the City:* "The armed youths made a sally into Roman territory."[10]

If knowledge of that language from which the translation is 27
made is necessary for a correct translation, as I mentioned, certainly it will be even more necessary to possess a knowledge of that language into which the translation is being made. For whoever wishes to translate correctly will by no means be able to accomplish his goal unless he has such command of that language into which the translation is being made that he is somehow master of it and has it, so to speak, so completely under control so that when a word has to be translated by a perfect match, which often

cogatur vel in aliena lingua ob crassam eius ignorantiam peregrinum extraneumque relinquat.

28 Vim quoque ac naturam verborum subtiliter et exacte noscat oportet, ne 'modicum' pro 'parvo,' ne 'fortitudinem' pro 'robore,' ne 'bellum' pro 'prelio,' ne 'urbem' denique pro 'civitate' inter transferendum exprimat. Consuetudines etiam figurasque loquendi calleat necesse est, quibus optimi scriptores crebro utuntur. Quod tertio inter interpretandi virtutes ponimus.

29 Quartum insuper requiritur ut omnis idoneus interpres habeat
aures teretes atque rotundas, ne forte illa, que eleganter concinne-
que dicta sunt, dissipet ipse atque perturbet. Hec cuicunque recto
proboque interpreti, quemadmodum superius dictum est, necessaria sunt. Que quidem omnia per certa quedam et expressa cuiuscunque traductoris vitia predictis virtutibus directe et e regione
contraria evidenter apparebunt. Manifesta enim cunctorum inter-
30 pretum vitia huiusmodi sunt. Nam si aut male capiunt quod inter-
pretantur, aut male reddunt aut si id, quod apte numeroseque
dictum fuerit, ipsi ita convertant, ut ineptum et inconcinnum et
dissipatum efficiatur, vitiosi interpretes non iniuria appellabuntur.
Si duo preterea usitata et nota exornationum — hoc est verborum
et sententiarum — ornamenta, quibus singula queque scripta precipue exornari illustrarique videntur, non ita expresserit, ut dignitas
ac maiestas primi auctoris si non usquequaque, saltem maxima ex
parte servetur, nequaquam boni interpretes habendi sunt.

31 Quocirca nisi et he interpretandi virtutes et ista de quibus diximus vitia, altere diligenter serventur, altera vero accurate evitentur,
nulla profecto interpretatio recta esse fierique poterit; quod unico
et quidem peregregio alicuius nobilis picture exemplo declarari
32 evidentissime ac manifestissime potest. Quemadmodum enim illi,

happens, he is by no means either forced to beg for it or leave it in an alien and foreign tongue because of his gross ignorance of the language.

He must also, subtly and accurately, know the force and nature 28
of words so that while translating he does not render "little" for "small," or "courage" for "strength," or "war" for "battle," or "city" for "state."[11] Over time he must come to know the idioms and figures of speech which the best authors use frequently. I consider this third among the virtues of translating.

The fourth virtue required is that every effective translator have 29
subtle and finely attuned ears so that he does not by chance destroy and confound what has been elegantly and artfully crafted. These attributes are necessary for every correct and proper translator, as I said above. All these attributes will evidently appear directly contrary to the above-mentioned virtues through definite and distinct faults of the translator. Indeed obvious faults of all
translators are of the following kind. For if they either imperfectly 30
understand what they are translating, or they translate it poorly, or they change something which has been precisely and sonorously said so that it is rendered awkward and ungraceful and tattered, they will justly be called poor translators. Moreover, if the two usual and familiar embellishments — that is, of words and of thoughts[12] — by which each individual piece of writing seems especially decorated and distinguished, are not expressed in a way that retains the dignity and grandeur of the original author — if not entirely, at least to a great extent — they can by no means be considered good translators.

Therefore unless, concerning the virtues and vices of translating 31
of which we have spoken, the former are carefully protected and the latter are diligently avoided, no translation will be able to be or become correct. This can be made clearly evident using the singular and extraordinary example of a famous painting. For just as 32

qui ad exemplar picture aliam picturam effingere conantur, nisi figuram et statum et ingressum ac totius corporis formam et liniamenta coloresque exinde probe apteque assumpserint, nec quid ipsi faciant, sed quid ille alter effecerit, ita ad unguem meditentur, ut cuncta predicta diligenter accurateque serventur, nequaquam de
33 recta expressione iure laudabuntur. Ita pariter quibuscunque interpretibus evenire necesse est. Nisi enim primo vim proprietatemque verborum, nisi deinde sententiarum gravitatem, nisi etiam digna utrorunque ornamenta, nisi insuper maiestatem dignitatemque primi auctoris suis interpretationibus bene eleganterque expresserint, nullatenus de recta interpretatione merito laudari poterunt.

34 Cum igitur quid sit interpretatio recta diffinierimus, consequens esse videtur ut ea quecunque ad verbum est traductio, recta esse non possit. Est enim triplex interpretatio: una ad verbum; altera, ut ita dixerim, ad sensum; tertia ubi aliqua interdum ornatus gratia omittuntur, non nulla pro arbitrio voluntateque interpretis superadduntur. Ad verbum interpretatio est ubi verbum verbo
35 redditur. Ad sensum vero ubi verbis tropisque dicendi omissis sententia tantummodo servatur. At si quando aliqua paulo obscuriora forte pretermitterentur, ne ob eorum positionem labefactaretur interpretatio, vel amplificandi gratia adderetur (quod altera ex duabus causis evenire necesse est), modo vel omissione vel additione primi auctoris sententia servaretur; profecto tollerabile esse videretur, ceu ab optimis scriptoribus non nunquam factum ac servatum fuisse legimus, ut paulo post manifestissime apparebit.
36 Quod autem ad verbum interpretatio facta, ut diximus, recta esse non possit, ex eo vel maxime patebit, quia tametsi in ea lingua, in quam traducitur, tot verba et paria et commoda reperirentur et

those who attempt to fashion a copy of an original, unless they carefully absorb the figure, pose, gait, and the shape of the lineaments and hues of the whole body, and do not think about what they themselves would do but study what the original artist has done down to the last detail, so that all the above-mentioned attributes are assiduously and carefully preserved, by no means could they be justly praised for the correctness of their copy.[13] The same 33
holds equally true for translators. For unless they imitate the strength and proper sense of the words, and unless they match the seriousness of the thoughts, and unless they imitate the ornaments worthy of each, and unless moreover they express in their translations the grandeur and dignity of the original effectively and tastefully, in no way can they deserve to be praised for producing a correct translation.

Since we have defined what a correct translation is, it seems to 34
follow that a word-for-word translation cannot be a correct translation. For there are three kinds of translation: one is word for word; a second is, as it were, according to sense; and a third occurs when some things are sometimes omitted because they are purely ornamental, while other things are added at the discretion of the translator. A word-for-word translation is one where each word is
translated by a word. A translation according to sense is one where 35
the thought alone is preserved while words and figures of speech may be omitted. But if sometimes a few obscurities should perhaps be omitted lest the translation suffer by their inclusion, or something be added to amplify the translation (each situation necessarily arises for two reasons), the thought of the original author would be preserved by omission or addition only. Certainly this would seem to be permissible, since we have read that the best
authors sometimes did this, as will become clear shortly. However, 36
that, as I said, a translation made word for word cannot be correct

que idem penitus significarent (quod evenire omnino impossibile est), adhuc restarent tropi ac methaphore figureque loquendi, que secundum verborum sonitum, ceu supra per plura et ea quidem nobilitata exempla probavimus, nullatenus probe converti possent.

37 Ad hanc tam validam prepotentemque rationem celebrate quedam non nullorum idoneorum scriptorum auctoritates bonorumque interpretum usus et consuetudines observationesque accedunt. Sed duabus duntaxat duorum optimorum auctorum, alterius prophani, alterius sacri, allegationibus brevitatis gratia contenti erimus. Oratius enim in *Arte poetica*, cum de recta interpretatione loqueretur, ita canit:

> nec verbum verbo curabis reddere fidus
> interpres.

38 Hieronymus etiam in prefatione libri *De temporibus*, cum de eadem re paulo exactius uberiusque dissereret, 'Dum ad verbum', inquit, 'interpretor, absurde resonat.' De usu vero bonorum interpretum dubitari non potest, qui semper ad sensum et non ad verbum interpretari consueverunt. Ut Cicero, optimus interpres, in transla-
39 tionibus suis plane aperteque testatur. Que etsi non reperiantur, sed incuria et negligentia maiorum nostrorum omnino periisse videantur, in prologo tamen interpretationis, quam de duabus illis famosissimis Eschinis et Demosthenis orationibus fecisse constat, apertissime asserit, et in aliquibus etiam que sparsim hinc inde ex Homeri et Sophoclis ac etiam ex Platonis et Aristotelis et non

will be especially clear for the following reason. Even if so many similar and appropriate words could be found in the target language and even if they fundamentally meant the same thing (which cannot ever be completely true), still the tropes and metaphors and figures of speech would be left over, which completely resist literal translation, as we proved above with many very well-known examples.

Several worthy writers lend their distinguished authority to this 37
compelling line of thinking, as do the customs, practices and habits of good translators. But for the sake of brevity, we will be content with the evidence of two of the best writers, one secular and one sacred. For Horace in his *Art of Poetry*, when discussing correct translation, says:

> Nor will you, as a faithful translator, care to render
> word for word.[14]

Jerome as well in the preface of his *Chronicle*, when discussing the 38
same thing more precisely and in more detail, says, "When I translate word for word, it sounds preposterous."[15] It is not possible to be in doubt about the practice of good translators, who were always accustomed to translate according to sense and not word for word, as Cicero, an extremely accomplished translator, clearly and
openly proves in his translations. Even if these translations are not 39
to be found and appear to be entirely lost through the carelessness and neglect of our ancestors, he nevertheless very clearly affirms this in the introduction to the translation which all agree he made of those two famous speeches by Aeschines and Demosthenes.[16] He is also perceived to have carefully and diligently observed this practice in his translations of the sayings of Homer and Sophocles and also of Plato and Aristotle and several other ancient writers,

nullorum aliorum vetustissimorum scriptorum sententiis in libris
40 suis posita videmus, diligenter accurateque servasse cernitur. Idem
pene et Hieronymus in sacris Scripturis, ubi minus ob dignitatem
maiestatemque divini eloquii sententiarumque gravitatem vel
potius divinitatem servandum fore videbatur, servasse novimus.

De hac nostra circa interpretationem rectam opinione, si quis
forte dubitaret, traductiones ad verbum factas in manus sumat. Ex
quibus quidem paulo diligentius accuratiusque perlectis omnis in-
41 ter legendum eius dubitatio ambiguitasque cessabit. Verba enim
inepta, peregrina et ambigua, sententias obscuras intercisasque et
interdum alienas falsasque reperiet. Quod ex duabus et Dyonisii
Ariopagite, Atheniensis episcopi, et plurimorum Aristotelis librorum veteribus interpretationibus intueri licet. Nam duo illi veteres
interpretes ad verbum ob sententiarum, alterius philosophi, alterius theologi, gravitatem interpretari conati, ita ambiguas, ita per-
plexas, ita denique obscuras traductiones suas reddiderunt, ut
absque certo quorundam explanatorum favore vix maleve ac perperam intelligi possint.

42 Et tamen non nulla eadem per duas alias duorum utriusque
lingue peritissimorum virorum, unius Bissarionis, reverendissimi
cardinalis Niceni, alterius Ambrosii, Camaldulensis ordinis patris
generalis, conversiones novas non ad verbum, sed ad sensum effectas, aperta, distincta et clara cernuntur. Bissarion enim Aristotelis
Methaphysice libros ex ambiguis ac perplexis et obscuris utcunque
latinis claros nimirum atque distinctos et apertos sua nova transla-
43 tione reddidisse conspicitur. Quod idem de Ambrosio sentimus et
dicimus, qui libris commemorati Dyonisii et *De celesti et De ecclesiastica hierarchia, De divinis* quoque *nominibus* et *De mystica* insuper

sayings which we see scattered here and there in his books.[17] We 40
know that Jerome maintained almost the identical practice in the
sacred Scriptures, where it seemed that this practice had to be followed less regularly because of the dignity and grandeur of the
divine style and the seriousness of the thoughts, or rather their
divinity.

If any one by chance should doubt our understanding of correct
translation, let him pick up translations made word for word. After reading them a little more carefully and closely, this reading
will dispel all doubt and uncertainty. For he will find words that 41
are poorly chosen, foreign, and ambiguous, thoughts which are
obscure, truncated, and sometimes alien and incorrect. It is possible to observe this in two old translations of Dionysius the Aer-
opagite, the bishop of Athens, and in old translations of many of
Aristotle's books.[18] For the two old translators, having tried to
translate word for word because of the seriousness of the thoughts
of both the philosopher and the theologian, produced translations
that were so ambiguous, confusing and obscure that, without the
support of some commentators,[19] they can scarcely or imperfectly
and wrongly be understood.

Nevertheless, many of the same things can be clearly and dis- 42
tinctly understood through two new translations made not word
for word but according to sense by two experts in both languages,
Bessarion, the most reverend cardinal of Nicaea, and Ambrogio,
abbot-general of the Camaldolese order. Instead of the ambiguous,
confusing and somehow obscure Latin, Bessarion translates the
books of Aristotle's *Metaphysics* in his new translation into truly
clear, distinguished, and accessible Latin.[20] We think and assert 43
the same thing about Ambrogio. He certainly does not appear incompetent in the books of the aforementioned Dionysius, especially given how esoteric, abstruse, and far removed from, not
to say alien to, common sense they are, namely the *Celestial and
Ecclesiastical Hierarchy*, also *The Divine Names* and in addition the

theologia, quos omnes ad Timotheum Ephesium episcopum in lingua greca eleganter conscripsit, non ineptus presertim in materia ita abstrusa, ita recondita, ita ab omni sensu remotissima et, ut ita dixerim, abhorrentissima evidenter ostenditur. Et in Laertii insuper Diogenis libris, qui *De vita et moribus philosophorum* inscribuntur, commemoratum Arnbrosium ad sensum, non ad verbum egregie eleganterque inter legendum convertisse cognovimus.

44 Quas ob res cum quid sit recta interpretatio et quomodo de una in aliam linguam ad verbum facta conversio perfecta et laudabilis esse non possit, hactenus pro facultate nostra breviter admodum disseruerimus, duo preterea ad ultimam huius nostri operis
45 consumationem restare videntur, de quibus pauca dicemus. Primum est quod, licet ad verbum interpretatio, ut supra diximus, sive secularibus et profanis sive religiosis sacrisque auctoribus recta atque idonea esse non valeat, inter traductiones tamen poetarum, oratorum, historicorum ex una parte, ex altera vero manifestam philosophorum ac theologorum differentiam non parvam illam quidem, sed magnam profecto et ingentem esse fierique oportet.
46 Tria enim illa antea posita in quavis conversione esse convenit, ut, sententia quodammodo servata, cuncta alia secundum evidentem primorum auctorum diversitatem varietatemque ornata et illustrata fuisse ostendantur. Reliqua vero duo graviorem quandam ac severiorem traductionem exigere et postulare videntur.

47 Nam, ut a poetis incipiam, Cecilius ac Terentius poete comici Menandri fabellas, atque Ennius et Pacuvius et Accius Euripidis et Sophoclis tragedias ita eleganter interpretati fuisse dicuntur, ut non minus ab utriusque lingue peritis illorum temporum hominibus nec minori etiam voluptate quam principales suarum celebra-
48 tarum fabularum auctores legerentur. Cicero nanque in commemorata prefatione quodam loco verba hec ponit:

> nec minus Terentium et Cecilium quam Menandrum legunt, nec *Andromacam* aut *Antiopam* aut Epigonos latinos recipiunt;

Mystical Theology, all of which Dionysius elegantly wrote in Greek to Timothy, the bishop of Ephesus.[21] In the course of our reading we have also learned that the aforementioned Ambrogio translated splendidly and elegantly, according to sense, not word for word, in the books of Diogenes Laertius' *The Lives of the Philosophers*.[22]

Therefore, since we have thus far, as best we can, very briefly 44
discussed what a correct translation is and how a perfect and praiseworthy translation cannot be made from one language into another word for word, there seem to be two things besides that remain before the final completion of our work. I will say a few words about these. The first is that, although a translation word 45
for word, as I said above, can be correct or suitable neither for secular and pagan authors nor for religious and sacred authors, nevertheless there ought to exist and be made no small—indeed an extremely sharp—distinction between translations of poets, orators, and historians on the one hand, and translations of philosophers and theologians on the other. It is fitting that the three 46
former kinds of writing just mentioned should appear in any given translation in such a way that, while somehow preserving the meaning, all the rest of the text be shown to have been decorated and adorned according to the distinct variety and diversity of the original authors. But the latter two kinds of writing seem to demand a much stricter and more disciplined translation.

For to begin with the poets, Caecilius and Terence are said to 47
have translated the plays of the comic poet Menander, and Ennius, Pacuvius and Accius are said to have translated the tragedies of Euripides and Sophocles so elegantly that they were read by men of those times expert in both languages with the same pleasure as the original authors of their own famous plays. For Cicero in some 48
passage in the aforementioned preface relates the following:

> Nor do they read Terence and Caecilius less than Menander, nor are they less receptive to a Latin *Andromache* or *Antiope*

> sed tamen Ennium et Pacuvium et Accium potius quam Euripidem et Sophoclem legunt. Quod igitur est eorum in orationibus e greco conversis fastidium, nullum cum sit in versibus?

49 De oratoribus quoque eadem ex ipsa Ciceronis prefatione deprehendere atque intelligere possumus, qui alicubi,

> quorum ego, inquit, orationes si, ut spero, ita expressero virtutibus utens illorum omnibus, id est sententiis et earum figuris et rerum ordine, verba persequens eatenus, ut non abhorreant a more nostro (que si de Grecis omnia conversa non erunt, tamen ut generis sint eiusdem elaborabimus), erit regula, ad quam eorum dirigantur orationes.

50 De historicis idem sentimus et dicimus, quorum excellentes priscosque a veteribus interpretibus nullatenus e greco latine traductos existimamus, cum id nunquam factum legerimus. Tuchididem tamen atque Herodotum, duos prestantissimos et elegantissimos cunctorum aliorum grecorum historicos, a duobus nostri temporis egregiis viris in latinum eloquium non ad verbum, sed ad sensum, quemadmodum fieri oportebat, conversos nequaquam
51 ignoramus. Atque de Iosepho et in libris *De antiquitate Iudeorum* et *De captivitate iudaica* et *De vetustate Hebreorum adversus Appionem*—illum grammaticum, cognomento Plistonicem, quod de multis diversarum rerum generibus scripserit; illum, inquam, Appionem grammaticum, qui ignobilitatem simul ac novitatem generis Iudeis scriptis suis vehementer obiciebat—quos omnes sive a Rufino, doctissimo viro, ut est quorundam eruditorum virorum non usquequaque contemnenda opinio, sive ab alio quocunque interprete traducti fuerint—; ad sensum, non ad verbum conversos haudquaquam ignoramus.

> or *Epigoni;* but nevertheless they read Ennius and Pacuvius and Accius rather than Euripides and Sophocles. What therefore is this distaste of theirs for speeches translated from Greek when there is no distaste for poetry?[23]

We are also able to perceive and understand the same points about orators from this same preface by Cicero, where he says somewhere: 49

> If, as I hope, I shall express their speeches by employing all their excellent qualities, such as their thoughts, their figures, and the order of the topics, and by following their words to the extent that they do not grate against our usage (and if they will not all be translated from Greek, we shall nevertheless endeavor that our words be of the same class), there will be a standard at which their speeches may aim.[24]

We hold and express the same view about historians, although 50
we suppose that the distinguished ancient historians were not translated from Greek into Latin by the ancient translators, since we read that that was never done. Nevertheless we are by no means ignorant of the fact that Thucydides and Herodotus, the two most outstanding and accomplished of all the Greek historians, have been translated by two extraordinary men of our time not word for word but according to sense, as they ought to have
been.[25] As for Josephus and his books *Jewish Antiquities* and *The* 51
Jewish Captivity and *On the Antiquity of the Jews against Apion*—Apion being a grammarian whose cognomen was Plistonices because he wrote about many different kinds of subjects and who strongly criticized Josephus' Jewish writings for the baseness and novelty of the genre[26]—we are well aware that, whether by Rufinus, a very learned man, as is the very respectable opinion of well-educated men, or by some other translator, all of those books [of Josephus] were translated according to sense and not word for word.

52 Ceterum de philosophis ac theologis, quanquam recte, ut diximus, in quibusvis interpretationibus ad verbum interpretari nequeamus, non ita tamen lata ac vaga et ampla cum verborum tum sententiarum quoque luminibus ornamentisque expolita, sed aliquando pressior ac gravior et exactior in predictis duobus quam in
53 tribus superioribus esse debet. Quippe ad gravitatem expressionemque sententiarum, quibus utraque commemorata facultas vel maxime abundat, in primis requiritur ut nec plura neque pauciora interdum verba reddantur, nisi quantum certa troporum et figurarum ac metaphorarum necessitas atque non nunquam nimia intelligentie obscuritas exigere et postulare videatur. Quod in sacris Scripturis precipue maximeque servandum iure existimamus et credimus.

54 Etenim Ciceronem duas predictas illas nobilissimas orationes aliter cum plura omiserit multaque addiderit, quam *Economicum* Xenophontis et Platonis *Prothagoram* traduxisse coniectura auguramur. In proemio quippe *De finibus bonorum et malorum*, ita scribit: namque

> si plane sic verterem Platonem aut Aristotelem, ut verterunt nostri poete fabulas, male, credo, mererer de meis civibus, si ad eorum cognitionem divina illa ingenia transferrem. Sed id neque feci adhuc, nec mihi tamen ne faciam interdictum puto. Locos quosdam, si videbitur, transferam et maxime ab iis, quos modo nominavi, cum inciderit, ut id apte fieri possit, ut ab Homero Ennius, Affranius a Menandro solet.

55 Quod utinam fecisses, Cicero! Non enim de illis qui tuo tempore neque etiam de posteris hominibus male, ceu ipse suspicari videbaris, sed vel potius optime meruisses, cum duorum gravissimorum philosophorum singularia quasi totius vere nobilisque philosophie

Although, as we said, we are not able to translate correctly word for word when it comes to translations of philosophers and theologians, nevertheless the translation should not be broad and rambling and decked out with brilliant words and opinions and ornaments, but in the end ought to be tighter, more serious, and more precise in these two areas than in the three mentioned above. For the dignity and expressiveness of utterance typical of the genre are especially required, so that sometimes neither more words nor fewer words are employed, unless a necessity for tropes, figures of speech, and metaphors or sometimes an overly obscure thought seems to call for them. We are justified in thinking and believing that this procedure ought to be especially and particularly maintained in the sacred Scriptures. 52 53

I would guess that when Cicero translated those two very famous speeches he left out and added a great deal, but translated the *Oeconomicus* of Xenophon or the *Protagoras* of Plato in a quite different way.[27] For in the introduction of his *On Ends* he writes the following: 54

> Clearly if I were to translate Plato and Aristotle as our poets translate plays, I would not deserve well, I think, of my fellow citizens, should I convey those divine geniuses to their understanding [like that]. But I have never yet done this, nor yet do I think myself forbidden from doing so. I shall translate some passages, if it seems right, and especially from those authors I just mentioned, when occasion arises, so that it might be done appropriately, as commonly Ennius does from Homer and Afranius from Menander.[28]

Would that you had done so, Cicero! For you would not have deserved badly of the men of that time, nor even of posterity, as you seemed to suspect, but rather you would have deserved the greatest commendation, since you would with your extraordinary and nearly unbelievable eloquence have marvelously adorned the 55

dogmata tua illa singulari ac pene incredibili eloquentia mirum in modum exornasses, atque ea ita latinis dilucida et ornata reddidisses, ut mali ac vitiosi interpretes, post multa temporum curricula, nulla optata nove traductionis oportunitate, nequaquam rursus convertere, quin immo vel potius pervertere et depravare ausi fuissent!

56 Quod si grecorum philosophorum latini interpretes ob sententiarum gravitatem preceptorumque ornatam traductionem exactius ac pressius quam aliorum secularium scriptorum traductores interpretari oportet, quidnam de sacrarum divinarumque Scripturarum conversionibus sentiemus, ubi cuncte queque sententie sacre ac divine sunt, in quibus omnis duntaxat humana salus vel
57 maxime consistere recondique videtur? Quod tametsi ita sit, excellentes tamen sacrarum Scripturarum interpretes usque adeo ab interpretatione ad verbum, utpote ab illa quam et sententias obscurare et interdum pervertere arbitrabantur, abhorruisse videntur, ut in medio sacri textus cum non nunquam amplificationibus, tum
58 alienis quoque interpretationibus utantur. Quod Hieronymum cum in libris Eusebii Cesariensis et *De temporibus* tum etiam et *De ecclesiastica historia* diligenter accurateque servasse inter legendum manifeste conspicimus; et id, quod ipse diligenter servavit, pluribus librorum suorum locis sic fieri oportere plane aperteque testa-
59 tur. Nam in prefatione commemorati *De temporibus* libri inter cetera verba hec ponit:

> Difficile est alienas lineas insequentem non alicubi excedere, et arduum ut que in aliena lingua dicta sunt, eundem decorem in translatione conservent. Significatum est aliquid unius verbi proprietate: non habeo meum quo id efferam;

unique doctrines of an almost completely true and noble philosophy derived from the two most authoritative philosophers. And you would have rendered them so lucidly and beautifully in Latin that incompetent and faulty translators after many ages, with no opportunity for a new translation to hope for, would never have dared to translate them again, or rather, to distort and pervert them.

But if, because of the profundity of their thoughts and pre- 56
cepts, Latin translators of Greek philosophers must produce an accomplished translation in a more exacting and closer manner than the translators of other secular writings, what will we think about translations of the sacred and divine Scriptures, where all the thoughts are sacred and divine, and wherein the entirety of all
human salvation seems to dwell and to be hidden? And although 57
this may be the case, nevertheless, distinguished translators of the sacred Scriptures seem to recoil from translating word for word (inasmuch as they thought such a translation shrouded and sometimes subverted the original meaning) to such a degree that in the middle of the sacred text they sometimes elaborate and at other
times employ unsuitable translations. In reading Jerome we clearly 58
see that he maintains this practice diligently and precisely in his translations of the books of Eusebius of Caesarea, both in the *Chronicle* and also in the *Church History*; and he himself indicates clearly and explicitly in many places in his own books that it
should be done this way. For in the preface of the above-mentioned 59
book, the *Chronicle*, he says the following:

> It is difficult for someone following another person's boundaries not to exceed them at some point, and it is hard to have what was said in another language preserve the same grace in translation. Something is signified by the proper meaning of one word: I do not have at my disposal a suitable translation;

> et dum quero implere sententiam, longo ambitu vix brevis vie spatia consumo. Accedunt yperbatorum anfractus, dissimilitudines casuum, varietas figurarum, ipsum postremo suum et, ut ita dicam, vernaculum dicendi genus: si ad verbum interpretor, absurde resonat; si ob necessitatem aliquid in ordine vel in sermone mutavero, videbor ab interpretis officio recessisse.

60 Et post multa ibidem ita scribit:

> Quod si cui non videtur lingue gratiam interpretatione mutari, Homerum ad verbum exprimat in Latinum. Plus aliquid dicam, eundem in sua lingua pro se verbis interpretetur: videbit ordinem ridiculum et poetam eloquentissimum vix loquentem.

Que quidem omnia cum in libro *De optimo genere interpretandi* ad suum propositum paulo latius et uberius commemorasset, statim in hunc modum subiungere non dubitavit:

> 61 Verum ne scriptorum nostrorum parva sit auctoritas (quanquam hoc tantum probare voluerim, me semper ab adolescentia non verba, sed sententias transtulisse), qualis super hoc genere ⟨praefatiuncula sit, in libro quo beati⟩ Antonii vita describitur, ipsius lectione cognosce. Ex alia enim in aliam linguam ad verbum expressa translatio, sensum operit et veluti leto gramine sata strangulat.

Et paulo post ita subdit:

> Dies me deficeret, si omnium qui non ad verbum interpre-
> 62 tati sunt, testimonia replicavero. Sufficit in presenti nomi-
> nasse Hilarium confessorem, qui *Homelias in Iob* et *In Psalmos*

> and while I seek to supply the meaning, I barely cover by a circuitous route the distance of a very short path. There are in addition the disjointedness of hyperbatons, the differences of cases, the variety of figures of speech, and finally the very idiom, so to speak, of the genre: if I translate word for word, it sounds preposterous; if out of necessity I change something in the order of the words or in the language, I will seem to be departing from the office of translator.[29]

And after much else, he writes in the same passage: 60

> But if it seems to someone that the beauty of language is not changed by translation, let him translate Homer into Latin word for word. I will add this as well: let him translate the same author into his own language for himself; he will see an absurd word order and the most eloquent of poets barely able to speak.[30]

When he had discussed all these points a little more fully and in more detail, in accord with his purpose in *On the Best Kind of Translating,* he did not hesitate at once to add the following:

> But in case the authority of our writings is too small (al- 61
> though I would wish only to prove only this: that from my youth I always translated not words but meanings) read and consider the short preface dealing with this kind of thing from the life of St. Anthony. For a translation squeezed word for word from one language into another buries the sense and strangles it as luxuriant grass strangles crops.[31]

A little later he adds the following:

> The day would be gone before I could recount all the testi-
> mony of those who have not translated word for word. For 62
> the moment it suffices to mention Hilary the Confessor, who translated many treatments of *Homilies on Job* and *Homilies on*

tractatus plurimos [ita interpretatus est, ut sensum, non verba sequeretur.] Nec hoc mirum in ceteris seculi aut ecclesie viris, cum Septuaginta interpretes et evangeliste atque apostoli idem in suis voluminibus fecerint. Legimus enim in Marco dicentem Dominum: *Ialda cumi,* statimque subiunctum est, 'Puella, tibi dico, "Surge,"' cum in Hebreo tantummodo sit 'Puella surge.' Sed ut id ipsum *emphaticoteron* faceret, ac sensum imitantis et interpretantis exprimeret, addidit: 'Tibi dico.'

63 Rursum in Mattheo, redditis a proditore Iuda triginta argenteis et empto ex eis agro figuli, scribitur: 'Tunc impletum est quod scriptum est per Hieremiam prophetam dicentem: "Et acceperunt triginta argenteos, precium appreciati quod appretiaverunt filii Israel: et dederunt eos in agrum figuli, sicut constituit mihi Dominus."' Hoc in Hieremia penitus non invenitur, sed in Zacharia, aliis multo verbis ac toto ordine discrepante.

64 Et ubi propria *Vulgate* editionis verba ad manifestam quandam tante et tam dissimilis discrepantie ostensionem posuit:

> Veniamus, inquit, ad illud eiusdem Zacharie testimonium, quod Ioannes sumit iuxta Hebraicam veritatem: 'Viderunt in quem compunxerunt,' pro quo in Septuaginta legimus ⟨*καὶ ἐπιβλέψονται πρὸς με, ἀνθ' ἐνωρχήσαντο*⟩, quod interpretati sunt Latini: 'Et aspicient in me, pro iis qui illuserunt vel insultaverunt.' Discrepat evangelista et Septuaginta, nostra quoque translatio, et tamen sermonis veritas spiritus unitate concordat.

the Psalms [in such a way that he followed the sense and did not translate word for word.][32] Nor is this astonishing in other secular writers and men of the Church, since the Seventy Translators and the evangelists and apostles did the same thing in their works. For in Mark [5:41] we read the Lord saying: *Ialda cumi* and immediately added to this is "Girl, I say to you: 'Rise,'" although in the Hebrew there is only "Girl, rise." But in order to make it more emphatic[33] and to communicate the sense of someone imitating and translating, he added: "I say to you."[34]

Again in Matthew [27:9], after the thirty pieces of silver are given back by the betrayer Judas and the potter's field has been bought with these, it is written: "Then was fulfilled what was written by Jeremiah the prophet when he said: 'And they received the thirty pieces of silver, the price which the sons of Israel paid: and they gave them for the potter's field, just as the Lord commanded me.'"[35] This is found nowhere in Jeremiah but in Zachariah and with far different words and in a completely different order.[36] 63

And after citing the very words of the Vulgate edition as clear evidence for so great and fundamental a divergence, he said: 64

Let us come to the testimony of this same Zachariah [12:10] which John understands according to the original Hebrew: "They will see whom they have pierced," for which we read in the Septuagint: ⟨"And they will look at me instead of those who danced among them,"⟩ which the Latins have translated: "And they will look at me instead of those who mocked or made sport."[37] The translations of the evangelist and of the Seventy, as well as our own translation, are divergent and yet the difference of the language is harmonized by the unity of the spirit.

65 In Mattheo quoque legimus Dominum predicentem Apostolis fugam, et hoc ipsum testimonio Zacharie confirmantem. Nam 'Scriptum est,' ait, 'Percutiam pastorem, et dispergentur oves.' At in Septuaginta et in Hebreo multo aliter est. Non enim ex persona Dei dicitur, sed ex prophete Deum patrem rogantis: 'Percute pastorem, et dispergentur oves.'

66 Sed quid pluribus exemplis opus est? Totum enim Vetus, ut dicitur, Testamentum a Septuaginta interpretibus in grecum eloquium conversum, partim additamentis, partim omissionibus, partim denique alienis interpretationibus ita referctum reperitur, ut horum omnium cumulus, si simul congereretur ita ut uno aspectu aspici viderique posset, profecto talium discrepantiarum numerus
67 pene incredibilis et quasi infinitus putaretur. Hanc tantam et tam ingentem varietatem antiqui doctores nostri evidentibus signis in codicibus suis per hunc modum notare consueverant. Nam que addita erant, signis quibusdam in stellarum modum factis, ad capita versuum notabant, et huiusmodi signa grece *asteriscos* vocabant. Ea vero que ommissa fuerant, ad capita eorundem versuum iacentibus virgulis quasi verubus signabant, que illi *obelos* vel cum dimi-
68 nutione *obeliscos* appellabant. Atque eandem ac multo maiorem inter alios celebratos Aquilam, Simachum et Theodotionem interpretes discrepantiam Origenis tempestate esse constabat. Que omnia cum ad manus illius prestantissimi viri ac grece et hebree lingue peritissimi pervenirent, novum quoddam et utile atque admirandum opus ad tollendam omnem, que ex multis tam diversis interpretationibus oriri videbatur, ambiguitatem ac contentionem
69 in hunc modum composuit. Nam cum lingue hebree virtutem ita mirabiliter didicisset, ut ea que a Iudeis hebraice legebantur, diligenter cognosceret, et qualia quoque essent ea que a diversis interpretibus traducta fuerant, plane et aperte intelligeret, per hunc, ut

In Matthew [26:31] also we read the Lord predicting the flight of the Apostle and confirming this with the testimony of Zachariah. For he says, "It is written, I will strike the shepherd and the sheep will be scattered." But in the Septuagint and in the Hebrew it is much different. For it is said not by God but by the prophet asking God the Father: "Strike the shepherd, and the sheep will scatter."[38] 65

But why is there need for more examples? The whole Old Testament, as it is called, as translated by the Seventy into Greek is 66
found to be so full of additions, omissions, and unsuitable translations that the accumulation of them all, if it could be gathered together in such a way as to be seen with one look, would be reckoned to be an almost incredible and practically infinite number of differences. Our ancient Doctors had been accustomed to indicate this 67
extraordinarily large degree of variation in their copies with clear signs in the following way. They would note what had been added at the heads of verses with certain signs that were made in the shape of stars, and they called signs of this kind "asterisks" in Greek. But those things that had been omitted they would indicate at the heads of the same verses with small horizontal rods like stakes that they called *obeli* or in the diminutive *obelisci*. [39] And it 68
was agreed that there was the same and even greater divergence among the famous translators Aquila, Symmachus, and Theodotion than at the time of Origen. When all of these differences came into the hands of this extraordinary man, an expert in both Greek and Hebrew, he constructed a new and useful and wonderful work for removing all the ambiguity and debate that seemed to emerge from many diverse translations in the following way. When 69
Origen had miraculously acquired so excellent a command of Hebrew that he knew in detail those things which were read by Jews in Hebrew and he clearly and plainly understood also the nature of the things that had been translated by the different translators,

diximus, modum singulare opus composuisse et compilasse tradi-
70 tur. Per singulas quippe columnellas separatim opus uniuscuiusque interpretis ita accurate descripsit, ut primo omnium ipsa hebrea verba hebraicis scripta litteris poneret; hebreis deinde caracteribus e regione greca verba signaret; tertio Aquile editionem subiungeret; quarto Simachi, quinto Septuaginta interpretum, sexto Theodotionis interpretationem collocaret, et ob hanc novi et admirabilis operis compositionem huiusmodi exemplaria *Exapla,* id est sexim-
71 plici ordine scripta, vocavit. Editiones autem, quas et Nicopoli et in Hierico et alibi sine certis auctoribus se invenisse testatur, sextam ac septimam editionem nominavit. Missos facimus duos excellentes Sacrarum Scripturarum de hebreo in caldeum idioma interpretes, quorum alter Unchelos, Calonici filius ac Titi nepos,
72 nescio quorum proselitus, appellatus est. Hic totum Moysi Pentatheucum ex hebreo in caldeum ita convertit, ut utrobique ob admirabilem quandam interpretationis sue excellentiam in summa, quin immo in tanta veneratione apud Hebreos Caldeosque habeatur, ut pro sacro ac divino textu consensu omnium existimetur, atque *Targum* caldaice nuncupatur. Alter vero, nomine Ionathan ben Oziel, digna superioris traductoris vestigia post trecentos circiter annos imitatus, reliqua omnia que ad Vetus Testamentum pertinebant, eodem modo pariterque convertit. Et tamen plerunque sensum secuti, a verbis interdum recessisse videntur.

73 Et ad idoneos quoruncunque tam profanorum quam sacrorum auctorum interpretes parumper redeamus, si prius unico ex multis memoratu dignis et quidem celebrate sacreque auctoritatis exemplo id quod dictum est, paulo dilucidius et evidentius ostenderimus. In illa nanque certa et decantata de expresso Messie adventu *Geneseos* sententia, in qua latinis litteris in hunc modum scriptum reperitur: 'Non auferetur sceptrum de Iuda, et dux de femore eius,

it is handed down that he compiled and created a unique work, as
I said, in the following way. In separate columns he wrote down 70
the work of each translator so precisely that, first of all, he placed the Hebrew words themselves written with Hebrew letters; then beside them Greek words with Hebrew letters;[40] third he added the edition of Aquila; fourth the edition of Symmachus, fifth the edition of the Seventy Translators, and sixth he placed the translation of Theodotion. Because of the organization of this new and admirable work, he called his manuscript the *Hexapla*, that is,
written in a sixfold design.[41] However, the editions which he indi- 71
cates he found at Nicopolis and in Jericho and elsewhere, without definite authorship, he called the sixth and seventh edition. We pass over two excellent translators of the Sacred Scripture from Hebrew into Aramaic. One of these men was called Onkelos, the son of Calonicus and the grandson of Titus, a convert to Judaism,
but I do not know by whom.[42] Onkelos translated the whole Pen- 72
tateuch of Moses from Hebrew into Aramaic in such a way that both the Hebrews and the Chaldeans, because of the excellence of his translation, considered it in the highest rank or rather, by agreement of all, as a sacred and divine text. It is called the *Targum* in Aramaic. But the other, a certain Jonathan ben Uzziel, following in the worthy footsteps of the previous translator about three hundred years later, translated all the remaining material which pertained to the Old Testament in the same way and with the same accomplishment. Nevertheless, while generally following the sense, they seem sometimes to have departed from the words.[43]

Let us return briefly to good translators of both profane and 73
sacred authors, if we can first prove more lucidly and visibly what has been said with a unique example, selected from many that are worthy of mention, an example that has renowned and sacred authority. In that precise and repeated idea from Genesis about the manifest arrival of the Messiah is found the following written in Latin letters: "The scepter will not be carried from Judah and the

donec veniat qui mittendus est, et ipse erit expectatio gentium,' in
Hebreo id quod ad propositum nostrum spectat, sic scribitur:
74 'Donec veniat scilo.' Quod commemoratus Unchelos evidenter
Messiam interpretatus est; licet verbum *scilo*, in textu sacro hebraice positum, a *scigla*, quod quidem secundinam significat, deri-
vatum atque infantem secundina involutum et inde denominatum
75 fuisse videatur. Nullam ad verbum factam traductionem laudabi-
lem ac perfectam esse posse quibusdam rationibus plurimisque
etiam prestantissimorum virorum auctoritatibus plane et aperte
superius probasse atque confirmasse meminimus, ac magnam quoque inter poetarum, oratorum ac historicorum traductores et inter
philosophorum ac theologorum interpretes diversitatem esse fie-
76 rique oportere manifestissime demostravimus. Nam illis primis
sive poetarum sive oratorum sive historicorum, ut ita dixerim,
conversoribus non nunquam elegantie et ornatus gratia arida
ieiunaque et exilia amplificare, et obscura pretermittere, et inter-
77 dum pro sua voluntate dilucidius interpretari licet. Fidi vero philosophorum theologorumque interpretes non ita pro suo arbitrio
vagi ac liberi, quasi per latos et apertos campos hinc inde discur-
rere et pervagari debent, sed arctioribus quibusdam interpretandi
legibus pressi et quasi certis cancellis astricti; modestius graviusque
iuxta severam quandam professionis sue normam incedere progre-
dique coguntur; nec ab incepto convertendi proposito longius eva-
gantes, nec primis etiam auctoribus omnino ac penitus ad verbum
adherentes, sed medium et tutum, ut dicitur, iter tenentes, inter
interpretandum ita se mediocriter habere decet, ut neutram in
78 partem declinare ac propendere videantur. Hoc enim ab eis, si diligenter et accurate quale et quantum sit hoc ipsum interpretandi
onus consideraverint, divina presertim omissis philosophis—

leader from his thigh, until he who must be sent comes, and he will be the nations' long awaited one."[44] As for what is relevant for our purposes, in Hebrew the following is written: "Until Shilo
comes." The above-mentioned Onkelos clearly interpreted this as 74
the Messiah, although the word *Shilo*, which occurs in the sacred text in Hebrew, seems to have been derived from *scigla*, which means afterbirth, and seems to have indicated an infant covered
with afterbirth, and it seems to have been named from this.[45] Re- 75
call that I proved and confirmed clearly and openly above, using the formidable reasoning and the authority of the most illustrious men, that no translation made word for word can be praiseworthy and complete, and I demonstrated very clearly that there is and ought to be a great difference between the translators of poets, orators, and historians [on the one hand], and the translators of
philosophers and theologians [on the other]. For it is permitted to 76
the first group of adapters,[46] so to speak, of poets or orators or historians sometimes to expand on dry, jejune, and meager material in the interest of elegance and decoration, to omit obscure points, and occasionally to translate more clearly according to their
inclination. But faithful translators of philosophers and theolo- 77
gians are not free to wander at will, as though obliged to run hither and thither and wander over wide and open fields, but are bound by the stricter laws of translating; and as it were restrained behind fixed bars, they are compelled to walk and proceed with greater reserve and sobriety, according to the exacting standard of their profession; neither wandering too far from the work taken for translation nor clinging entirely and completely word for word to the original authors, but hewing to a middle and safe way, as the saying goes,[47] it is fitting that in translating they stick to the
mean and do not incline to or favor either method. The divine 78
authority of the sacred Scriptures — leaving aside philosophers —

hoc inquam ab eis — Sacrarum Scripturarum auctoritas in primis non iniuria exigere et postulare existimabitur.

79 Quod si forte Septuaginta interpretes in sua illa tam celebri et tam famosa interpretatione, et apostoli quoque et evangeliste allegationibus suis aliter fecisse ac servasse comperiuntur, ob singularem quandam illorum tam prestantissimorum et tam excellentissimorum virorum auctoritatem — divinitus, ut ab idoneis auctoribus scribitur, concessam — id duntaxat talibus viris licuisse iure ex eo autumatur et creditur, quod divina sacrarum Scripturarum mysteria illis celitus innotuisse putentur, qua quidem abstrusarum rerum revelatione illustrati, ita interpretari posse videbantur, ut primos scriptores divinitus intellexisse et enuntiasse perceperant.
80 Atque ob hanc solam causam a recto idoneorum fidorumque interpretum officio tam procul recessisse non immerito excusantur, quanquam impiis quibusdam doctisque hominibus, utpote Celso, Porphirio ac Iuliano, manifestas quasdam calumniandi scripturas nostras ansas usque adeo prebuerunt, ut omnes tres commemorati auctores scriptis suis in vehementes Scripturarum nostrarum calumnias multum admodum prolaberentur.

81 Ego enim de cunctis aliarum rerum in alia idiomata interpretibus ita sentio, ut cuncta queque aliorum auctorum scripta, sacris
Litteris duntaxat exceptis, pro libero voluntatis suorum interpretum arbitrio, primorum scriptorum sensu tantummodo servato,
diversimode tamen, ut dictum est, traduci possint et valeant. Ceterum Sacra Scriptura ob divinam eius in omnibus auctoritatem,
que nec fallit nec fallitur, solemnem quandam et accuratam, gra-
vem atque affectatam interpretationem vel maxime et in primis
82 exigere et postulare videtur. Non tamen ita ad verbum fiat conversio, ut exinde declarationis et intelligentie gratia plerunque non

will especially be supposed to exact and demand this very procedure from them, if they weigh with care and precision the nature and scope of the translator's burden.

If by chance the Seventy Translators in their distinguished and 79
famous translation, and the apostles and the evangelists in their writings are found to have acted differently and observed a different policy, this is justly thought and maintained to have been permitted only to such men through their unique authority—divinely licensed, as is written by good authors—because the divine mysteries of the Sacred Scriptures are thought to have been known to them from a heavenly source. Enlightened by the revelation of hidden matters, they were seen to have been able to translate in the same way as they perceived the original authors to have understood and expressed it by divine inspiration. For this reason alone, 80
they are justly excused for having departed so far from the proper duty of good and faithful translators, although they provided to impious and learned men, like Celsus, Porphyry, and Julian, clear opportunities for traducing our Scriptures to such a degree that in their writings all three aforementioned writers were led on to fierce slander of our Scriptures.

For I believe the following about all translators of material into 81
other languages: that all the writings of other authors, leaving aside the Sacred Letters only, can be translated according to the unfettered discretion of the will of translators in a variety of ways, as has been said, provided only that the sense of the original authors is preserved. But the sacred Scripture, because of its divine authority in all things, which neither deceives nor is deceived, seems especially and above all to demand and require a solemn,
exact, serious, and studied translation. Let the translation not, 82
however, be word for word to the extent that it may not depart from the original in the interests of clarity and understanding. Nor

recedat; nec ita vaga ac lasciva sit oportet, ut procul abesse videatur atque nunquam cum nova addat, tum vetera pretermittat; nec plura alia diversimode, ut libuerit, interpretetur et exprimat, quemadmodum Hieronymus noster, optimus ae gravissimus interpres, hanc tam astrictam et tam severam ac tam accuratam de interpretandis Sacris Scripturis legem plerunque expressisse ac servasse
83 videtur. In hac enim sua universali et pernecessaria ac utilissima utriusque Testamenti, hebrei et greci, in latinam linguam traductione quandoque ita a verbo recedit, ut non solum sacer sensus ad unguem servetur, sed etiam dilucidior reddatur ac denique ornatior et illustrior habeatur.

84 Quapropter cum primo de cunctorum scriptorum obtrectatoribus ac secundo de diversis sacrarum Scripturarum interpretibus, et tertio et quarto de plurimis utriusque Psalterii iampridem conversi differentiis ac diversitatibus, atque postremo de recta interpretatione, et quemadmodum secularium auctorum omnium traductiones a sacris divinisque differre distareque videantur, pro
85 modulo nostro hactenus disseruerimus, reliquum est ut in calce totius voluminis paucis expediamus cur ecclesia Romana in orationibus suis privatis et publicis Septuaginta Psalterii interpretationem in diuturno et universali usu alteri Hieronymi de hebraica veritate traductioni usque adeo pretulisse videtur, ut altera quotidiano immo continuo et perpetuo usu approbetur, altera vero absque ulla consuetudine repudiata adeo torpescat, ut nunquam
86 fere vel raro in lucem prodeat, presertim cum in priori illa ac

should the translation be so wayward and self-indulgent that it seems to stray far off course, and it should never either add new material or neglect the old; nor should it contain too many inconsistencies. Here Jerome is our model, the best and most serious translator, who seems to have generally practiced and maintained this strict, severe, and exact law when translating the Sacred Scriptures. For whenever he departs from the letter of the text in his 83
universal, essential, and extraordinarily useful translation into Latin of each Testament, both the Hebrew and the Greek, he does so in such a way that not only is the sacred sense precisely preserved, but it is rendered clearer and in the end is thought to be more elegant and brilliant.

Therefore, since in the first book I have discussed to the limited 84
degree that I can the critics of all authors, and in the second book the different translators of the Sacred Scriptures, and in the third and fourth books the many differences and divergences between both of the old translations of the Psalter, and in the last book correct translation, and how the translations of all secular authors
seem to differ and diverge from sacred and divine translations, it 85
remains, at the end of this entire volume, that we explain why the Roman Church in its private and public discourses seems to prefer the Septuagint translation of the Psalter in its daily and universal use to the other translation of the Psalter by Jerome, one based on the original Hebrew. The preference is carried so far that one translation is favored through its daily and uninterrupted use and the other lies idle and unused, so completely spurned that it almost never or rarely sees the light, even though in the earlier 86

vetustiori multa addita, plurima ommissa, non nulla aliter conversa, certa quemadmodum supra tertio et quarto libro singillatim ostendimus; in altera vero vel nihil, vel pauca huiusmodi reperiantur. Mihi huius tam admirabilis et tam abstruse rei causas paulo diligentius et accuratius mecum ipse diutius perscrutanti ac crebrius animadvertenti, quatuor duntaxat fieri potuisse non iniuria videntur.

87 Una occurrebat quia inter omnes sacrarum Scripturarum traductiones, ut est communis omnium christianorum populorum ac universalis cunctorum pene eruditissimorum virorum opinio, prima fuerat, que ante Christi adventum in medium lucemque prodierat.

Secunda quia ab Evangelistis et ab Apostolis, in iis tamen in quibus ab hebraica veritate non discrepabat, usurpata cernebatur.

88 Tertia quia, ad communem ac vulgatam omnium christianarum gentium opinionem, [quod] singillatim quique ab aliis interpretandi collegis diversis cellulis et habitaculis separati, ita mirabiliter interpretati fuisse creduntur, ut una sola, et non plures, interpretatio videretur. Unde cum hoc humanis viribus fieri et provenire non potuerit, a Spiritu Sancto facta et celebrata fuisse creditur.

89 Ultimo propter carminum sonoritatem versuumque concinnitatem. Illa enim Septuaginta interpretatio carmina sonantiora ac concinniora et ecclesiasticis cantibus ac synphoniis accommodatiora quam altera Hieronymi consensu omnium continere videtur.

translation many things are added, many things omitted, and much is translated unsuitably, just as we showed certain examples above in detail in the third and fourth books. But in the other translation nothing or few things of this kind are found. As I investigate the causes of this surprising and complex matter a little more diligently and exactly and ponder it at greater length, there reasonably seem to be only four ways this situation could have arisen.

One explanation that came to me was that, among all the trans- 87
lations of the sacred Scriptures, the Septuagint had come first, as is the common opinion of all Christians and the universal opinion of almost all learned men, since it had been published before the advent of Christ.

The second explanation was that it was seen to be used by the evangelists and the apostles in those passages where it did not depart from the original Hebrew.

The third explanation, according to the common and wide- 88
spread opinion of all Christian people, was that each man, separated from his other colleagues engaged in translation in different cells and living quarters, is believed to have translated so miraculously that one translation alone appeared and not several. Therefore since this could not have happened as a result of human endeavor, it is believed that this had been done and made renowned through the Holy Spirit.

The last explanation was based on the sonority of the poems 89
and the elegance of the verses. For the translation of the Seventy seems by common consent to contain more sonorous and elegant poems and seems more suitable to Church hymns and choirs than the second translation of Jerome.

90 Atque hec habuimus, gloriosissime princeps, ut, ad maiestatem tuam tandem aliquando quasi longo quodam postliminio ex longa peregrinatione ad patriam reversi, in hoc adversus obtrectatores nostros *Apologetico* pro certa quadam sacrarum Scripturarum latinarum catoliceque veritatis defensione diligenter accurateque ad perpetuam et eternam nominis tui gloriam congereremus.

EXPLICIT LIBER QVINTVS ET VLTIMVS
APOLOGETICVS IANNOZII MANETTI
AD ALFONSVM CLARISSIMVM ARAGONVM
ET SICILIE REGEM FELICITER

I have accomplished this, most glorious prince, namely that, 90
upon returning at long last to Your Majesty, as if reestablishing my rights upon returning to my homeland after an extended journey abroad,[48] I have diligently and carefully assembled, in this *Apologeticus* against my detractors, this material to be a sure defense of the sacred Scriptures in Latin and of Catholic truth for the perpetual and eternal glory of your name.

THE FIFTH AND LAST BOOK OF
THE APOLOGY OF GIANNOZZO MANETTI,
DEDICATED TO ALFONSO,
THE FAMOUS KING OF ARAGON AND SICILY,
ENDS WITH GOOD FORTUNE

Note on the Text

For Giannozzo Manetti's *Apologeticus,* we have followed for the most part Alfonso De Petris' excellent edition. He explains his editorial decisions in his introduction (xliii–xlv). The three chief manuscripts are:

A Vatican City, Biblioteca Apostolica Vaticana, MS Pal. lat. 40
B _____ MS Pal. lat. 41
C _____ MS Urb. lat. 5

A is the autograph copy of Giannozzo Manetti. It is a working copy that has corrections by Manetti himself, his son, Agnolo Manetti, and a third scribe. *B* is the dedication copy for King Alfonso and is written by Pietro Ursuleo da Capua. Both manuscripts are now digitized and can be accessed at the Vatican Library's site: vaticanlibrary.va. Each of these Palatine manuscripts contains a preface, tricolumnar Psalter, and the *Apologeticus.*

C functions somewhat like Manetti's *Selected Works.* It was written, sometime after the mid-1460s, for Federico da Montefeltro, the duke of Urbino, by an inaccurate scribe who worked for Vespasiano da Bisticci. De Petris considers it an inferior copy. The most detailed description can be found in *Codices Urbinates Latini,* ed. Cosimo Stornaiolo (Rome: Typis Vaticanis, 1902), 8–9. Additional information is presented in De Petris' edition (xlix–li) and in the introduction to Elizabeth R. Leonard's edition of Manetti's *De dignitate et excellentia hominis* (Padua: Antenor, 1975). Notably, Urb. lat. 5 contains only Manetti's translation of the Psalter, without the versions by Jerome.

There is no edition of Manetti's translation of the Psalms. There is, however, a Latin edition of the preface (based on *B*) in Paul Botley's *Latin Translation in the Renaissance,* 179–81, where he lists further editions of the Psalter. Fuller manuscript information on Manetti's translation of the Psalms can be found in Christoph Dröge's *Giannozzo Manetti als Denker und Hebraist.*

The most significant changes we make to the text are at 2.22, where De Petris prints *Ad hec Eleazarus rescripsit,* and at 2.24, where he offers *Multa deinde hac . . . subiungit,* as if they were Manetti's words. These words actually derive from George of Trebizond's translation of Eusebius' *De praeparatione evangelica* (*Preparation for the Gospel*), not identified as such by De Petris. We have formatted them accordingly as part of the long citations from George's translation. As this version differs materially from the Greek text, we have cited it according to the book, chapter, and section divisions established in John Monfasani's forthcoming edition in the series "Edizione Nazionale delle Traduzioni dei testi Greci in età umanistica e rinascimentale." (We thank Professor Monfasani for verifying the citations from his edition.) We have also cited two other versions of Eusebius: (1) the only available English translation, E. H. Gifford's *Preparation for the Gospel,* although it is antiquated; (2) the standard contemporary scholarly version of Eusebius' work, in the *Sources chrétiennes* series. For invaluable information on the forty-seven manuscripts and sixteen printed editions of George's version of Eusebius, see John Monfasani, *Collectanea Trapezuntiana: Texts, Documents, and Bibliographies of George of Trebizond* (Binghamton: MRTS, 1984), 721–26.

We note as well the following changes from De Petris' edition:

1.13. *e contrario* in place of e *contra*

1.32. *potius quam* should be deleted

2.18. *nec a poetis* emended from *nec a portis*

2.21. *re gesta* corrected from *regesta*

2.22. *quantam* emended from *quam nam*

2.25. *inquinanti* corrected from *inquinantis*

2.38. *doctorum* corrected from *docti*

2.52. *constat* corrected from *constati*

2.66. *solis* emended from *soli*

3.18. *humilitate* corrected from *humiliata*

3.19. delete: *In eodem 'Voluntarie sacrificabo tua disperde illos,' abundant 'et'* (typesetting error)

3.36. ⟨*non*⟩ added before *declinavi* (cf. Ps. 119)

3.54. *principum* corrected from *principium*

3.57. *post antepenultimam deficit 'ipsa'* emended from *post penultimam deficit 'ipse'*

3.57. *loquar* emended to *loquebar*

3.58. ⟨*pen*⟩*ultima* corrected from *ultima*

3.58. *suas* corrected from *sua*

4.4. *exaltatur* corrected from *exaltator*

4.9. *tripudians* emended from *tripudiantis*

4.14. *cooperiantur* corrected from *cooperiuntur*

4.15. *spectati* corrected from *spetiei*

4.17. *surgentur* corrected from *sugentur*

4.28. *cenomia* corrected from *cynomia*

4.39. *poterunt* corrected from *potuerunt*

4.68. ⟨EXPLICIT LIBER QUARTUS⟩ has been added at the end

5.7. ⟨*nati sunt*⟩ added after *hominibus*

5.11. *nominis tui* corrected from *nominis tuis*

5.31. *si* emended to *nisi*

5.31. *nobilitate* emended to *nobilis*

5.55. *nobilitate* emended to *nobilis*

5.55. *pervertere* corrected from *pervetere*

5.61–64. De Petris sometimes silently corrects Manetti's quotations from Jerome to harmonize them with modern editions of the *De optimo genere interpretandi*. We restore here Manetti's readings (verified from online manuscript images), but fill in a few lacunae in angle brackets ⟨/⟩ from Bartelink's edition where the passage would otherwise be untranslatable.

5.61. *non ad verbum* Manetti: *non ad sensum* De Petris: *ad sensum* Jerome

5.62. *ita interpretatus est . . . sequeretur*: Manetti paraphrases Jerome

5.63. *discrepante* corrected from *discrepans*, following Jerome

5.64. *sumit* B: *summit* A

5.64. *nostra quoque* A: *nostraque* B

So as not to multiply reference systems without necessity, we have preserved De Petris' numbering of sections within Books I, II, and V but have made our own decisions about paragraph divisions. (De Petris gives no section numbering in Books III and IV.) For the Notes to the Translation, we have provided references to English translations of the Latin texts referred to wherever possible or, failing that, translations into other modern languages. We are much indebted to De Petris' edition, to which we direct the readers who want fuller information on sources, possible sources, parallels, and secondary literature than we have been able to include here. We are indebted as well to Stefano Baldassarri's notes to his abridged translation of Book V.

Notes to the Translation

ABBREVIATIONS

Bruni, *DRI*	Leonardo Bruni, *De recta interpretatione,* in Leonardo Bruni, *Sulla perfetta traduzione,* ed. P. Viti (Naples: Liguori, 2004), 73–123. English version in *The Humanism of Leonardo Bruni,* ed. G. Griffiths, J. Hankins, and D. Thompson (Binghamton, NY: MRTS, 1987), 217–29.
CSEL	*Corpus Scriptorum Ecclesiasticorum Latinorum* (Vienna: Verlag der Österreichischen Akademie der Wissenschaften, 1866–).
DBI	*Dizionario biografico degli italiani* (Rome: Fondazione Treccani, 1960–).
Eusebius, *Ev. Praep.*	Eusèbe de Césarée, *La Préparation Evangélique,* Sources Chrétiennes, 9 vols., trans. J. Sirinilli et al. (Paris: Cerf, 1974–91). Latin text with French translation. English version: *Preparation for the Gospel,* trans. E. H. Gifford (Oxford: Oxford University Press, 1903).
Jerome, *DOGI*	Jerome, *Liber de optimo genere interpretandi (Epistula 57),* edited with a commentary by G. J. M. Bartelink (Leiden: Brill, 1980). English translation: *On the Best Kind of Translating,* trans. Kathleen Davis, in *The Translation Studies Reader,* ed. Lawrence Venuti, 3rd ed. (London: Routledge, 2012), 24–34.
PL	*Patrologiae cursus completus series latina,* ed. J. P. Migne, 221 vols. (Paris: Migne, 1844–64).

Trebizond, *EEP* — Eusebius Caesariensis, *De evangelica praeparatione*, trans. George of Trebizond, ed. John Monfasani (forthcoming in the series "Edizione Nazionale delle Traduzioni dei testi Greci in età umanistica e rinascimentale"). See also Note on the Text.

Vulgata — *Biblia sacra iuxta Vulgatam versionem*, ed. R. Weber and R. Gryson, 5th ed. (Stuttgart: Deutsche Bibelgesellschaft, 2007).

BOOK I

1. The rubric at the beginning of the work in the manuscripts is as follows: PREFATIO IANNOZII MANETTI AD ALFONSVM, CLARISSIMVM ARAGONVM REGEM, IN V LIBROS ADVERSVS SVE NOVE PSALTERII TRADVCTIONIS OBTRECTATORES APOLOGETICOS, INCIPIT FELICITER (THE PREFACE OF GIANNOZZO MANETTI TO ALFONSO, DISTINGUISHED KING OF THE ARAGONESE, TO THE FIVE BOOKS DEFENDING AGAINST THE CRITICS OF HIS NEW TRANSLATION OF THE PSALTER, BEGINS HAPPILY). As De Petris (lxi–lxiii) notes, the presence of this rubric is puzzling, since the work contains no separate preface; Manetti's prose continues without break to the end of Book I. It is possible, as De Petris suggests, that a break was intended at the end of §21, but there is no indication of it in the manuscripts (and compare also 5.19, a passage that must also weigh against this suggestion). The scribe of C seems to have recognized the problem, since he replaces PREFATIO with LIBER, deletes IN V LIBROS, and writes, in place of FELICITER, the words LIBER PRIMUS DE DIVERSIS CUNCTORUM AUCTORUM OBTRECTATORIBUS (BOOK ONE ON THE VARIOUS CRITICS OF ALL AUTHORS). De Petris concludes that the puzzling rubric is evidence that Manetti was unable to make up his mind whether to write a separate preface or not.

2. A reference to schoolmasters; the anecdote is from Plutarch, *Sayings of Kings and Commanders*, in Plutarch's *Moralia* 175c.

3. Luscius Lanuvinus was an older playwright to whose criticisms Terence replied in some of his prologues. The first point appears to be a

misunderstanding of *Self-Tormentor,* Pr 17, the charge that Terence "contaminated many Greek plays," i.e., that he combined several Greek models in a single comic plot. The charge of turning good Greek plays into bad Latin ones is quoted at *Eunuch* Pr 8, that about diction and matter at *Phormio* Pr 5.

4. References to the first four critics derive from Donatus' *Life of Vergil,* 43–44. A Latin text with English translation can be found in *The Virgilian Tradition,* ed. Michael Putnam and Jan Ziolkowski (New Haven: Yale University Press, 2008), 181–99. On Evangelus, see Macrobius, *Saturnalia* 1.24.21, and on Cornutus, see Aulus Gellius, 2.6.1–6. These two passages are reproduced in *The Virgilian Tradition,* 640 and 65–66, respectively.

5. Vergil, *Eclogues* 6.75–6. Manetti has selected this Vergilian quotation, along with the six following ones, from Aulus Gellius, 2.6.1.

6. Vergil, *Georgics* 3.4–5; Aulus Gellius, 2.6.3.

7. Vergil, *Georgics* 4.479, *Aeneid* 6.438; Aulus Gellius, 2.6.13–14.

8. Vergil, *Aeneid* 10.314; Aulus Gellius, 2.6.4.

9. Vergil, *Aeneid* 8.187–88; Aulus Gellius, 5.8.1.

10. Vergil, *Aeneid* 6.278–79.

11. Vergil, *Aeneid* 6.14–15; Aulus Gellius, 7.6.1.

12. Donatus, *Life of Vergil* §46, in Putnam and Ziolkowski, *The Virgilian Tradition,* 186 (Latin), 194 (English translation).

13. Cicero criticizes Hortensius for neglecting his art after his consulship and failing to change his style to fit the persona of a senior statesman (*Brutus* 320 and 325–26); Hortensius criticized Cicero for resorting to demagoguery and inciting envy of the upper class (*Against Verres* 2.1.151) and for propounding riddles (for example, in his defense of Verres, since he offered only a very brief summation of the case before calling witnesses: Quintilian, *Institutes* 6.3.98). Cicero responds to Atticist criticism of his style as too lush in *Brutus* and *Orator.*

14. Cicero, *On Ends* 1.1.

15. Cicero, *On the Laws* 1.5.

16. Manetti perhaps has in mind the strictures on mythologizing at Thucydides 1.21.1, albeit Herodotus is not mentioned by name.

17. Aulus Gellius, 10.26, Title and 1.

18. See Asinius Pollio cited in Quintilian, *Institutes* 1.5.56 and 8.1.3.

19. Diogenes Laertius, 5.11.

20. Diogenes Laertius, 2.109.

21. Aulus Gellius, 12.2.1–2.

22. Aulus Gellius, 10.12.1–7.

23. Jerome, "The Apology Against the Books of Rufinus," in *Saint Jerome, Dogmatic and Polemical Works,* trans. J. Hritzu (Washington: Catholic University of America Press, 1965), 146.

24. Jerome, *Praefatio . . . in libro Iosue,* in *Vulgata,* 285.

25. Jerome, *Praefatio . . . in librum Psalmorum,* in *Vulgata,* 768.

26. For an English translation, see *The Correspondence (394–419) between Jerome and Augustine of Hippo,* trans. Caroline White (Lewiston: Edwin Mellon Press, 1990). The Latin text can be found with French translation in *Lettres croisées de Jérôme et Augustin,* trans. Carole Fry (Paris: Les belles lettres, 2010).

27. On Francis of Meyronnes (ca. 1288–1328), the now little-known medieval Franciscan theologian, see William Duba's article in *The Encyclopedia of Medieval Philosophy* (Dordrecht: Springer, 2011), 1:364–66. In 1455, Meyronnes' name appeared on a list of authors that King Alfonso's chief librarian was to purchase. See Alan Ryder, *Alfonso the Magnanimous* (Oxford: Oxford University Press, 1990), 320.

28. See n. 12 above.

29. Most of these names derive from the doxography at *Metaphysics* 1.3–5. Anaximander is named later (1069b 22). Aristotle polemicizes against Melissus (and Parmenides) at *Physics* 1.2. He does not mention the philosopher Archelaus by name; he may be alluded to at *On the Soul* 404a 26 (so John Philoponus *ad loc.*).

30. For Chaerephon's consultation of the oracle of Apollo at Delphi and the famous response that no one was wiser than Socrates, see Plato, *Apology* 21a. The Socratic paradox, "No one willingly does wrong," is criticized at *Magna Moralia* 1187a5 ff.

31. See below.

32. Aristotle, *Nicomachean Ethics* 1.4, a text Manetti had translated.

33. Perhaps a reference to *Against the Jews and the Gentiles,* planned as a treatise of twenty books but never completed; see above, xvii.

34. See §26.

35. Elijah's revival of the widow's son is narrated at 1 Kings 17:17–23; for Amittai as Jonah's father, see Jonah 1:1.

36. Malachi means "messenger" (*angelos* in Greek, borrowed into Latin as *angelus*).

37. *Divrei ha-Yamim* is the Latinization of the Hebrew term for Chronicles and means *Words of the Days* (*verba dierum*).

38. Manetti elaborates on this point at 5.25–28.

39. Rabbi Salomon is more familiarly known as Rashi (1040–1105 CE), the medieval biblical commentator. He composed a *Commentary on the Psalms,* ed. and trans. Mayer Gruber (Leiden: Brill, 2004).

40. The implicit point of comparison is Cicero's *On Ends* (*De finibus bonorum et malorum*), where such a debate is, in fact, conducted among a variety of speakers.

41. Jerome, *Praefatio . . . in librum Psalmorum,* in *Vulgata,* 768.

42. Jerome, *To Paulinus (Letter 53),* trans. W. H. Fremantle (Grand Rapids: Eerdmans, 1996), 94–106; Latin text in *CSEL* 54, 442–65.

43. Psalm 119. On Psalm titles, see *The Book of Psalms: Composition and Reception,* ed. Peter Flint and Patrick Miller (Leiden: Brill, 2005).

44. Or: "on various occasions."

45. See Eusebius, *Ev. Praep.* 9.6 (trans. Gifford, 175) = Trebizond, *EEP* 9.3.12–14.

46. Eusebius is referring to the Neo-Pythagorean philosopher Numenius (mid-second century CE); see *Ev. Praep.* 9.6.9, 11.10.14, citing Clement of Alexandria, *Stromateis* 1.22.150 (fragment 8 in Des Places' edition of Numenius fragments).

BOOK II

1. Arrian, *History of Alexander,* Pref. 1; see also Eusebius, *Historia Ecclesiastica* 7.32.

2. On Manetti's evolving views on the creator of the Septuagint, see Smith and O'Connor, *Building the Kingdom,* 97.

3. The story of the creation of the library of Alexandria and the origins of the Septuagint translation is ultimately dependent on the *Letter of Aristeas* (or the *Letter to Philocrates*), which survives in over twenty Greek manuscripts; it was translated into Latin before 1403 and was well known in Florence after that date. See R. Weiss, *Medieval and Renaissance Greek* (Padua, 1977), 244–45 n. 117, 254, 277. Manetti could have easily known the original letter in this Latin translation or the later one of Mattia Palmieri (see Book V, n. 25, below), but here he appears to follow the extracts in Eusebius, *Ev. Praep.* 8.2–5, 8.9, 9.38, 13.12, according to De Petris; for further details on Manetti's sources, see De Petris' elaborate *apparatus fontium* to §§1–11 on 28–31.

4. Eusebius, *Ev. Praep.* 8.1.6–8.2.3 (trans. Gifford, 348) = Trebizond, *EEP* 8.1.5–10.

5. Aulus Gellius, 7.17.1.

6. Aulus Gellius, 7.17.2–3.

7. Eusebius, *Ev. Praep.* 8.3.1–4 (trans. Gifford, 351) = Trebizond, *EEP* 8.1.12–15.

8. Eusebius, *Ev. Praep.* 8.4 (trans. Gifford, 352–54) = Trebizond, *EEP* 8.1.18–26.

9. The connection between the Septuagint and the Pisistratan redaction of Homer may have been suggested by Josephus, *Against Apion* 1.2.12.

10. Taking *rhapsodia* from *rhapto* (sew together) and *aoide* (song).

11. Compare §28 above.

12. Manetti's source for the Pisistratan edition of Homer must have been the *Scholia on Dionysius Thrax*, ed. A. Hilgard (1901), in *Grammatici Graeci*, ed. G. Uhlig (Leipzig: Teubner, 1883–1901), 3.29.17–3.30.17 (see F. A. Wolf, *Prolegomena to Homer*, ed. A. Grafton, G. W. Most, and J. E. G. Zetzel [Princeton, 1985], 140n), though how he came by this knowledge is difficult to say.

13. Cicero, *On the Orator* 3.34.137

14. See Diogenes Laertius, 1.57.

15. See Jerome, *Commentary on Daniel*, trans. G. L. Archer (Grand Rapids: Baker, 1958), 120–21.

16. I.e., both the translation and the original.

17. Augustine, *City of God* 18.43 (*CSEL*, 40:2, 336–37).

18. Augustine, *City of God* 18.44 (*CSEL*, 40:2, 338–40).

19. Augustine, *City of God* 18.44 (*CSEL*, 40:2, 340).

20. Jerome, *Praefatio in Pentateuchum Moysi ad Desiderium*, in *Biblia sacra Vulgate editionis Sixti V et Clementis VIII . . . auctoritate recognita* (Antwerp: apud J. B. Verdussen, 1716), cols. xix–xx.

21. Eusebius, *Historia ecclesiastica* 7.32.

22. Josephus, *Jewish Antiquities* 12.57.

23. Ibid.

24. On the later translators of the Septuagint, known as the *recentiores* (more recent ones), see the useful introduction by Jennifer Dines, *The Septuagint* (London: Clark, 2004), 84–90.

25. Eusebius, *Historia Ecclesiastica* 6.16.

26. Jerome, *De viris illustribus* 54. See also the preface to Jerome's translation of the Gospels (*PL* 29:525–30).

27. Jerome, *Praefatio in librum Psalmorum* (*PL* 28:1124–25).

28. Manetti's biographical material on Jerome appears to be mostly excerpted from the twelfth-century life by Nicolò Maniacutia (*BHL* 3873 = *PL* 22:183–202; on Nicolò himself, see Paolo Chiesa in *DBI* 69 [2007]).

On medieval and Renaissance lives of Jerome, see Eugene Rice, *Saint Jerome in the Renaissance* (Baltimore: The John Hopkins University Press, 1985), chapter 2.

29. Aristotle, *Nicomachean Ethics* 1.3.

30. Manetti indicates his intention that the *Apologeticus* was to follow his translation of the Psalms, as it in fact does in the three manuscripts used by De Petris as the basis for his edition.

31. See Josephus, *Jewish Antiquities* 1, proem; idem, *Contra Apion* 2.4.26, alluded to by Jerome in *Liber Hebraicarum quaestionum in Genesim*, preface (*PL* 23:937).

32. Evidently Sophronius meant his love for Christianity by which, in disputation with the Jew, he fell into possible error in the interpretation of the Psalms.

33. *Vulgata*, 285 = *PL* 28:1124–25.

34. Compare §16, above.

BOOK III

1. Manetti is mistaken; there is no second "and."

2. I.e., the second "my."

3. I.e., the second instance in the English text.

4. I.e., the "your" modifying "lightning."

5. I.e., it should go before "vain" in the English version.

6. I.e., it should go after "helper" in the English.

7. The phrase is repeated in the singular ("Direct the work of our hands"); Manetti presumably meant for "itself" to follow this phrase.

8. I.e., before "slumber" in the English text.

BOOK IV

1. The difference, purely grammatical, does not appear in the English translation: *an*, as in the second version, is used in indirect questions.

2. See Robert Alter, *The Book of Psalms. A Translation and Commentary* (Norton: New York, 2007), for helpful notes on the Hebrew titles of many of the Psalms.

BOOK V

1. Terence, *The Self-Tormentor* 1.1.25.

2. Plato, *Epistle* 358a, quoted by Cicero, *On Ends* 2.45, *On Duties* 1.22.

3. Cicero, *For Marcellus* 25.

4. Cicero, *On Duties* 1.7.

5. Aramaic is referred to in the Latin as *Caldeus* (Chaldean).

6. From 5.23 to 5.32, Manetti cites liberally from his mentor's work on translation. The most significant borrowings will be cited from Bruni, *DRI*.

7. Compare Bruni, *DRI*, 78 (*The Humanism*, 218).

8. Manetti borrows all but the last example from Bruni, *DRI*, 78 (*The Humanism*, 218).

9. Examples from Vergil, *Aeneid*, 5.398 and 7.162–63 are drawn from Bruni, *DRI*, 219.

10. The example from Livy 1.14.4 (also at 3.8.7) is drawn from Bruni, *DRI*, 80 (*The Humanism*, 219).

11. Compare Bruni, *DRI*, 82 (*The Humanism*, 220). Here, Manetti uses four of Bruni's five examples.

12. The distinction is observed by Cicero, *On the Orator* 3.148–209, and elsewhere; they are sometimes referred to as "schemes" and "tropes."

13. Compare Bruni, *DRI*, 84 (*The Humanism*, 220).

14. Horace, *The Art of Poetry*, 133–34. Manetti borrows these verses from Jerome, *DOGI*, V, 21.

15. Jerome, *Preface to the Chronicle*, in *A Translation of Jerome's "Chronicon" with Historical Commentary*, trans. Malcolm Donaldson (Lewiston: Mellen, 1996).

16. Cicero's translations were meant to appear at the end of his short work or preface, *On the Best Kind of Orator.* The translations are not extant. Manetti repeats Jerome's citation from *DOGI,* V, 24.

17. Cf. J. G. F. Powell, "Cicero's Translations from Greek," in *Cicero the Philosopher,* ed. J. G. F. Powell (Oxford: Clarendon Press, 1995), 273–300.

18. On medieval translations of Pseudo-Dionysius the Areopagite, see Walter Berschin, *Greek Letters and the Latin Middle Ages* (Washington, DC: Catholic University of America Press, 1988), 239–42. In fact, there were four medieval translations of the pseudo-Dionysius, those of Hilduin (ca. 838), John Scotus Eriugena (ca. 862), John the Saracen (ca. 1165), and Robert Grosseteste (ca. 1240). On the debate between medieval and humanist translations of Aristotle, see Botley, *Latin Translation,* 53–54.

19. Pseudo-Dionysius' texts were commented on by many medieval philosophers, including Scotus Eriugena, Hugh of St. Victor, Grosseteste, Albert the Great, Thomas Aquinas, Bonaventure, John Clichtove, Meister Eckhart, John Tauler, and others.

20. On Bessarion's translation of Aristotle's *Metaphysics,* see Dieter Harlfinger, "Zur Überlieferungsgeschichte der *Metaphysik,*" in *Études sur la Métaphysique d'Aristote.* Actes du VI Symposium Aristotelicum, ed. P. Aubenque (Paris: Vrin, 1979), 7–36.

21. See Charles Stinger, *Humanism and the Church Fathers: Ambrogio Traversari (1386–1439) and Christian Antiquity in the Italian Renaissance* (Albany: SUNY Press, 1977), 158–61 and 281–82.

22. See Stinger, *Humanism,* 35–75. The praise of Traversari here is almost identical to that in *Against the Jews and Gentiles,* 6.32. See, in this I Tatti series, Giannozzo Manetti, *Biographical Writings,* trans. Stefano Baldassarri and Rolf Bagemihl (Cambridge, MA: Harvard University Press, 2003), 158–61.

23. Cicero, *On the Best Kind of Orator,* 18.

24. Cicero, *On the Best Kind of Orator,* 23. Compare Jerome, *DOGI,* V, 21.

25. The unidentified translators are Lorenzo Valla and Mattia Palmieri (to be distinguished from Matteo Palmieri [1406–75], author of *On Civil*

Life). On Valla's translation of Thucydides, see Marianne Pade, "Thucydides," in *Catalogus Translationum et Commentariorum*, ed. Virginia Brown, vol. 8 (Washington, DC: The Catholic University of America Press, 2003), 113, 120–28. For Valla's translation of Herodotus (after 1457) and Palmieri's earlier translation, see Stefano Pagliaroli, *L'Erodoto del Valla* (Messina: Centro interdipartimentale di studi umanistici, 2006), and idem, "Il Proemio di Mattia Palmieri alla traduzione latina delle *Storie* di Erodoto," in *Hérodote à la Renaissance*, ed. S. Gambino Longo (Turnhout: Brepols, 2012), 23–43. Among other works, Mattia translated the *Letter of Aristeas* on origins of the Septuagint.

26. Apion was a controversial Greek grammarian whose anti-Semitism provoked Josephus to write *Against Apion*. On Apion, see Cynthia Damon, "'The Mind of an Ass and the Impudence of a Dog': A Scholar Gone Bad," in *Kakos: Badness and Anti-Value in Classical Antiquity*, ed. I. Sluiter and R. Rosen (Brill: Leiden, 2008), 335–64.

27. Compare Jerome, *DOGI*, V, 23. The testimonies and fragments of Cicero's translations of the *Oeconomicus* and the *Protagoras* are printed at *M. Tulli Ciceronis Fragmenta ex libris philosophicis, ex aliis libris deperditis, ex scriptis incertis*, ed. I. Garbarino (Mondadori: Turin, 1984), 65–85. It is surprising that Manetti says nothing of Cicero's translation of the *Timaeus*, a substantial fragment of which is extant (*editio princeps* Venice, 1474).

28. Cicero, *On Ends*, 1.7.

29. Jerome, *DOGI*, V, 24.

30. Ibid.

31. Jerome, *DOGI*, VI, 24–25.

32. Manetti paraphrases Jerome in the bracketed phrase. For Hilary's commentary on the Psalms, see the parallel French-Latin edition, Hilaire de Poitiers, *Commentaires sur les Psaumes*, trans. J. Doignon (Paris: Editions du Cerf, 2008).

33. Modern editions of Jerome's text have here the Greek word ἐμφατικώτερον; Manetti's quotation transliterates the Greek.

34. Modern texts of Jerome have "calling and commanding" (*vocantis et imperantis*) rather than "imitating and translating." Compare Jerome, *DOGI*, VII, 25. Discussion in Botley, *Latin Translation*, 98.

35. Compare Jerome, *DOGI*, VII, 25.

36. Jerome, *DOGI*, VII, 25. Compare Zachariah 11:12–13.

37. See the discussion in Stefano Baldassarri, *Umanesimo e traduzione da Petrarca a Manetti* (Cassino: Università di Cassino, 2003), 231 n. 4.

38. Jerome, *DOGI*, VII, 25.

39. On Origen's editorial conventions, see Jennifer Dines, *The Septuagint* (London: Clark, 2004), 96–101. Further discussion in *Origenis Hexaplorum quae supersunt*, ed. F. Field (Oxford: Clarendon Press, 1875; repr. Olms: Hildesheim, 1964), lii–lx.

40. A mistake: Manetti should have said Hebrew words with Greek letters.

41. On Origen's hexaplaric recension, see Dines, The *Septuagint*, 96–102, and Anthony Grafton and Megan Hale Williams, "Origen's Hexapla: Scholarship, Culture and Power," in *Christianity and the Transformation of the Book* (Cambridge, MA: Harvard University Press, 2009), 86–133.

42. "Targum Onkelos," in fact, means "The translation of Aquila." See *Targum Onkelos to Numbers*, trans. Israel Drazin (Hoboken, NJ: Ktav Publishing House, 1998), 3.

43. This is the targum to the Prophets, commonly attributed to Jonathan ben Uzziel. See Dines, *The Septuagint*, 84.

44. Genesis 49:10.

45. Shiloh can refer to both the Messiah and the city of the same name (1 Samuel 1:3).

46. *Conversores*, a word Manetti seems to have invented in order to indicate those who render freely into another language, as opposed to *interpretes*, translators properly so called, who stick closer to the original.

47. Ovid, *Metamorphoses* 2.136 (Daedalus to Icarus), by Manetti's day a trite proverb.

48. Manetti refers to his arrival at Alfonso's court after his activity in Florence and Rome metaphorically as *postliminium*, the legal process by which a Roman citizen reestablished his rights after a sojourn abroad; see A. Berger, *An Encyclopedic Dictionary of Roman Law* (Philadelphia: American Philosophical Society, 1953), s.v.

Bibliography

TEXTS AND TRANSLATIONS

Manetti, Giannozzo. *Apologeticus*. Edited by Alfonso De Petris. Rome: Temi e testi, 1981. The sole complete critical edition of the Latin text.

Manetti, Giannozzo. "*Apologia, libro V, a Sua Altezza Serenissima Alfonso d'Aragona.*" In Stefano Baldassarri, *Umanesimo e traduzione da Petrarca a Manetti*, 219–36. Cassino: Università di Cassino, 2003. Abridged Italian translation of Book V of the *Apologeticus* with notes.

Manetti, Giannozzo. *Giannozzo Manetti y la traducción en el siglo XV. Edición Critica del Apologeticus, Libro V.* Edited and translated by Maurilio Pérez Gonzaléz. León: Ediciones Universidad de León, 1999. Critical edition of Book V of the *Apologeticus* with Spanish translation.

Ruiz Vila, José Manuel. *En defensa de su traducción: estudio introductorio, traducción y notas*. Madrid: Escolar y Mayo, 2014. Abridged Spanish translation of Books I, II, and V.

SELECTED LITERATURE

Baldassarri, Stefano. "Teoria e prassi della traduzione nell'*Apologeticus* di Giannozzo Manetti." *Journal of Italian Translation* 3 (2008): 7–36.

Bergquist, Anders. "Christian Hebrew Scholarship in Quattrocento Florence." In *Hebrew Study from Ezra to Ben-Yehuda*, edited by William Horbury, 224–33. Edinburgh: Clark, 1999.

Botley, Paul. *Latin Translation in the Renaissance: The Theory and Practice of Leonardo Bruni, Giannozzo Manetti and Desiderius Erasmus*. Cambridge: Cambridge University Press, 2004.

Den Haan, Annet. "Giannozzo Manetti's New Testament: New Evidence on Sources, Translation Process and the Use of Valla's *Annotationes*." *Renaissance Studies* 28 (2014): 731–47.

———. "Giannozzo Manetti's New Testament: Translation Theory and Practice in Renaissance Italy." PhD diss., University of Groningen, 2014.

———. "Translation into the *Sermo Maternus*: The View of Giannozzo Manetti (1396–1459)." In *Dynamics of Neo-Latin and the Vernacular: Language and Poetics, Translation and Transfer*, edited by Tom Deneire, 163–76. Leiden: Brill, 2014.

De Petris, Alfonso. *Ripercorsi filosofici e letterari da Platone a Ficino*. Spoleto: Fondazione Centro italiano di studi sull' alto medioevo, 2012. Collected studies on various figures, including Manetti.

Dröge, Christoph. *Giannozzo Manetti als Denker und Hebraist*. Frankfurt am Main: Verlag Peter Lang, 1987.

———. "*Quia morem Hieronymi in transferendo cognovi . . .*: Les débuts des études hébraïques chez les humanistes italiens." In *L'Hébreu au temps de la Renaissance*, edited by Ilana Zinguer, 65–88. Leiden: Brill, 1992.

Fubini, Riccardo "L'ebraismo nei riflessi della cultura umanistica." *Medioevo e Rinascimento* 2 (1988): 283–324. Reprinted in Riccardo Fubini, *Storiografia dell'umanesimo in Italia da Leonardo Bruni ad Annio da Viterbo*, 291–334. Rome: Edizioni di Storia e Letteratura, 2003.

Garofalo, Sebastiano. "Gli umanisti italiani del secolo XV e la Bibbia." *Biblica* 27 (1946): 338–75.

Hermans, Theo. "Concepts and Theories of Translation in the European Renaissance." *Übersetzung: ein internationales Handbuch zur Übersetzungsforschung*, ed. Harald Kittel et al., 2:1120–129. Multiple volumes. Berlin: De Gruyter, 2004–11.

Monfasani, John. "Criticism of Biblical Humanists in Quattrocento Italy." In *Biblical Humanism and Scholasticism in the Age of Erasmus*, edited by Erika Rummel, 15–38. Leiden: Brill, 2008.

Norton, Glyn P. "Humanist Foundations of Translation Theory (1400–1450): A Study in the Dynamics of Word." *Canadian Review of Comparative Literature* 8 (1981): 173–203.

———. *The Ideology and Language of Translation in Renaissance France and Their Humanist Antecedents*. Geneva: Droz, 1984. Section on Manetti, 44–54.

Rener, Frederick. *Interpretatio: Language and Translation from Cicero to Tytler.* Amsterdam: Rodopi, 1989.

Reventlow, Henning Graf. "Rediscovering the Hebrew Original: Giannozzo Manetti." In idem, *History of Biblical Interpretation,* vol. 3: *Renaissance, Reformation, Humanism,* 5–10. Atlanta: Society of Biblical Literature, 2010.

Smith, Christine, and Joseph F. O'Connor. *Building the Kingdom: Giannozzo Manetti on the Material and Spiritual Edifice.* Tempe, AZ: Arizona Center for Medieval and Renaissance Studies, 2006.

Trinkaus, Charles. *In Our Image and Likeness: Humanity and Divinity in Italian Humanist Thought.* 2 vols. Chicago: University of Chicago Press, 1970. Section on Manetti, 2:578–601.

Vanderjagt, Arjo. "*Hebraica veritas* and Humanism: Giannozzo Manetti and the Debate on Hebrew and the Jews." In *Hebrew Bible/Old Testament: The History of Its Interpretation from the Renaissance to the Enlightenment,* edited by Magne Saebø, 167–73. Göttingen: Vandenhoeck and Ruprecht, 2008.

Index

Publication of this volume has been made possible by

The Myron and Sheila Gilmore Publication Fund at I Tatti
The Robert Lehman Endowment Fund
The Jean-François Malle Scholarly Programs and Publications Fund
The Andrew W. Mellon Scholarly Publications Fund
The Craig and Barbara Smyth Fund
for Scholarly Programs and Publications
The Lila Wallace–Reader's Digest Endowment Fund
The Malcolm Wiener Fund for Scholarly Programs and Publications